I Love the Work, But I Hate the Business

Mel Proctor

Blue River Press
Indianapolis, IN

Cover designed by Phil Velikan
Cover art © Chris Pechin
Edited by Mark Bast, MB Ink
Packaged by Wish Publishing

Printed in the United States of America
10 9 8 7 6 5 4 3 2 1

Published by Blue River Press
Distributed by Cardinal Publishers Group
Tom Doherty Company, Inc.
www.cardinalpub.com

This book is dedicated to the memory of my dad, who taught me to love, appreciate, and respect the world of sports.

Foreword by Ron Darling, Broadcaster TBS, SNY, and WPIX-TV

Two days before the 2005 Major League Baseball season began, I was home in Lake Tahoe when my agent called and said the Washington Nationals wanted to hire me to do commentary on their telecasts during the team's first season. I don't know why they called me. I hadn't even auditioned for the job. I had some experience doing studio shows for Fox and pre- and postgame shows for the Oakland A's, but I'd never been a game analyst. I had two hours to make a decision and decided to go for it. I caught a redeye to Philadelphia where the Nationals were opening the season. I arrived at the Four Seasons Hotel and went straight to bed. I received a message that I'd be working with play-by-play announcer Mel Proctor. When I woke up, I called Mel and we agreed to meet in the hotel lobby. I'd never met Mel and didn't know what he looked like. At noon, just three hours before the Nationals' first-ever pitch, we met. It was the beginning of a great friendship as we endured the most difficult season imaginable.

When I think of Mel I always break out in a big smile. Broadcasting has become so competitive that sometimes the "newbies" forget that at some point you're watching a game and getting paid for it. Mel has never forgotten that.

I would not have the career I enjoy today without Mel's mentoring. My first lesson was that I used to play sports at a high level, but I didn't anymore. All the hard work that had been put into sports would now have to be put into broadcasting. It's a blue-collar job that takes a great degree of work and concentration.

Another lesson: you are around the royalty of sports, but your existence can sometimes be minimally tolerated. Mel taught me that you and your broadcast partner are each other's best friend and when the game is done it's all right to celebrate a job well done. You will enjoy this read because it is impossible to not enjoy Mel's company and his anecdotes.

Many of us do not live a life worthy of a book. That is not Mel Proctor. He has many more stories, some too risqué for publication. Mel is one of the golden voices of our generation, and I have been so lucky because he and I bonded one hot summer in D.C. Enjoy his hilarious and compassionate life.

Prologue

The idea for this book was conceived at Warwick's Bookstore in La Jolla, California, in 2007. I had gone to say hello to Cal Ripken Jr., who was there for a book signing for his autobiography *The Only Way I Know*. With Cal was John Maroon, former public relations director for the Baltimore Orioles. After saying hello to Cal and John, we reminisced as Cal sat at a table autographing books. We were joined by Ron Donoho of *San Diego* magazine, who was going to write a feature story on Ripken and San Diego Padres' star Tony Gwynn, who would both be inducted into baseball's Hall of Fame in July. As the three of us talked, we figured out that I was the only person on earth who had broadcast the games when Cal broke Lou Gehrig's consecutive-games streak in 1995 and Tony Gwynn's 3,000th hit in 1999 and final game in 2001.

I realized how fortunate I was. As a television play-by-play announcer for the Baltimore Orioles for 12 years, I had watched Cal Ripken become the best all-around shortstop in baseball history. And for five years as a broadcaster for the San Diego Padres, I'd seen one of the game's most remarkable hitters, Tony Gwynn, who won eight batting titles.

The accomplishments of Cal Ripken and Tony Gwynn may never be equaled. Not only the numbers they put up, but the fact that both of them played for the same team their entire careers. Both played the game the way it was supposed to be played; were loyal to their cities, teams, and fans; and understood they were role models.

I had been in the middle of baseball history, describing the careers of Cal Ripken and Tony Gwynn. The enormity of what I'd been part of hit me squarely between the eyes. I decided I was going to Cooperstown.

Acknowledgments

Thanks to all the people who've helped shape my career, including Ed and Steve Sabol at NFL Films, Ernie Tannen at WEEZ Radio and Bob Brinker. Special thanks to Earl McDaniel and KGMB for bringing me to Hawaii. He and his wife Ellie have been friends and mentors for 40 years.

Thanks to Abe Pollin, Bob Ferry, Jerry Sachs, and WTOP Radio, who helped me become the voice of the Washington Bullets. Thanks to John Chanin and Luke Griffin at Mutual Radio; Randy Bongarten, Jack O'Rourke, Rich Bonn, Rich Hussey, and Ted Nathanson at NBC; and Ted Shaker at CBS. At Turner Sports I would like to thank Don McGuire, Rex and Mike Lardner, and Don Ellis.

I was fortunate to have spent 14 years at Home Team Sports working with wonderful people like Bill Aber, Jody Shapiro, Bill Brown, Bill Bell, and Chris Glass, who gave me the freedom to grow creatively and to expand my career.

Without my talented broadcast partners, there would be no stories and no book. I was blessed to have worked with John Lowenstein, Jim Palmer, Mike Flanagan, and Rex Barney on Baltimore Orioles telecasts; Phil Chenier, Wes Unseld, and Kevin Grevey on Washington Bullets games; Rick Sutcliffe and Mark Grant on San Diego Padres games; and Ron Darling, my partner with the Washington Nationals.

Thanks to my agent and friend Martin Mandel for believing in me, and thanks to Tom Doherty of Blue River Press, Mark Bast of MB Ink, and Wish Publishing for helping make this book a reality.

Thanks to the producers, directors, and broadcast crew members who've put up with me all these years. Most of all thanks to my incredible wife Julie, who has lived with my crazy lifestyle, and to my kids Billy and Maile, to whom I have passed along my love of sports.

May all of you enjoy this book.

Contents

National Baseball Hall of Fame, Cooperstown, New York, July 29, 2007
(photo courtesy of Mel Proctor)

Chapter 1
Cooperstown

Cooperstown, New York, is a quaint village with a population of roughly 2,000, but in late July 2007, 75,000 fans flooded the town to pay homage to Cal Ripken and Tony Gwynn, as they were inducted into baseball's Hall of Fame. The crowd saluted the players' character as much as their accomplishments. Both had spent their entire careers with one team: Ripken a Baltimore Oriole for 20 years and Gwynn a San Diego Padre for 19. They had earned their adulation not only through excellence, but through example—showing loyalty to their cities, teams, and fans. Richard Gere and John Travolta and wife Kelly Preston were among the Hollywood stars who attended, along with a record turnout of 53 Hall of Famers. Cooperstown's few hotels, motels, and bed and breakfasts were filled; some residents left for the weekend, renting homes to visitors. Many who remained turned their lawns into parking lots, charging $25–$50 a pop while hawking hot dogs and lemonade on the sidewalk.

On the day before the induction ceremony, I joined the crush of humanity, like a slow-moving glacier, inching down Main Street, past the Doubleday Café, the Cooperstown Diner, and memorabilia shops like the Cooperstown Bat Company, the Seventh Inning Stretch, and Where It All Began. Since I'd broadcast for both the Orioles and Padres, I saw old friends, who waved, many asking, "Who are you broadcasting for now?" or shouting, "We miss you in Baltimore," or "Come back to the Padres." It was good to be remembered, but I felt like a worn-out baseball glove, tossed aside for a newer model. I wasn't working and had no job prospects in sight.

At Tony Gwynn's party at the Fennimore Art Museum, I congratulated "Mr. Padre" and reminisced with Padres announcers Jerry Coleman, Ted Leitner, and Bob Chandler. At Cal Ripken's bash at the Hoffman Lane Bistro, I thanked "the Iron Man" for the thrills he'd provided, said hello to his family, and swapped memories with former Orioles, including Brady Anderson and B.J. Surhoff. As someone led a chant of "O-R-I-O-L-E-S," I realized how much I missed baseball.

On the morning of July 29, dark clouds hovered ominously over the mass of fans walking to the Clark County Sports Center, many holding umbrellas; carrying coolers, food baskets, and folding chairs; and ready to pounce on a prime spot on the expansive grassy field, site of the induction ceremony. As I found my chair in the media section near the stage, I looked back at a sea of Orioles orange and black sprinkled with Padres brown and gold; fans wearing jerseys, Ripken's No. 8 and Gwynn's No. 19; and people holding signs reading, "My son is named for you Cal," and "Tony, I drove 3,000 miles for my hero."

It began to drizzle, but it was as if the baseball gods mandated there would be no rain on this special day. By noon the storm clouds dissipated, giving way to billowy white fluffs set against a bluer than blue sky, with the sun beating down on my whiter than white skin. Since I'd forgotten sun screen, I borrowed some from the man sitting next to me. After I rubbed white cream onto my face and hands, we introduced ourselves. He was Richard Sandomir, the acclaimed sports and television writer for the *New York Times.*

"Ron Darling speaks highly of you," Sandomir said. "He said he wouldn't have survived in Washington without you." Darling, the ex-New York Mets pitcher, had been my broadcast partner on Washington Nationals telecasts in 2005, the team's first year—an historic season but a year from broadcasting hell and my last job. Ronnie had survived our year in Washington, landing a lucrative analyst's job with Mets TV and then being hired by Turner Sports for national telecasts. Adversity had forged our friendship, and I was proud of him.

As the festivities began, highlights of Cal Ripken's career appeared on the video screen, and I heard a familiar voice— *mine*—booming from the loudspeakers: "Cal Ripken has just played in his 2,131st consecutive game, eclipsing the Iron Horse Lou Gehrig and setting a major league record for the most consecutive games played." I wanted to scream, "That's me!" but held back. As Ripken completed his eloquent speech, the crowd roared. Then Tony Gwynn appeared on the screen, and

I heard my voice again: "Gwynn facing Dan Smith... a drive to center field...there it is! Number 3,000 for Tony Gwynn! In his first at-bat of the night, in a foreign country, in Canada and Olympic Stadium, Tony Gwynn has done it." I wanted to hug Richard Sandomir and yell, "That's me," visualizing my name in the *New York Times*, but I knew it was just my ego screaming, and besides, this day belonged to Cal and Tony.

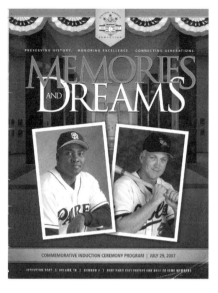

Image courtesy of the National Baseball Hall of Fame

A tidal wave of emotions overwhelmed me. How fortunate I'd been to follow the amazing careers of Cal Ripken and Tony Gwynn, describing some of the greatest moments in baseball history. How lucky I was to have teamed with broadcast partners like Ron Darling, John Lowenstein, and Rick Sutcliffe, knowing that I'd contributed to their success. Although I yearned for the satisfaction my career had provided and wondered what the future held, that day in Cooperstown I realized how fortunate I'd been and recalled how it all began.

Hall of Fame employees about to mount plaques of Cal Ripken and Tony Gwynn (photo by Mel Proctor)

Chapter 2
Go East Young Man

Juan Reid, the dean of men, said, "Proctor, I've been at Colorado College for 40 years. I've known academics, athletes, and assholes. I've known you for four years and still can't figure out which one you are," he said, sending me into the real world in 1968. Now what?

Sports had been my life. My dad was a successful high school baseball coach, and I became his batboy when I was five. We shared our love for the game and often went to Bears Stadium to watch the Denver Bears, the New York Yankees AAA affiliate, featuring future major leaguers like Tony Kubek, Bobby Richardson, Norm Siebern, and Marv Throneberry. I dreamed of becoming one of them.

When the Bears were on the road and I was supposed to be asleep, I lay in bed, a transistor radio pressed to my ear, a pillow covering my head, as I listened to Bill Reed, the Bears' radio announcer. "Welcome to Denver Bears baseball," he said, "tonight the Bears meet

Photos courtesy of Mel Proctor

The Coach—my dad, Bill Proctor (photo courtesy of Mel Proctor)

the St. Paul Saints at Nicolet Park in St. Paul, Minnesota." I pictured the park, the fans, and me, roaming center field for the Bears. I didn't have a single thought about becoming an announcer. I also didn't know Bill Reed wasn't in St. Paul but in a Denver studio doing a re-creation, which I'd learn more about later.

I wanted to work in sports but doing what? A high school coach like Dad? No thanks, too much work and little pay. A sportswriter? Come on, I was a business major. An umpire? I had a problem with authority figures. A jockey? I was too big. Finally, in need of any job, I found a position in the advertising department at the C. A. Norgren Company—coat and tie, punch the time clock at 7:30 a.m., two coffee breaks and a half hour for lunch. I hated it.

"Lionel Taylor," said an athletic looking black man, extending a ham-sized hand. Taylor had just retired from the Denver Broncos, where he'd led the AFL in receiving for six straight years and had become the first receiver in pro football history to have 100 catches in a season. Lionel was C. A. Norgren's public relations ambassador, shaking hands, hugging visitors, and rehashing Broncos memories. Lionel and I often ate lunch together, and both of us, bored, vowed to get back into sports.

"My friend, you're looking at the new wide receivers coach for the Los Angeles Rams," Lionel announced one day. We hugged and wished each other well. I was happy for Lionel, but how was I going to escape corporate hell?

At halftime of a game between the Phillips 66'ers and Peoria Cats in the National AAU Basketball Tournament at the Denver Auditorium, I watched sportscaster Fred Leo interview

*Photo courtesy of Mel
Proctor*

Michigan All-American Cazzie Russell. Cool job. Maybe I could do that. As Leo finished the interview, I introduced myself and said I might be interested in becoming a sportscaster.

"Mel, where did you go to school?"

"Colorado College."

"Great school. Use your degree. Don't get into this crazy business."

"Why not?"

He leaned closer and said quietly, "Mel, I'm going to tell you the truth. If you're going to make it as a sportscaster, you've got to be black, a Mexican, or a woman." He flicked his cigarette aside, said goodbye, and walked away.

Then I thought of Steve "Sudden Death" Sabol, who'd played football at Colorado College. His dad, Ed Sabol, founded NFL Films, and they ran the company. I wrote to Ed Sabol, only to be told jobs rarely opened up. But I was determined. By day, I wrote installation instructions for air pumps and hydraulic valves; at night I created program ideas for NFL Films and bombarded Ed Sabol with my mailings. No answer. I kept sending them.

Finally, a position opened up at NFL Films, and I flew to Philadelphia for an interview. "You want to work here?" asked "Big Ed" Sabol, 50ish, with salt and pepper hair, wearing a plaid sport coat and full of bluster.

"Yes, I'll work for free to show you . . ."

"Bullshit, I'm tired of you sending me all those ideas. Actually, some of them are good. You're hired."

I moved to Philadelphia in time for a kickoff party before the 1970 NFL season. Howard Cosell, the most famous sportscaster in America, was there along with Ed and Steve Sabol, NFL executives, and Philadelphia Eagles players, including Gary Pettigrew and Bill Bradley.

As the party ended, I heard Ed Sabol tell Howard Cosell that a limo was waiting to move partiers to a Philly hot spot. Party on! I'd graduated summa cum laude in partying. I'd seen the long black stretch in the parking lot, so I ran down the stairs and jumped into the passenger's seat.

"Damn it, Stanley, take him home," bellowed Big Ed as he opened the limo door and saw me.

Stanley Leshner, NFL Films MVP, shot camera, edited film, made travel reservations, was the designated driver, and eventually became my roommate. He deposited me on the front steps of my apartment building. The next morning, when I pulled the pillow off my aching head, I thought, *oh shit, I'm fired.*

"Have too much to drink?" asked Big Ed Sabol.

"Yes, sorry."

He slapped me on the back, told me not to worry, and added, "Always finish like a pro."

I produced highlight films for the Miami Dolphins, Cincinnati Bengals, and Chicago Bears. The rookie was always thrown to the Bears. Owner George Halas sent a couple of cronies, left over from the Al Capone days, to oversee the film's production. Smoking cigars and wearing wide ties and 1920s pinstriped suits, Halas' boys dictated every shot in the film, but I tried to slip in a little creativity.

Despite a 1–13 record in 1969, the Bears' worst season ever, running back Gayle Sayers had returned from knee surgery to lead the NFL in rushing. Editing the film, I flashed back to Sayers' 1968 injury and then dissolved to a montage of spectacular runs in 1969.

"Take it out," barked one of Papa Bear's guys.

"Are you kidding? Gayle Sayers might be the greatest running back ever. He gives Bears fans hope."

With Charlie Jones (L) and Pat Summerall (R) (photos courtesy of Mel Proctor)

"It's too positive. If our fans see this, they'll expect us to win. Just show one or two of Sayers' runs." I felt like I was banging my head against the Liberty Bell.

"Okay, okay. Check this out," I said, watching defensive end Ed O'Bradovich jumping up and down, waving his arms and screaming at an official.

"Out."

"But it's hilarious."

"Look, if O'Bradovich sees this, he'll want speaking engagements and a raise. Take it out." I thought about naming the film "Take It Out" but figured it might be mistaken for a porno film.

Game films arrived Sunday evening, and we stayed up all night editing and writing. The next morning, CBS's Pat Summerall and NBC's Charlie Jones narrated *This Week in Pro Football*. Summerall's CBS partner, Tom Brookshier, eventually replaced Charlie Jones. "Brookie," a star defensive back with the Philadelphia Eagles, was the most popular sportscaster in Philly. Through strange circumstances, we bonded.

Brookshier's brother had died in Roswell, New Mexico, so Brookie flew to his hometown for the funeral. The mortuary's owner was my uncle, Bob Coons, who mentioned that his nephew, me, worked for NFL Films. When Brookie returned, he told me how he'd met my uncle. We soon became friends, and Tom Brookshier became one of my biggest supporters.

Besides Tom Brookshier, Pat Summerall, and Charlie Jones, I met team announcers like Jack Brickhouse of the Bears, Marty Glickman of the Giants, Phil Samp of the Bengals, and Van Miller of the Bills. I heard their voices so often, I could imitate them. One voice I couldn't master was the voice of God, John Facenda.

The longtime news anchor at WCAU-TV, John Facenda was a kind man and during narration sessions, always paid for Philly cheesesteaks from nearby Fireman Junior's. During a lunch break, Facenda described how he became the voice of NFL Films. "I was in a bar watching an NFL Films production," Facenda recalled, "and I started to rhapsodize about how beautiful it was. Ed Sabol was in the same bar, heard what I said, and asked, 'If I give you a script, can you repeat what you just said?'"

John Facenda (photo courtesy WCAU-TV)

"I'll try," said Facenda, who got the job.

It was "a bitterly cold day in Baltimore," as John Facenda might have said, as I stepped off the NFL Films bus at Memorial Stadium to watch the Colts play the Miami Dolphins. Wearing a fake fur coat that made me look 30 pounds heavier, I must have been mistaken for a player because several kids asked for my autograph.

"Who do you guys think I am?" I asked, walking away.

"You're the Mad Dog, Mike Curtis."

"No I'm not."

"Curtis, you suck," one kid yelled, "and so do the Colts."

Standing on the Colts' sideline, I watched a drunk, long-haired hippie stumble onto the field and pick up the football. A goofy smile on his face, he tried to run away, but Baltimore's All-Pro middle linebacker, Mike Curtis, bolted out of the Colts' huddle and cold-cocked this idiot as the football shot 15 feet in

Vince Lombardi coaching the Washington Redskins (photo courtesy the Washington Redskins)

the air. After the game, more kids asked for my autograph. "Best of luck, Mike Curtis," I signed. I didn't want to disappoint them.

In 1969, Vince Lombardi came out of retirement to coach the Washington Redskins. After the Skins beat the Eagles at Philadelphia's Franklin Field, I interviewed some Philly players and then rushed to the Redskins' locker room, where only the great Lombardi remained, standing in front of his locker, pulling on his slacks.

"Coach Lombardi?"

He looked up.

"Mel Proctor, NFL Films. Could I ask you a few questions?"

Lombardi stared at me. The crocodile had spotted dinner. "Damn it. What the fuck do you want? I've done every fucking interview I'm doing. Why didn't you come in here with the reporters? Get the fuck out of here." I later worked with former Green Bay Packers Paul Hornung, Jerry Kramer, and Max McGee, who convinced me that I'd seen only one side of their beloved coach.

Sometimes, NFL Films productions needed a shot of "oomph." Viewers assumed the sideline voices they heard were players, but "Take his head off" might have been yelled by Ralph Caputo, Ed Sabol's limo driver; "Kill him," may have come from cameraman Jack Newman. Thus began NFL Film's "Theater of the Absurd."

I produced a CBS halftime feature about hot dog vendor Charley Frank—yes, that's his real name—who worked at Franklin Field. Like Alfred Hitchcock, I put myself in the film, and my coworkers loved it.

Then I created *Superfan*, a film about Jim Ondrus, a General Motors assembly line worker, who on Sundays became the Detroit Lions' "Superfan." His Volkswagen bug and Airstream trailer, both silver, each had a blue stripe painted down the middle, resembling a Lions helmet. His trailer was a Lions museum, stuffed with jerseys, helmets, signed footballs, pennants, and pictures of Lions legends like Mel Farr, Joe Schmidt, Alex Karras, and Bobby Layne.

With the Lions hosting the Packers, I played Jim's cousin Melvin from Green Bay. Sitting in Jim's front-row seats at Tiger Stadium, he blew an air horn and cheered maniacally for the Lions, while I wore a yellow Packers hard hat and shouted, "The Pack is back!" As I edited *Superfan*, I knew this was my entree into both the Director's Guild and the Actor's Studio.

Superfan was supposed to air during CBS's Sunday NFL telecast. At a viewing party at my apartment, my NFL Films friends and I drank beer and waited for halftime, to hear Brent Musburger say, "Folks, there are fans and 'Superfans,'" but when Brent said, "Let's go back to the stadium for the second half," there was silence. Then, "Hey, Cecil B. DeMille, where's your Academy Award winner?" yelled a coworker as everyone but me laughed.

"I guess they saved it for the Super Bowl," added another wiseass.

"What the fuck?" I yelled, bursting into head of production John Hentz's office the next morning. "What happened to *Superfan*?"

Hentz explained that CBS had grown weary of NFL Films employees' recurring faces and voices in our features, and when the network saw *Superfan*, CBS brought the curtain down on the NFL Films players.

John Hentz gave me another chance, assigning me to produce a film about the 1971 College All-Star game, at Soldier Field in Chicago, pitting the best college players against the

NFL champion Baltimore Colts. If this film was even mediocre, I was toast, unless NFL Films somehow kept me as a janitor because I starred on the company softball team.

Quarterbacks Jim Plunkett of Stanford and Dan Pastorini of Santa Clara were the marquee names, and I wanted to contrast these stars with an obscure player from a little-known school. I scanned the All-Stars roster: Penn State, Wisconsin, Ohio State, USC, and then, bingo, Yankton (S.D.) State. Lyle Alzado, defensive end, 6'-4", 240 pounds.

Fate made Lyle Alzado an All-Star. A Denver Broncos assistant coach was driving through Montana when his car broke down. While a mechanic repaired his car, the coach watched game film of Montana Tech playing Yankton State, whose aggressive defensive end, Lyle Alzado, terrorized the opposing quarterback. The Denver Broncos drafted Alzado in the fourth round in 1971.

Dripping sweat and breathing hard, Alzado sat on the hood of a car waiting for me. His teammates had left the practice field. I apologized for imposing and asked if he'd do an interview.

"Let's do it my man," he said.

In a Brooklyn accent with lots of *dese* and *dose,* Alzado said he'd grown up in a tough neighborhood, learned to fight at an early age, received no scholarship offers, went to junior college and then to Yankton State, an NAIA school. After the interview, I asked Alzado to pose in front of a tackling sled. "I'll do better than that," he said.

I stood on the back of the sled as Alzado charged, hitting the pads so hard he nearly knocked me over backward. "OK, Lyle, that'll do it."

"Bullshit. Keep the camera running." He backed up, snorted, and attacked. I heard metal on metal as a piece of the sled flew through the air. "I broke the motherfucker," he said, proudly.

The Baltimore Colts won 24–17, but Lyle Alzado had a great game and was the star of the film. "Damned good work," John Hentz said after NFL Films critics watched *The 1971 College All-Star Game,* produced and directed by Mel Proctor. I'd still bat third on the company softball team.

Years later, I walked into a Denver sports bar, where Lyle Alzado sat, regaling friends with stories. As I approached and started to speak, Alzado dug into his wallet, pulling out my old NFL Films business card. "Mel Proctor, you made me a star. Sit your ass down." For two hours, I sat with Lyle and his buddies, guzzling Coors beer and reminiscing. Alzado played 15 years in the NFL but died at 43 of a brain tumor, his death attributed to years of steroid abuse.

Despite the All-Star film's success, I was restless. I laugh now, but back then this was serious. I thought there was "an answer" or "a purpose" to what I should do with my life. I'm still searching.

I wanted to try broadcasting so I convinced a small suburban radio station that because I worked at NFL Films, I was a football expert. So for $15 a game, I joined Bob Brinker, the voice of the Upper Perkiomen Indians, broadcasting high school football.

"Mel, I've got the flu," Brinker said, a few weeks into the season. "You'll have to do the game tonight."

"Bob, I've never done play-by-play."

"You'll do fine," he said.

I was so scared I don't remember anything I said during the broadcast.

"You were good but mention your name more often," Tom Brookshier said. "You never know who's listening."

"Great," said Bob Brinker. "This is what you should be doing." Brinker left sportscasting for the financial world, and for over 20 years he's hosted *Money Talk* on ABC Radio.

In the *Philadelphia Inquirer*, I read that the Chester High School Clippers, ranked number one in the state, had won their league basketball championship and were headed to the 1971–72 PIAA State Tournament in Harrisburg.

In the yellow pages, I found one radio station in Chester, WEEZ. Isn't that a respiratory condition? I called station owner Ernie Tannen and said, "My name is Mel Proctor. I'm a sportscaster. Why aren't you carrying Chester High's games in the state tournament?"

"Mel, if you can sell the advertising, you can broadcast the games." I had a Kool-Aid stand once, the extent of my sales experience.

Chester was 99 percent black. I was the 1 percent. I went door to door in poverty-ridden downtown to find advertisers. "How about sponsoring the Clippers?" I asked the owner of Man's World, a men's clothing store. "They're in the state tournament."

"My man, why should I?" he said. "Chester's broke and dem kids don't buy nothin'. They just come in and steal things."

School colors were orange and black so I asked the owner if he had anything in those colors that he could give away. "Orange and black stockin' caps," he said. "Shee-it, we tried to give 'em away a couple of years ago, but nobody wanted 'em."

"All right."

I recorded a commercial at WEEZ's studio. "Man's World congratulates the Chester High Clippers for making the Pennsylvania State High School Basketball Tournament. We're a proud sponsor of Clippers basketball. To show our loyalty, any Chester student who comes into our store will get, free, an official Clippers stocking cap."

"Mel, you da man," gushed the store owner, giving me a high five. "We've been swamped with kids who want those damned stockin' caps."

"Are they buying?"

"Some are, but moms or pops or an older brother comes in with 'em and they're buyin' bell-bottoms or Super Fly shirts. Man, sign us up."

"Yes!" I said, pumping my fist in the air. A start, but I needed to hook a whale.

I called the advertising manager at the Scott Paper Company, who invited me to his office. He mentioned a girl I occasionally dated. I knew she only saw me when she was on the outs with her boyfriend. This was the boyfriend. As I imagined his hands around my neck, he said his girlfriend thought I was a good guy, and Scott agreed to sponsor the games. Along with Scott Paper and Man's World, I added

Southeast National Bank and B & J Sporting Goods, selling the available commercial time. The tournament was one and done, so if Chester lost their first-round game, they were out, but if they went deeper into the tournament, WEEZ and I would make money.

Basketball is king at Chester. NBA star Tyreke Evans of the Sacramento Kings, the 2009–2010 Rookie of the Year, and All-Star Jameer Nelson of the Orlando Magic played at Chester. Alums include former NBA player Horace Walker; Bo Ryan, the head coach at Wisconsin; and playground legends like Emerson Baynard and Granny Lash.

I borrowed my roommate's TV, found a basketball game, turned down the volume, and substituting Chester players' names, did play-by-play. "Gordy passes to Harris . . . 15 footer good . . . and the Clippers take the lead."

Chester had reached the finals six times but had never won. The Clippers won their first four tournament games by an average of 23 points per game. I could hear the *cha-ching* of the cash register as the Clippers marched into the championship game against the Farrell High Steelers.

Coach Juan Baughn (photo courtesy of Delco Times)

Farrell's Ed McCluskey was the winningest high school basketball coach in Pennsylvania history, with 502 victories and six state championships. Farrell ran a disciplined, structured offense and played take-no-prisoners defense.

"Controlled playground basketball," is how Chester coach Juan Baughn described his team's offense. Baughn, a young black man—my age—with a huge Afro, was coach, psychiatrist, and father confessor. Most of his players were poor—many from single-parent families—and several had fathered children. Coach Baughn made sure his kids had food to eat, a place to sleep. and someone to confide in.

Farrell had walloped Chester 74–54 in December. Chester's star Herman Harris missed the game with a foot injury and had played sparingly since. Coach Baughn didn't know if "Herm the Germ" could play in the championship game.

The smaller but more aggressive Farrell Steelers took a 17-point lead in the second quarter. After Coach Baughn chewed out his team at half-

Herman Harris (photo courtesy of Delco Times)

time, the Clippers sprinted out of their locker room, kept running, and wiped out Farrell's lead. With six minutes left in the game, Chester led by one. Despite Chester's comeback, Farrell held on to win, 56–55, the Steelers' seventh state championship. Chester was now 0–7 in the finals.

The broadcasts created a community buzz, WEEZ made money, and Ernie Tannen offered me a full-time job as sports director. One night, I sat for hours on the back steps at NFL Films, wondering whether I should stay in a secure, prestigious job, surrounded by good friends, or jump to a struggling 5,000-watt radio station. I trusted my gut and dove into the murky waters of broadcasting.

Chapter 3
WEEZ . . . 1500 on Your Radio Dial

I walked into WEEZ, paint peeling off the walls, a threadbare carpet, and radio equipment left by Marconi. On pay day, employees raced to the bank to cash paychecks before the money ran out. What the hell had I gotten into?

I hosted an afternoon sports talk show, stared at the switchboard, and prayed for calls. Sometimes I primed the pump, asking coworkers to call. Finally the red switchboard lights flashed and the show caught on.

Then, Ernie Tannen asked me to host *Mel at the Mall,* a one-hour show from a near-bankrupt shopping center. I stood in the middle of the mall with a microphone, chasing the occasional shopper and asking questions like, "What do you think of Watergate?" Finally the mall closed and so did *Mel at the Mall.*

"Mel, I've got the perfect show for you," Ernie Tannen said, *The Feminine Forum.* Hosted by smarmy West Coast D.J. Bill Balance, the show was a national hit. Each day, Balance talked sex with women, no men allowed.

"Hi, welcome to *The Feminine Forum,*" I said. "Our question tonight is Where is the most unusual place you've ever had sex?"

A man's voice. "Sorry sir, women only."

"Wait," he pleaded. I could hear cars whizzing by in the background.

"Where are you?"

"Don't hang up. We're in a phone booth off the interstate. My wife and I were driving to the Poconos, heard your question, started laughing, and had to call."

Since the switchboard was dark, I said, "OK, I'll make an exception. Where's the most unusual place you've ever made love?"

"On the roof of the church where we got married," he said, describing the juicy details.

As I left WEEZ one night, a beautiful blonde sat in a white Corvette by the front door. The car's motor was idling and so was hers. "Get in," she said. As I closed the door, envisioning a night of ecstasy, lights bounced wildly off the rearview mirror as a tanker truck pulled in behind us.

"Oh shit, my husband."

She floored it and the Corvette took off. After a chase through the suburbs, her Corvette won and she dropped me at WEEZ. Fortunately, I never saw either one of them again.

The show was a hoot, and my social life perked up, but since I talked sex with mothers in the morning and described their sons' athletic exploits at night, I was number one on the P.T.A's most wanted list. Under community pressure, Ernie Tannen sent *The Feminine Forum* to join *Mel at the Mall* in broadcasting's junkyard.

With five starters back from the state runner-up team, the 1972–73 Clippers were favored to win their first championship. Crushing opponents by an average of 40 points a game, in December, the Clippers boarded a yellow school bus and headed 374 miles north for a rematch with the state champion Farrell High Steelers.

Snow fell as we drove, and 100 miles from Farrell, a blizzard hit. Roads were icy, visibility terrible. Normally a six-hour drive, it took 10 hours to reach Farrell. The players were oblivious as music blared from a boom box and they danced in the aisles, exchanging high fives and getting psyched. We reached the gym at 6:30 p.m. for a 7:00 p.m. game.

I've broadcast the NBA Finals, NCAA tournaments, and thousands of college and pro games, but that first quarter in Farrell is still the damndest thing I've ever seen on a basketball court. A blur of orange and black, Chester seemed like the only team on the floor. Herman Harris buried turnaround jumpers, Hank and Phil Mann couldn't miss, and Len Gordy led a suffocating defense that blanked Farrell 14–0 in the first period, the only time I've seen a basketball team shutout for a quarter. The Clippers buried the state champs 71–38, the worst loss in Farrell's history.

When Chester played at Aliquippa the next night, there was no press table so I broadcast from the stands among hostile fans. When I took a punch in the head, I figured the guy next to me didn't like my commentary. I kept talking and counter-punched, landing two solid left jabs. Soon, security arrived. I was awarded a TKO victory and the Clippers also won.

The next day, another blizzard canceled our bus ride home and all flights out of Pittsburgh. We slept overnight on airport benches. Killing time, Coach Baughn read from a local paper, "Aliquippa coach Tony Farnell said, 'Mel Proctor of radio station WEEZ made us sound like animals. He said we were pushing and shoving. I wish people listening could've seen where he was broadcasting from. At the top of the gym, in a corner. He said a fan slugged Phil Mann when he went after a loose ball. I didn't see it. The police didn't see it. I don't think Mel was close enough to see anything.'" Coach Baughn and I laughed and exchanged high fives.

Len Gordy (photo courtesy of Delco Times)

The Clippers breezed through their schedule, won another league title, and again entered the state tournament. In the 1972–73 PIAA Tournament, the Clippers beat Lancaster by 31 points, Northampton by 29, and Easton by 8. Then they faced the 27–1 Reading Red Knights, led by 6'-5" star Stu Jackson, who had a huge Afro with a white spot in it. Reading's all-time leading scorer, Jackson averaged 27 points per game. The Clippers entered the semifinals with a 26–2 record, one of those losses at Reading, 75–55, earlier in the year.

Chester trailed for most of the game but tied the score at 38–38 as the third quarter ended. With Reading ahead 46–42 in the fourth quarter, Chester's Len Gordy and Reading's Stu Jackson exchanged punches and both were ejected. Then

Herman Harris fouled out with three minutes left after scoring 25 points. Reading won 59–53. A photo in the *Delaware County Times* showed Chester's Phil Mann lying facedown on the Farm Show Arena floor, crying. That said it all. Reading won the state championship, while Chester lost a meaningless consolation game to future Hall of Fame quarterback Joe Montana and Ringgold, 74–65.

Herman Harris broke the county scoring record. He and Len Gordy had stellar careers at Arizona, and Hank Mann played at Florida State.

Stu Jackson starred at Oregon, became head coach at Wisconsin, and later coached the New York Knicks and Vancouver Grizzlies. Ironically, Stu Jackson, who was ejected from the Chester game for fighting, is now the NBA's vice president of basketball operations, in charge of handing out fines and suspensions to NBA players.

I also broadcast Widener College basketball on WEEZ. Widener's legendary coach C. Alan Rowe won more than 500 games and owned two successful Dairy Queens on the Jersey Shore. I usually rode the team bus to road games, but in 1973 when Widener traveled to Lebanon Valley College, Ed Gebhart, my broadcast partner and sports editor of the *Delaware County Times,* convinced me to join him and another writer on the two-and-a-half-hour drive to Annville, Pennsylvania. I told Ed I had to get there two hours before tipoff, to set up my broadcast equipment, establish a phone line, and talk to the coaches.

"No problem," Ed said, as he drove leisurely and we talked basketball. When he stopped for lunch, I started to worry, and when we hit heavy traffic outside of Annville, I began to sweat. An hour before game time, we weren't even close.

We arrived 20 minutes before tipoff. The gym was packed. This was a big rivalry, and fans had also come to watch Lebanon Valley's All-American Don Johnson, who averaged 25 points per game and was drafted by the ABA's Virginia Squires.

I dragged my heavy equipment suitcase into the gym, looked up, and saw a mountain of people blocking my climb to the broadcast table in the top row. Sensing my dilemma, a front-row fan said, "We'll pass you to the top and then we'll send up your suitcase."

I lay down and stiffened my body, like a corpse. Each row of fans passed me to the row behind them, all the way to the top, and as promised, my suitcase also arrived. I plugged in my equipment, tested the phone line, and got on the air minutes before tipoff. Ed Gebhart walked up, sipping coffee. "Well partner, I told you we'd get here on time." I wanted to strangle him. To make matters worse, Lebanon Valley beat Widener 78–66.

By 1972, Coach Bill Manlove had built Widener's football program into a small-college dynasty, led by running back Billy "White Shoes" Johnson, a 5'-9" dynamo who ran a 4.3 forty, could dunk a basketball, paralyzed defenses, and pioneered the end zone dance. As a sophomore against Drexel, Johnson accepted his teammates' dare to dance if he scored a touchdown. Touchdowns weren't a problem. He scored 62 in his college career. Inspired by soul singer Rufus Thomas' "Funky Chicken," when Johnson scored, he went to a corner of the end zone, put his hands on his knees, and swayed back and forth as he held the football aloft.

Billy "White Shoes" Johnson's touchdown dance (photo courtesy of Widener College)

At Dr. Watson's pub in Philly, I talked sports with big-time columnists Dicky Weiss of the *Philadelphia Daily News* and Jim Barniak of the *Philadelphia Bulletin*, who ranted about the Phillies, Eagles, and Sixers, while I mumbled into my beer about Billy "White Shoes" Johnson.

"I'm tired of hearing about 'White Shoes,'" Jim Barniak said, after double-figure Rolling Rocks. "Nobody is that good, but I need a column." On a crisp fall afternoon, I made sure Jim Barniak had a program, hot dog, Coke, and the best seat in the press

Billy Johnson as a Houston Oiler
(photo courtesy Houston Oilers)

box. Billy Johnson ripped off two long runs. Then, on a sweep right, he dropped the handoff but without breaking stride wrenched his body sideways, caught the ball as it bounced off the turf, and raced for a 19-yard touchdown. But that incredible move set off back spasms, and Johnson, aided by the trainer, walked painfully down the hill to the locker room.

Jim Barniak rolled his eyes and closed his steno pad. I hoped Billy Johnson would return and had to keep Barniak there, so I asked him to be my halftime guest, bribing him with two gift certificates for hoagies, instead of one. As the third quarter ended, still no Billy Johnson. As Jim closed his briefcase and stood up to leave, the crowd roared and the stadium shook as Billy Johnson limped over the hill toward the field. Jim sat down.

As the fourth quarter began, Billy Johnson jogged in place. As he entered the huddle, the crowd went berserk. After a couple of five-yard runs, "Johnson takes the handoff and runs to his right," I told WEEZ listeners, "He hurdles a tackler, cuts back to his left, to the sideline. Nobody will catch him. He's to the 30, the 20, the 10. Touchdown. An amazing 75-yard run!" A few plays later Johnson caught a screen pass, ran 54 yards to the 1, and then dove into the end zone for the clinching touchdown. On 17 carries Johnson ran for 201 yards and three touchdowns as Widener rallied to beat Swarthmore 21–8. Jim Barniak wrote a glowing column, and KYW-TV sportscaster "Big Al" Meltzer produced a feature about White Shoes, who was suddenly a national story.

After a stellar final season in 1973, Billy Johnson left Widener with 22 school records and 9 NCAA marks. Despite Houston's general manager Sid Gillman saying, "We don't want to draft a midget," the Oilers took Johnson in the 15th round of the 1974 NFL Draft. After his first touchdown and end zone dance, the Oilers rookie approached the sideline. "Son, if you keep scorin' touchdowns," drawled Coach Bum Phillips, "you can dance all you want."

White Shoes danced for 14 NFL seasons plus two more in Canada. He scored 35 NFL touchdowns, eight of them on kick returns, was named to the NFL's 75th Anniversary All-Time Team as a punt returner, and was inducted into the College Football Hall of Fame. Billy "White Shoes" Johnson is still the most exciting college football player I've ever seen.

I became a regular at Big Five Conference luncheons and at Phillies, Eagles, Flyers, and 76'ers games. With a talk show, sports reports, and high school and college games, I was getting a cram course in broadcasting. Fun, yes, but I was just a Mike Schmidt homer away from four pro teams and was still working for a 5,000-watt radio station. I needed a vacation. Little did I know that it would change my life.

KGMB Radio, 1973 (photo courtesy KGMB Radio)

Chapter 4
Aloha from Hawaii

In *Broadcasting* magazine, I read that Honolulu radio station KGMB had acquired broadcast rights for high school football, and the article mentioned station general manager Earl McDaniel, to whom I sent a resume and tape of my work. No answer. I decided to vacation in Hawaii anyway. After checking into a Waikiki hotel, I called McDaniel, who apologized for not answering my letter and invited me to KGMB.

Since I hadn't expected a job interview, I left my blue blazer in Philly, instead wearing my disco outfit: a red and white checked sport coat, red bow tie, pink shirt, red bell-bottoms, and red platform shoes, with hair almost to my shoulders. Earl McDaniel wore an expensive Aloha shirt, white slacks, shined shoes, and a Rolex watch. I felt like an idiot. After lunch, Earl took me to KGMB-TV to meet Gene Erger, an Abe Lincoln lookalike and general manager of Channel 9.

Earl and Gene explained that broadcasting in Hawaii presented a unique challenge because of the different ethnic groups: Hawaiians, Japanese, Chinese, Samoans, Tongans, Filipinos, Portuguese, Caucasians, and African Americans. Wondering if I could handle the diverse pronunciations, they asked me to do a mock high school football broadcast the next day. I went to one of the many ABC Stores in Waikiki and bought a Hawaiian pronunciation guide. I holed up in my hotel room, opened the phone book, and spent all night pronouncing name after name. I fell asleep on "Shimabuku."

The next morning at KGMB's studio, Earl McDaniel handed me a script. I sat down in front of a microphone, put on a headset, took a deep breath, and read, "Punahou's ball, third-and-5 at Iolani's 35-yard line. Handoff to Rocky Borges. He runs over Nakamura and Chun and is brought down by Rezentes and Kaloia. Red Raiders' coach Eddie Hamada sends in three subs, Rocky Ah Yat, Brendan Ta'amu, and Kaena Penesa." I kicked ass. After 15 minutes of pronouncing every name from Ane to Zulu, I pictured the crowd cheering and the judges holding up 10s.

But as I came out of the booth, neither Earl nor Gene looked at me. Finally, Gene said, "I'm sorry Mel . . ."

Fuck.

"Just kidding, you're hired."

Earl McDaniel hugged me and took me to dinner at the Ilikai Hotel. Earl said he'd hired me because "anybody who has the balls to show up wearing that outfit you wore has to be good." After cocktails, Earl slid down the rubber banister on the hotel escalator, yelling, "Aloha, Mel Proctor, welcome to Hawaii!" How could you not love a boss like that?

Earl McDaniel was more than a boss. For nearly 40 years he's been my friend, mentor, cheerleader, and psychiatrist. Tall and imposing, with a strong handshake, warm smile, and boundless enthusiasm, Earl had been a big-time disc jockey in L.A. and a TV sportscaster in Hawaii before becoming a management guru. "My job is to create the perfect atmosphere for talented people like you to succeed," Earl said. He also told my wife Julie to "put aside 10 percent of every check," because everyone hits hard times in this business. Thank God for Earl's advice.

Mosi Tatupu (photo courtesy of Hawaii Sports Hall of Fame)

Earl started me off broadcasting high school football for the ILH, the private schools, and for the OIA, the public schools on Oahu. High school football games regularly drew more than 20,000 fans at Honolulu Stadium. In one of my first broadcasts, Mosi Tatupu, Punahou's 220-pound, manchild Samoan running back, took the opening kickoff and, at full speed, flattened a St. Louis High tackler and ran for a touchdown. Mosi Tatupu shattered every Hawaii high school record, became a star at USC, and then enjoyed a 15-year NFL career.

I thought I'd handled pronunciations well, until Lavender Lealaitafea, a Kahuku High School running back, seemed to carry the ball on every down. I was proud that I hadn't mangled his name, enunciating "lay-a-lie-ta-fay-ah" every time.

"Hello, KGMB sports," I said, answering the phone after the broadcast.

"Hey brah, da way you say Lavender Lealaitafea means *soft shit* in Samoan," said a tribal chieftain. Eh tanks brah.

I was having a ball but was broke. I couldn't afford a car so I borrowed a bicycle, pedaled to Holiday Mart, and bought a futon to sleep on and some pineapples, since they were on sale. Forget the Pineapple Diet. Canker sores don't help a single guy in Waikiki. Feeling sorry for me, several KGMB secretaries helped me break in the futon.

I saw Gene Erger in the hallway at KGMB. "Gene, I can't make it on $750 a month."

"Do you deserve more?" he asked, as he kept walking.

"Yes."

"I agree," he yelled, over his shoulder. "We'll give you $1,000 a month."

With more money came more work. As sideline reporter on KGMB's radio broadcasts of University of Hawaii football, when I had an injury update or a story, I'd wave my arms, trying to catch the attention of play-by-play announcer Joe Moore. Sometimes Joe saw me, sometimes he didn't. Fans started chanting, "Hey Joe," and finally one made a huge "Hey Joe" sign, which I held up when I needed airtime. The next year I became the radio play-by-play announcer for both UH football and basketball.

UH Rainbow basketball had become enormously popular in the 1970s, thanks to the "Fabulous Five." Coach Red Rocha and assistant Bruce O'Neil recruited junior college stars Bob Nash, Dwight Holiday, Al Davis, and Jerome "Hook" Freeman to go with Air Force vet John Penebacker. "The Fab Five" went 47–8 the next two years and received an NIT invitation in 1971 and the school's first NCAA tournament bid in 1972. Wearing

UH coach Bruce O'Neil (photo courtesy University of Hawaii)

green and white floral-print shorts and averaging 91 points per game, the Rainbows forced sports fans nationwide to notice that there was more to Hawaii than Don Ho.

After the Fab Five left, the Rainbows went 16–10 and UH fired Red Rocha and made his assistant, 30-year-old Bruce O'Neil, the youngest head coach in the nation. Tall, blonde, and handsome, O'Neil wore colorful Hawaiian shirts and puka shell necklaces. Since high school basketball was weak in the Hawaiian Islands, O'Neil imported players from another island, Manhattan.

The New York pipeline delivered All-American guard Tom Henderson, a 1972 Olympian, who led the Rainbows to a 19–9 record and an NIT berth in O'Neil's first year. One of O'Neil's New York connections asked him to take forward Keith Bowman, a two-time high school All-American and junior college dropout. Bowman's skills had eroded after he was shot multiple times and left for dead on a New York street corner, a drug deal gone bad.

Interviewing University of Hawaii All-American Tom Henderson (photo courtesy of Mel Proctor)

"Bowman, head injury, officers on the way," I heard on KGMB's police scanner, as I prepared for the Sunday night sports. I called HPD and was told it wasn't Keith Bowman but a Kent Bowman who'd been injured. The next day as we met at Honolulu Airport to begin a road trip, Keith Bowman arrived with a bandaged head.

"Keith, what happened?" I asked.

"Oh, I passed out last night and hit my head on a coffee table."

"Did you see a doctor?"

"Yes."

"What'd he say?"

"He said it was either epilepsy or a brain tumor." Bowman played in 27 of the Rainbows' 28 games.

At practice the 6'-8" Bowman and 5'-6" Victor Kelly got into a fight. After they were separated, Bowman left but returned with a baseball bat and chased Kelly around Klum Gym. Fortunately Kelly was faster.

For the second time in school history, Hawaii was invited to the NIT. The Rainbows beat Fairfield but then were eliminated by Purdue. After the game, Bruce O'Neil asked me to join him at P.J. Clarke's restaurant to meet basketball guru Howie Garfinkel, founder of the Five-Star Basketball Camps, along with one of his protégés who wanted to coach.

"Bruce, I'd like you to meet Rick Pitino," Garf said. "He was a point guard at UMass." I watched as Pitino sold himself; he was personable, street-smart, and loved basketball. Bruce hired him as a graduate assistant, the first rung on Pitino's ladder to a celebrated coaching career.

Rick Pitino (photo courtesy University of Hawaii)

The bidding war for UH basketball television rights was fierce, and in 1974 KGMB-TV won, offering nearly $100,000. Earl McDaniel, who'd become GM of Channel 9,

UNIVERSITY OF HAWAII
RAINBOW
BASKETBALL
AT HOME AND AWAY ON
KGMB-TV 9

KGMB Television brings Hawaii the entire season of Rainbow Basketball games, in town and on the road.

HAWAII'S FINEST SPORTS
PRODUCTION TEAM IS AT KGMB-TV!

KGMB Production teams have been responsible for:
• The Hula Bowl
• The Hawaiian Open Golf Tournament
• Championship Boxing
• Sports Satellite feeds from around the world
• Major Independent College Football

HAWAII IS KGMB-TV

YOUR BROADCAST CONTACT IN HAWAII IS KGMB-TV
Phone (808) 941-2011
P. O. Box 581 · Honolulu, Hawaii 96809

9kgmbtv

Photo courtesy KGMB-TV

poked his head into my office and said, "Let's go." Recalling his sometimes acrimonious negotiations with UH and ever the showman, Earl was going to pay in cash, to the penny. I followed Earl, who was carrying a bulging money bag, as he boldly walked up to a UH secretary, announced our arrival, and emptied the bag. Stacks and stacks of long green landed on her desk, and coins spilled onto the floor. "Come out here now," the girl shouted to her boss on the intercom.

Earl and I laughed and high-fived all the way back to KGMB. Then Earl said, "By the way Mel, you'll be the TV announcer for UH basketball this year." Wow. Rainbow basketball was the hottest show in town. Home games sold out, and UH basketball was the highest-rated show on TV, eclipsing even *Hawaii 5-0*.

Although Tom Henderson was gone, the first-round pick of the Atlanta Hawks, the 1974–75 Rainbows returned 6'-9" Melton Werts, joined on the front line by 7-footer Tommy Barker and 6'-9" Jimmy "Bad Boy" Baker.

Jimmy Baker came to Hawaii in the first trade in college basketball history. Baker had starred for two years at UNLV, playing for Jerry Tarkanian. Although Baker averaged 19 points and 10 rebounds, he'd fallen out of favor with Tark the Shark.

Boyd Batts, a 6'-6" forward who liked his steaks "well, well, well done with lots of ketchup," had averaged 13 points a game his first year at Hawaii but was on the verge of being declared ineligible.

So, Bruce O'Neil and Jerry Tarkanian made a trade: Jimmy Baker for Boyd Batts. Since Hawaii and UNLV were independents and not subject to conference rules requiring transfers to sit out a year, both played immediately for their new schools.

How the hell was Bruce O'Neil luring top players to Hawaii, wondered many big-time coaches. At that time, recruits were allowed unlimited visits, and who didn't want a free trip to paradise? UH got a lot of publicity when high school All-American Moses Malone visited, although O'Neil knew Malone had no intention of playing for the Rainbows.

The capper was Tommy Barker, who played one year at Minnesota and then was a JC All-American at Southern Idaho. North Carolina State head coach Jim Valvano was sure he had Barker wrapped up, and Jimmy V was incensed when Barker forsook Tobacco Road for Waikiki Beach.

Guard Victor "Tiny" Kelly, a 5'-6" New Yorker, had also been a JC All-American at Southern Idaho after leaving USC. Freshman Henry Hollingsworth, still another New Yorker, joined Kelly in the backcourt. In one of the best performances I've ever seen, Victor Kelly went under, over, and around 7'-1" All-American center Robert Parish to score 26 points as Hawaii upset Centenary 79–78.

With the Boston Celtics, Robert Parish, Larry Bird, and Kevin McHale formed the greatest front line in NBA history, winning three NBA titles. Parish, "the Chief," was selected as one of the 50 greatest players of all-time and was inducted into the Hall of Fame.

Tommy Barker (photo courtesy University of Hawaii)

Reggie Carter (photo courtesy University of Hawaii)

Victor Kelly was a 10th-round pick of the Atlanta Hawks but didn't make the team. The Harlem Globetrotters wanted Kelly, but he only wanted to play "serious" basketball.

Jimmy Baker was a first-round pick of the ABA's Kentucky Colonels and a third-round pick by the Philadelphia 76'ers.

After the Rainbows finished a disappointing 16–11 season, Baker came to KGMB to say goodbye; his grandmother had died and he was flying home to Philadelphia. We shook hands and hugged, and then Baker said, "Oh Mel, can you loan me 20 bucks to help with airfare?" "Bad Boy" hit up half of Oahu for $20, and a teammate said this was Baker's fifth grandmother who'd passed away.

In 1975–76, Rick Pitino became a full-time assistant, in charge of recruiting. Pete Gillen and Al Menendez, two successful New York high school coaches, joined Bruce O'Neil's staff.

With their tentacles firmly imbedded in New York, the Rainbows extracted high school All-Americans Reggie Carter and George Lett. With Carter and Lett joining Tommy Barker, Melton Werts, and Henry Hollingsworth, this looked like the best team in Hawaii's history.

The Rainbows won their first four games and then hosted the 12th-ranked University of San Francisco Dons, with future NBA players Winford Boynes, James Hardy, and 7-footer Bill Cartwright, who played on three Chicago Bulls NBA championship teams.

Before the first of two games, I went to USF's shootaround. Coach Bob Gaillard told his players to double-team Reggie Carter and not worry about Henry Hollingsworth, who he said wasn't a good shooter. Are you kidding me? Henry H was a great standstill shooter. I'm assuming the statute of limitations for basketball espionage has expired because I revealed USF's game plan to Bruce O'Neil.

Henry Hollingsworth scored 24 points, Reggie Carter set a school record with 19 assists, and Hawaii won, 81–80. USF bounced back the next night to win a double-overtime thriller, 105–103.

The Rainbows were 7–3 and ranked in the top 20 as we began the first road trip at Arizona State. Then, KGMB-TV's owner Cec Heftel called and told me that four UH players had appeared in a commercial for Cutter Ford, a violation of NCAA rules. Although the players weren't paid or named in the commercial, it was still a violation. Henry Hollingsworth, the only starter, and reserves Gary Gray, George Ritter, and David Knight were suspended and became known as "the Cutter Four."

Hoping to minimize the damage, Heftel dictated every question and told me to interview Bruce O'Neil at a Phoenix TV station. But it was too late. The Cutter Ford commercial focused media attention on the UH basketball program. Under the dark cloud of an NCAA investigation, the Rainbows lost all five games on the road trip.

UH fired Bruce O'Neil. We eased our pain at a downtown bar. As we stumbled out, I pulled a *Honolulu Star Bulletin* out of the newspaper rack. Bruce's picture was on the front page, his firing the headline. Rick Pitino became interim coach and went 2–4. The Rainbows finished the season 11–16.

Pitino left to become an assistant at Syracuse and then became head coach at Boston University, Providence, and Kentucky, where he won an NCAA championship in 1996. Pitino is the only coach in history to take three different teams to the Final Four. Pitino also coached the New York Knicks and Boston Celtics in the NBA. After an unsuccessful four years in Boston, he returned to college coaching at Louisville, where he's been since 2001.

Pete Gillen and Al Menendez also bailed. Gillen later became head coach at Xavier, Providence, and Virginia, and Menendez was an NBA assistant and a longtime scout for the Indiana Pacers.

Wilt Chamberlain (photo courtesy the Wilt Chamberlain collection)

Reggie Carter transferred to St. John's and George Lett to Centenary, and both had outstanding college careers. Tommy Barker was drafted by the Atlanta Hawks in the fourth round of the 1976 draft and played in the NBA for five years.

Centenary's coach Larry Little, a friend of Bruce O'Neil's, replaced Bruce as coach. The two-year NCAA probation crippled the UH basketball program. In 1977–78, the Rainbows were 1–26 and lost their last 22 games. Since I played on a Colorado College team that won its first game and then lost 19 straight, I was the right guy to announce the games.

Hawaii was a celebrity haven. Wilt Chamberlain owned a Waikiki apartment, befriended Bruce O'Neil, and played basketball at Klum Gym. At night, the Dipper dipped in discos, especially Rex and Eric's. The best-looking women, all "10s," waited in line to hand their phone numbers to Wilt. It became ridiculous. The local disco kings were pissed, and a couple of "Big Buggahs" warned Wilt to tone down his act. Wilt claimed he made love to 20,000 women. I can't vouch for 19,999 of them, but Wilt did do the deed in my apartment one night. I considered mounting a plaque on the wall, "Wilt Chamberlain scored here," hoping it would increase the apartment's value.

O. J. Simpson had won the 1975 Superstars, an ABC Sports all-around competition resembling a decathlon, and returned to Hawaii as an ABC commentator. Track and field competition was held at Punahou School, and between events, us local media types, including some fine-looking wahines (Hawaiian for *women*), sat in a circle on the football field "talking story." O. J. joined us. When my contact lens popped out, disappearing into the long grass, I was on all fours, crawling around, looking for it. A couple of the girls joined the search and then O. J. Simpson was on his hands and knees. Are you kidding? A Heisman Trophy winner, Hall of Famer, movie star, trying to help the common man?

"Found it," O. J. said proudly, holding up his index finger with my lens resting on it.

"O. J., thank you," I said, retrieving the lost lens. "That was really nice of you."

"What? That was yours?"

"Yes, Juice, thanks again."

"Ah shit, I thought it was hers," he said, pointing to one of the girls. Disgusted, he walked away, muttering, "It was the dude's lens, Juice. Come on O. J, what are you doing? Damn ..."

Bill Bradley was my idol, an All-American, College Player of the Year, Rhodes Scholar, and member of two New York Knicks championship teams. Bradley was part of a group of NBA players coming to Honolulu for an exhibition game. My cameraman and I waited on the airport tarmac as Bradley disembarked.

"Bill, Mel Proctor from KGMB-TV," I said. "How about an interview?"

My idol kept walking and over his shoulder said, "It's been a long flight, I'm tired and boring. Talk to Don Nelson."

Shit. Bill Bradley had blown me off. I interviewed other players but was still pissed, when after the exhibition game, I went to Nick's Fishmarket.

Bill Bradley sat at the bar. He saw me. "Aren't you the guy from the airport?"

"Yes, and when I asked you to do an interview, you blew me off."

"Sit down," Bradley said, pointing to an empty bar stool. For two hours, I shared beer and conversation with Bill Bradley, discussing everything from basketball to politics.

Years later, when I was the New Jersey Nets' announcer, Bradley was running for the Senate and was in the Meadowlands parking lot, shaking hands, talking to people

Joey Heatherton (photo courtesy fanpix.net)

and trying to win votes. As I approached, he yelled, "Mel Proctor, voice of the New Jersey Nets. I remember you from Hawaii. I listen to the Nets' games. You're doing a great job."

Singer-dancer-actress Joey Heatherton was a star in the 1970s, best remembered for her sexy Serta Mattress commercials. The sultry blonde was in Hawaii for a performance, and KGMB-TV reporter Linda Coble did a feature on her. That night, Linda and anchor Tim Tindall invited me to meet them at Rex and Eric's. I walked in and joined Tim at the bar. "Where's Linda?" I asked.

Tim pointed to a table where Linda Coble visited with Joey Heatherton. When Linda returned to the bar, she said, "Joey thinks you're cute and wants to meet you."

"Right Linda," I said.

Several beers later, Linda convinced me that Joey Heatherton was serious. I stood up, threw back my shoulders, puffed out my chest, sucked in my stomach, and macho-walked to Joey Heatherton's table. She was in the midst of telling a joke, so I knelt next to her chair.

As Joey delivered the punch line, her friends obligingly laughed, but the smile slid off her face as she looked down at me. "What the fuck do you want?"

I babbled something about Linda Coble, KGMB-TV, the feature, but then I saw Linda and Tim at the bar, convulsed in laughter. I'd been had. I sheepishly apologized and slinked away as someone muttered, "asshole."

I also made my acting debut, playing a tour guide in an episode of *Hawaii 5-0* called "Tour de Force, Killer Aboard." I met star Jack Lord, had a scene with James McArthur, who played Danno, and had several scenes with guest star Cliff Gorman, who played the killer and became a lifelong friend. I still get residual checks, now down to about $6.00.

In 1974, pro football arrived with the Hawaiians and the World Football League. Chris Hemmeter, a Honolulu hotel developer, and Sam Battistone, owner of the Sambo's restaurant chain, were the principal owners of the Hawaiians. Mike Giddings, a San Fran-cisco 49'ers assistant, was named head coach and brought with him former 49'ers All-Pros Matt Hazel-tine and Billy Wilson. Bob Schloredt, the legendary one-eyed quarterback from the University of Washing-ton, was on staff along with former USC assistants Damon Bame and Marv Marinovich.

With Hawaii 5-0 *guest star Cliff Gorman (photo courtesy of Mel Proctor)*

Marinovich, who'd played at USC and with the Oakland Raiders, was a health food freak who brought bags of fruits, nuts, and vegetables on flights. Today, he's best known as the father of "Robo Quarterback" Todd Marinovich. When Todd was born, Marv programmed his son to be a quarterback: no candy bars, no junk food, stretching while still in the crib, weight lifting after a diaper change, push-ups at age three, a four-mile run at four. The best high school quarterback in America and a star at USC, Todd Marinovich left college early to join the Raiders, but drug addiction destroyed his career.

To drum up publicity, the Hawaiians held a tryout camp at the University of Hawaii. Lawyers, doctors, dentists, teamsters, ex-cons, and anybody who'd ever played football— from Pop Warner to the pros—showed up.

The team didn't expect to find any prospects, but when 6'-4", 250-pound Karl Lorch won every 40-yard dash, the coaches stared in disbelief at their stopwatches. A local kid, Lorch had starred at Kamehameha School, played at USC, and was drafted by the Miami Dolphins. Homesick, he came back to Hawaii. Lorch was the only player signed out of the tryout camp.

Karl Lorch (L), Levi Stanley, Ron East, and Lem Burnham (R) (photo courtesy of WFL)

After the WFL folded in 1975, Lorch spent six years with the Washington Redskins and is still a legend in the nation's capital, remembered more for his dietary choices than his career. On a Monday night talk show from the Dancing Crab Restaurant, sportscasters Glenn Brenner and Sonny Jurgensen interviewed Lorch and teammates John Riggins and Coy Bacon. As they talked football, Lorch reached into a tank of water, pulled out a live crab, and ate it. Big, tough Coy Bacon ran to the restroom and threw up. Although Karl Lorch returned to Hawaii, he's still part of Redskins lore.

In brutal summer heat and smog, the Hawaiians trained at the University of California at Riverside. Players stayed cool by dipping into a wealthy divorcee's swimming pool. If I needed an interview, I went poolside.

When camp ended, we flew cross-country to open the WFL season against the Florida Blazers. As our bus arrived, workers had just finished welding in the goal posts and rewiring the Tangerine Bowl scoreboard. Only 18,625 showed up as the Blazers won, 8–7.

Then we flew to Anaheim where the Southern California Sun thumped the Hawaiians, 38–31.

After seven weeks and 12,000 miles of travel, we finally flew home. On a cold, rainy night, maybe 5,000 fans showed up at Honolulu Stadium for the home opener. Rookie quarterback Norris Weese threw two touchdown passes in a 36–16 victory over the Detroit Wheels.

Coin toss before the first home game (photo courtesy of WFL)

Trainer George Kamau was the Hawaiians' biggest cheerleader. When the other team had the ball, George stalked the sideline yelling, "Watch out for da run. Watch out for da pass. Watch out for da screen. Oh, watch out for everyting."

After the Chicago Fire scorched them, 53–29, the Hawaiians embarked on a grueling three-game road trip to Jacksonville, Birmingham, and Memphis. After losing in Jacksonville, the team had an off night in Birmingham, and my friend, defensive end Lem Burnham, and I agreed to meet for dinner. I sat at the hotel bar nursing a beer. "How ya'll doin'?" I turned and saw a bulbous red nose; attached to it

Hawaiians' cheerleaders (photo courtesy of WFL)

was a guy wearing a red University of Alabama baseball cap, tipped back on his head, with a toothpick between his teeth. "What brings y'all to Birmin'ham?"

I said I was there for a WFL game between the Hawaiians and Birmingham Americans. We shot the shit over a beer, and then this cracker asked, "How many nigguhs y'all 'ave on your team?"

Just then, Lem Burnham, a 6'-4", 240-pound ex-marine, sat down next to me.

"I guess you didn't hear me," repeated Rudolph the Red Nosed Bigot. "How many nigguhs y'all 'ave?"

"I don't know, ask him," I said, leaning back so he could see Lem. I walked away, covering my mouth to stifle laughter.

Within five minutes, Lem and the redneck became buddies, patting each other on the back and swapping jokes. No wonder my friend became Dr. Lem Burnham, psychologist and eventually vice president of player development for the NFL.

After a game, when the media asked about his team's performance, the perpetually tan and always smiling coach Mike Giddings said, "We won't know until we watch the game film." When the Birmingham Americans blitzed the Hawaiians 39–0, Giddings didn't need to see film. He blew off reporters, and assistant Matt Hazeltine told the media, "We'll make some changes."

In the final game of the trip, former Heisman Trophy winner John Huarte threw four touchdown passes in the first half as the Memphis Southmen won, 60–8. The Hawaiians were 1–6 and had been outscored 99–8 in two games. Despite the Hawaiians' pitiful start, whenever George Najarian, the team's director of player personnel, saw me, he gave me two thumbs up, a goofy grin, and said, "Stay positive."

WFL teams had signed many NFL stars to future contracts for 1975. The Hawaiians big catch was Calvin Hill, the former running back with the Dallas Cowboys and Washington Redskins. Midway through the WFL's 1974 season, NFL teams started releasing these "lame ducks." On the flight from Memphis, Mike Giddings and his staff stood in the aisle and talked all night. George Najarian waved his address book, shouted players' names, and circled phone numbers. The Hawaiians were about to undergo a facelift.

After losing two of their next three, the Hawaiians were 2–8—last place—but then added quarterbacks Randy Johnson and Edd Hargett, running back Vince Clements, and defensive backs Willie Williams and Otto Brown, all released by the New York Giants. Linebackers Jim Sniadecki, Dave Olerich, and wide receiver John Isenbarger were let go by the 49'ers, and defensive back Chuck Detwiler was cut by the Cardinals. The WFL's youngest team added badly needed experience.

I was a juggler, keeping track of daily roster changes and updating my spotting boards. Working by myself, I was play-by-play announcer and analyst. Although I felt like a split personality, I became a better announcer as I learned the intricacies of pro football.

In Houston, Edd Hargett threw two touchdown passes, Derrick Williams returned a kickoff 80 yards for a touchdown, and the Hawaiians beat the Texans, 33–15.

We returned to Oahu for three straight home games. Before the game against the New York Stars, Hawaiians kicker R. A. Coppedge dropped his only pair of eyeglasses on the locker room floor, and a 250-pound teammate's foot turned them into ground glass. Sure enough, Coppedge was called on to kick a game-winning field goal. Squinting as he lined up, Coppedge kicked the ball. "I couldn't see a thing without my glasses," he said. "I didn't know it was good until I heard the crowd." The Hawaiians won, 17–14.

A week later, the Philadelphia Bell intercepted four passes and beat the Hawaiians, 21–16. The Hawaiians were 4–9, but as new players became acclimated, the team began to jell. Randy Johnson connected on 10–19 passes and led two long scoring drives as the Hawaiians upset Birmingham 14–8, avenging an earlier 39–0 loss to the Americans.

Then it was back on the road as the inhumane schedule continued. At 100,000-seat JFK Stadium, longtime home of the Army-Navy game, the Hawaiians upset Philadelphia, 25–22.

Despite new glasses, in Portland, R. A. Coppedge missed four field-goal attempts, but the Storm's Booth Lusteg connected on a 37-yarder as Portland won, 3–0.In Chicago, Randy Johnson threw four touchdown passes in a 60–17 Hawaiians win.

The *Honolulu Advertiser* claimed the Hawaiians lost $200,000 every home game, and team owners said they needed an average attendance of 25,000 per game to break even. Attendance of 11,000 a game wasn't cutting it.

The entire WFL was headed for a slip next to the Titanic. The New York Stars moved to Charlotte. Detroit and Jacksonville filed for bankruptcy, and Chicago eventually folded. There was strong sentiment to end the season after 17 games and declare the Memphis Southmen champions.

Instead, the league reduced the number of playoff teams from eight to six and announced that besides divisional winners, the two teams with the best second-half records would also make the playoffs. Although 7–10 overall, the Hawaiians were 3–1 in the second half to enter the playoff picture.

The largest home crowd of the season, 20,544, celebrated Halloween and "10 cent beer night" at Honolulu Stadium, but Memphis won, 33–31.

The next week, Randy Johnson completed 17 of 30 passes for 259 yards and two touchdowns in a 29–8 romp over the Southern California Sun.

At Honolulu Stadium, the Hawaiians shut out the Portland Storm, 23–0. During the game a fight broke out. As players slugged it out, Mike Giddings ran onto the field yelling, "Whoever isn't back on the sideline in five seconds is going to be fined!"

"Fined? You're kidding. We're all broke," shouted a player, as everyone started laughing so hard they stopped fighting.

The Hawaiians finished the regular season 9–11 and 5–2 in the second half, putting them in the playoffs against the Southern California Sun in Anaheim. Claiming they hadn't been paid, three of the Sun's best players, running backs Kermit Johnson and James McAlister and offensive lineman Booker Brown, boycotted the game. Weakened by the players' absence and low morale, Southern California was no match for the Hawaiians. Randy Johnson shredded the Sun defense, completing 14 of 24 passes for 148 yards and two touchdowns as Hawaii advanced with a 32–14 win.

Next, a road game against the Birmingham Americans. Birmingham had thrashed the Hawaiians at home 39–0 earlier in the season, but the Hawaiians, fortified by ex-NFL'ers, had won in Honolulu, 14–8.

Birmingham rushed for over 300 yards and ended the Hawaiians' season, 22–19. The Americans went on to win the first WFL championship by beating Florida. Three Hawaiians players were named to the WFL's all-time team: wide receiver Tim Delaney, a super-glue-fingered pass catcher who had 132 receptions in two years, guard John Wilbur, and defensive tackle Karl Lorch. The WFL folded after the 1975 season, the same year I accepted a new challenge.

Tim Delaney, #82, led the WFL in receptions (photo courtesy of WFL)

Photo courtesy of Mel Proctor

Chapter 5
The Hawaii Islanders

In 1975 Jack Quinn, president of the Hawaii Islanders baseball team, hired me to do play-by-play for the San Diego Padres' AAA affiliate. I drove to empty Honolulu Stadium one night, climbed the stairs to the broadcast booth, sat in the dark, and imagined following former Islanders announcers Harry Kalas and Al Michaels to the big leagues.

The Islanders invested a lot of money and effort into ticket promotion and advertising, assuming they'd be moving to new Aloha Stadium. But in December 1974, the state announced that the new stadium wouldn't be finished until late summer 1975, at the earliest, and Honolulu Stadium's owners planned to close the old park. The Islanders had no place to play. Finally, the team and state signed a lease, enabling the Islanders to play the 1975 season at Honolulu Stadium.

Undaunted by the distractions, Jack Quinn signed big-league veterans, including pitchers Jerry Johnson, Jim Shellenback, and Frank Linzy; infielders Sonny Jackson and Carmen Fanzone; and outfielder Jim Fairey. Roy Hartsfield had a strong nucleus as he began his third year as Islanders skipper.

On the last day of spring training, the Padres had left camp in Yuma, Arizona, to begin the 1975 National League season, and most of the AAA players were headed home. The few remaining Islanders played an intrasquad game. Since we weren't broadcasting, manager Roy Hartsfield let me sit in the dugout with him and pitcher Jerry Johnson, the only extra player.

Islanders manager Roy Hartsfield (photo by Leonard Nakahashi)

In the sixth inning, a pitcher got wild and began walking hitters. "Shit, J. J., get warm," Hartsfield grumbled, looking around for someone to warm up Johnson. All of the available players were in the game.

"Roy, I'll warm up J. J.," I said, grabbing a catcher's mitt and mask. "I played college baseball. No problem."

"Do you have a cup?" Roy asked.

"Roy, the only cup I've had was a cup of beer last night in the bar." I knew Roy meant a plastic protective cup.

Roy thought for a moment and then said, "Podnah, go ahead but be careful."

I ran to the bullpen wearing the perfect catcher's outfit: a short-sleeved Izod shirt, Dockers, and penny loafers. Jerry and I played catch until he got loose. "You ready?" he asked, toeing the pitcher's rubber.

I tightened my shin guards, pulled the catcher's mask over my face, and crouched. *Pow, pow, pow.* I loved the sound as J. J. buried fastballs into the pocket of my catcher's mitt. When the popping began to sound like Orville Redenbacher's popcorn, my thumb began to throb.

"You okay?" Roy Hartsfield asked.

"No problem skip. J. J. throw the damn ball."

He pounded my mitt with more fastballs. My hand felt like hamburger. As I removed the catcher's mitt and shook my hand, J. J. covered his face with his glove. In the dugout, Roy Hartsfield turned away.

"Are you okay?" asked J. J.

I punched my fist into the mitt. "J. J., is that the best shit you've got?"

J. J. flicked his glove, indicating he was going to throw sliders. The first one hit in front of the plate and nailed me on the thigh. I took pitches off my ankles and knees. I was hurting, but I wasn't going to quit. Finally, one of J. J.'s sliders dove into the dirt, bounced up, and hit me squarely in the balls.

"I'm ready," J. J. said.

"Nice job, rookie," said Roy.

As J. J. ran to the mound, I slipped ice cubes down my pants to soothe my pulsating testicles. In my hotel room, I iced my knees, ankles, and thumb.

Jerry Johnson and I became friends. Years later, sitting at the bar at Bully's in Del Mar, J. J. said, "I've never told you this, but that day I wasn't really throwing as hard as I could."

"J. J., you son of a bitch."

Located in the Moi'ili'ili district at the corner of King and Isenberg streets, Honolulu Stadium was known as "the Termite Palace" because the pests had eaten away at the wooden structure since it was built in 1926.

Where else could you find saimin, boiled peanuts, and corn on the cob at the concession stands? The Columbia Inn restaurant sponsored a sign in right field with a puka, or hole, in it. If a player hit a home run through the puka, he received a thousand dollars. Only the Islanders' Walt "No Neck" Williams accomplished the feat in 1968. In the crowd, men wore Aloha shirts and women, colorful muumuus. "The Manoa mist," a light rain, fell on Honolulu Stadium in late afternoon, and fans either brought hats or fashioned them out of the just-delivered *Honolulu Star Bulletin*.

When I heard that Mickey Mantle was coming to Hawaii, I nearly pissed my pants. As it turned out, my hero pissed his. Fingers fluttering, forearms bulging, the switch-hitting Hall of Famer drove pitches deep into the Hawaii night as the crowd roared. Later, my idol joined me for an interview. Mick was hammered. I asked him a few questions, but between his

Columbia Inn puka (photo courtesy Columbia Inn)

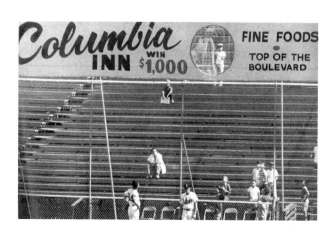

Oklahoma drawl and massive quantities of alcohol, he was unintelligible. I lost interest in getting his autograph, thanked Mickey, and watched my hero stumble down the stairs, shaking hands with fans and pausing to hit on an Islanders ballgirl. When I walked into the clubhouse after the game, Mickey leaned against a wall, passed out, a dark spot circling his crotch. I blinked, fighting off tears.

As Tucson Toros manager Hank Aguirre and Roy Hartsfield met at home plate to exchange lineup cards, Aguirre refused to reveal his lineup and was ejected. When the Honolulu Stadium PA announcer informed the crowd that Aguirre wouldn't announce his starting lineup, fans booed. Many of them kept score, and we needed the lineups to broadcast the game.

With Aguirre gone, player-coach Ramon Webster took over. He came to home plate wearing a batting helmet, on backward, with a piece of the bill chipped out. When the plate umpire asked him to turn his helmet around, Webster refused and got thrown out. Apparently, he and Hank Aguirre had early reservations at the best Mexican restaurant in Honolulu.

The Islanders held on to first place despite a seven-inning no-hitter by Salt Lake City's Chuck Dobson in the first game of a doubleheader at Honolulu Stadium. My first no-hitter! I grabbed my tape recorder and sprinted to the Gulls' clubhouse. Dobson was attacking the clubhouse spread, a hot dog in each hand and mustard on his face. "Chuck, Mel Proctor, Islanders announcer," I said sticking a microphone in his face. "You just pitched a no-hitter; how does it feel?"

"I don't give a shit," he said," I should have pitched in the big leagues today. The California Angels screwed me by sending me down." So much for the excitement of a no-hitter.

When the Islanders played road games, we rarely traveled, instead re-creating away games. Several major league teams did re-creations in the 1940s and 1950s, but the Islanders were the only team still doing them in the 1970s. In my first year, I worked with veteran Hank Greenwald, later the longtime voice of the San Francisco Giants.

Here's how a re-creation worked. If the Islanders were in Tucson, a sportswriter called before the game with lineups, bare facts, and play-by-play of the first three innings:

Tucson, Arizona . . . 103 degrees . . . a crowd of about 4,000 at Hi Corbett Field.

RHP Lew Krausse (4–1, 3.60 ERA) pitching for Tucson.

TOP OF THE FIRST . . . HAWAII AT BAT

Rod Gaspar . . . hit by pitch.

Sonny Jackson . . . struck out swinging. One out.

Jerry Turner . . . home run to right field. Hawaii 2, Tucson 0.

Steve Huntz . . . struck out. Two outs.

Carmen Fanzone . . . fouled out to catcher. Three outs.

Hawaii 2, Tucson 0.

Jerry Turner's home run became "Jerry Turner steps in to face veteran right-hander Lew Krausse with Rod Gaspar at first and one out. Krausse checks the runner and delivers. A high fly ball to deep right field . . . going, going, and gone. Home run! Jerry Turner has given the Islanders a 2–0 lead."

Ron Wiley, a bronzed, long-haired surfer, was our MVP, engineering games and taking phone calls from road correspondents. In the studio, Ron had a stack of cassettes, tapes of real crowds booing, cheering, and everything in between. Depending on the situation, he shoved one into the tape player.

After three innings, we waited for the next call. If the phone didn't ring, we stalled. "There's a problem with the mound. The groundskeeper has come out to fix it." Or, "Morganna the kissing bandit has run onto the field and is smooching the shortstop." Or, "The stadium lights just went out, a power failure."

When Ron Wiley gave us a thumbs-up and fresh play-by-play sheets, we'd resume our play-by-play. One time as Hank Greenwald and I sifted through the slips of paper, a half inning was missing. The top of the fifth was there but not the bottom of the fifth. We stalled as Ron phoned Tucson. No answer. Hank and I looked at each other and in unison said, "Fuck it." We went from the top of the fifth to the top of the sixth. Nobody noticed.

Another time, the Islanders were in Portland. Our reporter had made two phone calls, but with Hawaii leading 3–2 going to the bottom of the ninth, our guy never called again, probably on his second martini.

So we faked the bottom of the ninth, praying that Portland went down in order. In the morning, the *Honolulu Advertiser* reported the final score: Hawaii 3, Portland 2. Thank you, God.

By the end of July, Hawaii had opened up a 13-game lead over Tacoma and maintained their advantage into late August. As the Islanders began their final road trip, needing one win to clinch the PCL West, they lost three straight. If the Islanders were going to win the division title, they'd have to do it at home, against the Tacoma Twins.

Jim Shellenback scattered seven hits, Sonny Jackson hit a two-run double, and Steve Huntz blasted a two-run homer as Hawaii won 6–3 to clinch the PCL West. The Islanders finished 88–56 with a 14-game lead over Tacoma and faced the Eastern Division champion Salt Lake City Gulls in the finals.

With the Islanders leading the series three games to two, 7,731 fans watched the final game in Honolulu Stadium's 50-year history. Twenty-two-year-old Dave Wehrmeister shut out Salt Lake City 8–0 as the Hawaii Islanders won their first pennant in 15 years in the PCL.

I loved my work but was making little money. KGMB owner Cecil Heftel wasn't going to throw hundred dollar bills at me, so I went to see him. Making $18,000 a year, I tried to convince Cec that I was an up-and-comer, loved my work, and would stay in Hawaii forever. Always suntanned and smiling, Cec said, "Mel, guys like you are a dime a dozen. Every day I get letters from people who would work for free at KGMB. If you're not happy, go somewhere else."

Back in the newsroom, I kicked my desk and threw papers in the air. My desk was behind Joe Moore's. Joe turned around. "What's the matter?"

I explained my failed salary negotiations. Joe smiled.

"Did Cec tell you that guys like you are a dime a dozen?"

"Yes."

"Did he say he gets letters from people who'd work for free?"

"Yes."

"Welcome to the club," Joe said as he resumed typing.

Then I thought of KHON-TV. Veteran Les Keiter was Channel 2's sports director, but maybe they needed a weekend guy. I called KHON's owner George Hagar.

Over lunch, Hagar knocked me off my feet, offering me the sports director's job.

"What about Les Keiter?" I asked.

"We'll move him to weekends."

George Hagar offered a $1,000 signing bonus, a $25,000 salary with full benefits, a three-year contract, and a new car. I asked him to give me a day to think about my decision.

About to grab Channel 2's offer, I knew that I really wanted to be a play-by-play announcer for a pro team, and at KGMB, I was getting the best possible experience with UH football and basketball, Hawaii Islanders baseball, and TV sports.

With one foot in KHON's front door and the other in Cec Heftel's office, I told Cec I loved my work but couldn't turn down Channel 2's offer. He asked what KHON had offered.

After I told him, Cec said, "Come back in an hour."

"I'll match everything Channel 2 offered," Cec Heftel said as I returned to his office. "What kind of car do you want?" Heftel obviously had a spy at Channel 2 who had validated their offer.

George Hagar accused me of using him to get more money. Hell, I wasn't experienced or smart enough to know that's how the negotiation game worked. If Cec hadn't matched the offer, I would have gone to Channel 2.

The defending PCL champion Hawaii Islanders opened the 1976 season in new 50,000-seat Aloha Stadium. Jim Leahey replaced Hank Greenwald as my broadcast partner. Roy Hartsfield began his fourth year as Islanders manager and his 34th season in baseball with a veteran team loaded with characters.

Joe Pepitone as an Islander (photo by Leonard Nakahashi)

Joe Pepitone, former Yankee first baseman and playboy, attempted a comeback. Wigs and a hair dryer hung in his locker. Pepi hit the first home run in Aloha Stadium's history, but his skills had eroded, and he was making a lot of money. He was released in mid-May.

Bobby Valentine had once been a Dodgers prospect. Playing outfield for the California Angels, Valentine tried to catch a drive off the bat of Oakland's Dick Green. He raced to the warning track and planted his foot on the wall to climb higher, but his spikes caught. Snap, crackle, and pop. Done. He'd badly broken his leg, robbing him of his speed. By the time he got to the Islanders he was 27 years old and trying to return to the big leagues as a utility man.

Left-hander Jim Shellenback returned for 1976. In his first major league start, Shelly beat the Dodgers 2–1 in 11 innings. Six days later he was in a near fatal automobile accident and still limped on a misshapen right leg.

Dave Roberts had been the Padres' first-round pick in 1972 out of the University of Oregon. A great athlete, he was rushed to the big leagues as a third baseman and was back at AAA, trying to regain his confidence and become a catcher.

Jack Quinn strengthened the pitching staff, adding reliever Eddie Watt, who pitched in three World Series with the Baltimore Orioles; side-armer Chuck Hartenstein, rescued from civilian life; and 39-year-old Diego Segui, coaxed out of retirement to join prospects like left-hander Bob Shirley, an All-American at Oklahoma, and the hyperactive Mike Dupree.

Outfielder Rod Gaspar, who had played for the Miracle Mets in the 1969 World Series, began his sixth season with the Islanders.

Other prospects included Gene Richards, the Minor League Player of the Year in 1975; shortstop Bill Almon, the number-one pick in the 1974 draft; second baseman Mike Champion; and outfielder John Scott.

The tone for this bizarre season was set in May when Aloha Stadium execs said that Monsanto, makers of the AstroTurf field, had said no baseball spikes could be worn on the turf. I knew this was bullshit. There were AstroTurf fields in Houston, Philadelphia, Cincinnati, St. Louis, and Pittsburgh. The

With Islanders pitcher Chuck Hartenstein (photo by Leonard Nakahashi)

first few opponents who played at Aloha Stadium abided by the rule, wearing rubber cleats.

Then, the Islanders' archrivals, the Tacoma Twins, arrived in May. Their parent club, the Minnesota Twins, insisted that AAA players would wear spikes. Why should players wear one type of shoe in the minors and another in the majors? The Twins also felt rubber cleats contributed to injuries.

This was personal. Aloha Stadium manager Mackey Yanagisawa and Jack Quinn, once friends and co-owners of the Islanders, had become adversaries. This was "stick it to Jack" time. In the bottom of the first inning, Tacoma pitcher Bill Butler walked to the mound wearing spikes. As Butler warmed up, the umpires inspected his footwear and suggested he change. No, said the Twins. Mackey Yanagisawa had the stadium lights turned off, and the Islanders forfeited the game because, according to the rule book, the home team hadn't provided suitable playing facilities. Surely one loss wouldn't make a difference.

The next night, doing Channel 9 sports, I called Monsanto's CEO. "Those idiots," he said, referring to Aloha Stadium executives. There are no restrictions about shoes on AstroTurf. Shit, I'll call them tomorrow."

After reporting Monsanto's reaction, I ripped the Stadium Authority for their stupidity. When the newscast ended, my phone rang. "If you don't retract that story, you'll never work in Hawaii again," said someone claiming to be a member of the Stadium Authority. When I asked for his name and offered equal time, he hung up.

By July, the Islanders led Tacoma by seven games and "Spikesgate" was rarely mentioned. But then the Islanders began to win one, lose one, while Tacoma caught fire. During August, the Islanders and Twins played leapfrog for the division lead. The race on the field was nothing compared to the Islanders' challenges off the field.

Despite home attendance that would exceed 300,000, the club had serious financial problems. The IRS padlocked team offices because the Islanders owed $30,000 in back taxes. After

Islanders' president Jack Quinn is locked out by the IRS (photo by Leonard Nakahashi)

a week of negotiating, Jack Quinn convinced the IRS to reopen the doors. Then the Islanders were hit with an avalanche of lawsuits. Creditors lined up, players' paychecks bounced, and wives complained they couldn't pay grocery bills.

"No pay. No play," said Diego Segui, the team's ace pitcher with an 11–5 record, saying he was suing the team.

Despite the distractions, the Islanders hung on and on September 1 had a two-game lead with six games to play, at home against Sacramento. Tacoma had eight games left, all at home against the last-place Spokane Indians.

Hawaii and Sacramento split the first two games. Normally this would have been Diego Segui's turn to pitch, but Roy Hartsfield handed the baseball to Jim Shellenback, who hadn't won since mid-June, hadn't started in two months, and hadn't pitched at all for two weeks. Shelly allowed four hits and shut out Sacramento, 1–0.

The Islanders lost the next two games, while Tacoma won six of its first seven against Spokane, to take a one-game lead over Hawaii with one game to play.

September 6, 1976. Labor Day. Amazingly, Spokane beat Tacoma 8–7 in an afternoon game at Cheney Stadium. On their way to the gallows, the Islanders had been granted a reprieve.

That night, Hawaii hammere1d Sacramento 11–3 to tie Tacoma for the PCL's Western Division lead. If "Spikesgate" hadn't forced the Islanders to forfeit that game to Tacoma in May, Hawaii would have won the division outright.

Normally, home field for a one-game playoff was decided by a coin flip. Since the Islanders were broke, PCL president Roy Jackson ruled that the game would be played in Tacoma, with the winner to meet Eastern Division champion Salt Lake City. The league would pay Hawaii's travel expenses.

During a layover in Los Angeles, we sat in the airport bar where Jim Shellenback said, "We're cutting our own throats. If we keep winning and keep playing, we'll have to pay for our own meals."

"I started playing this game for fun and no money," said pitcher Tom Dettore, "and I'll wind up the same way."

"It took me 16 years, but I've regained my amateur standing," cracked Eddie Watt.

After traveling for nine hours and 3,500 miles, we arrived at our Tacoma hotel, only to find a No Vacancy sign; the Islanders were being shut out because they owed money from previous trips. Somehow, the hotel, the Islanders, and the PCL worked out a deal that kept us all from sleeping in a nearby park.

Finally, the Islanders caught a break. A coin toss made them the home team even though they were playing in Tacoma's Cheney Stadium, before a hostile crowd. The Islanders would bat last.

Rod Gaspar led off the bottom of the first with a triple. A brisk, chilling wind blew in from left field as Bobby Valentine stepped to the plate. Bobby V hit a low line drive to left that cleared the fence, giving Hawaii a 2–0 lead. In the sixth, Valentine was hit by a pitch, stole second, took third on a sacrifice, and scored on John Scott's sacrifice fly to make it 3–0.

Tacoma put men on second and third with one out in the ninth. Eddie Watt relieved starter Jim Shellenback and shut down the Twins' rally. Hawaii won, 3–1. Western Division champions. Once again, with the cards stacked against them, the Islanders had turned over a winning hand.

In the jubilant Hawaii clubhouse, Roy Hartsfield handed a $50 bill to Tacoma general manager Stan Naccarato and asked to have champagne, on ice in Tacoma's clubhouse, delivered to the Islanders.

Bobby Valentine (photo by Leonard Nakahashi)

"Nobody's going to stop us," yelled Rod Gaspar during the postgame celebration. "They could throw Sandy Koufax at us and we'd still win."

On the ride from Cheney Stadium to the hotel, a black cat ran in front of the bus. "Hey fellas, there's our team mascot," said Roy Hartsfield.

Normally, the PCL Championship Series would have been best of seven, with the series split between Salt Lake City and Honolulu. Because of the Islanders' financial problems, the series was shortened to best of five, with all games to be played at Salt Lake City's Derks Field, where the Gulls had gone 52–21.

The Islanders took another hit when first baseman Adrian Garrett, the team's best power hitter, left to join his ailing father in Florida. First, their ace pitcher. Now their best slugger. What next?

The next morning at 5:00 a.m., we straggled onto the bus to the airport and flew to Utah. Not only did the Islanders drink Tacoma's champagne, they also took the Twins' plane reservations and hotel rooms in Salt Lake City.

When we landed in Utah, there was no team bus. We grabbed our bags and put

Steve Huntz (photo by Leonard Nakahashi)

coins in the slot as we boarded a city bus that stopped several blocks from the hotel. Dragging luggage, we walked the rest of the way.

Roy Hartsfield moved versatile Bobby Valentine to first base to replace Adrian Garrett and started erratic right-hander Dave Wehrmeister in Game 1. Salt Lake City's starter was nine-year major league vet Wayne Simpson, a 6'-3", 220-pound right-hander, once a phenom with the Cincinnati Reds. As a 21-year-old rookie in 1970, Simpson won his first 10 games, pitched a one-hitter against the San Francisco Giants, and made the National League All-Star Team. Then he suffered a torn rotator cuff and continued to pitch for seven years with marginal results.

Salt Lake City was heavily favored, having galloped home 14 games in front in the Eastern Division, with a 90–54 record, compared to Hawaii's 78–67 mark. The Gulls, the California Angels' AAA affiliate, were loaded with outstanding hitters and exceptional team speed.

Batting practice before Game 1 (photo by Mel Proctor)

Salt Lake City's Carlos Lopez hit a three-run homer off Wehrmeister in the third inning, but the Islanders' Dave Hilton answered with a two-run shot off Simpson in the sixth. It was 4–4 as they headed to the ninth.

Quietly watching from the end of the Hawaii dugout was 30-year-old utility man Steve Huntz. Huntz had told Roy Hartsfield that he was thinking of leaving the team. Huntz had suffered through a frustrating season and was worried that his wife and two small daughters might be stranded in Hawaii. Hartsfield reminded Huntz that he'd been an important part of two winning teams and convinced him there might be more to come. "Stick it out, Huntzy," the manager told him. "You might regret it if you don't."

With one out in the ninth, Huntz watched Rod Gaspar light a spark with a single to left and saw Gulls skipper Jimy Williams bring in left-hander Skip Pitlock to face left-handed-hitting Gene Richards. Richards walked, and designated hitter Jim Fairey, another left-handed hitter, approached the plate. "Huntzy," Roy Hartsfield yelled, "go hit for Fairey." The switch-hitting Huntz grabbed his bat and walked to the plate. Pitlock grooved a pitch, and Huntz drilled a long high drive down the left-field line, a game-winning home run as the Islanders won, 7–4. In the clubhouse, the normally stoic veteran was close to tears. "I guess that makes me one-for-two," Huntz said, "one for two months."

While the teams were deciding issues on the field, club owners voted 7–0 to terminate the Islanders' membership in the PCL for failure to fulfill financial and contractual obligations. Although up 1–0 in the championship series, the Hawaii Islanders were kicked out of the Pacific Coast League.

"Since we're not the Hawaii Islanders," said Bobby Valentine, "we need a new name."

"The IRS All-Stars," suggested Bill Almon.

"The Bad News Bears," said Dave Roberts.

Since I was the broadcaster and enjoyed the sound of my voice, I referred to the team as "the Destitute Darlings." The nickname caught on. The Islanders received a telegram signed by 2,000 Hawaii fans, wishing them good luck.

Since none of the games would be played in Hawaii, Cec Heftel, owner of KGMB Radio and TV, announced that Channel 9 would televise the remaining playoff games.

With no room in the press box, I broadcast from the stands, behind the backstop, with a monitor and Salt Lake City fans surrounding me.

The Gulls won the second and third games to take a 2–1 lead in the series and were one win shy of a pennant.

The Islanders had lost their best pitcher and their best power hitter. The team's office doors had been padlocked, and they had been kicked out of hotels and the league. Had the miracles run out for the Destitute Darlings?

Pregame pressure? From left to right — Tom Dettore, Jim Shellenback, Eddie Watt, and Rod Gaspar (photo by Mel Proctor)

Before Game 4, starting pitcher Jim Shellenback, who had pitched for three consecutive PCL pennant winners, said, "I haven't completed a game in Salt Lake City in four years." Then he leaned his chair back against the wall and resumed reading *Breakfast of Champions.*

Shelly went the distance, Dave Hilton hit a three-run homer, and Hawaii won, 7–2. With the series tied 2–2, the scene was set for the final game of the 1976 Pacific Coast League Championship Series.

With Islanders pitching depleted, Roy Hartsfield named Mike Dupree as the starting pitcher for the final game. Hartsfield hoped the Gulls didn't know that his catcher Dave Roberts had a sprained thumb and sore right shoulder. If they knew, the Gulls would run at will.

Salt Lake City manager Jimy Williams came back with Wayne Simpson as his starting pitcher.

As Dave Hilton struck out to end the Islanders' third inning, for the second time in the game his bat sailed past the mound. Simpson snarled at Hilton, who snapped back. Hilton charged the mound and Simpson met him halfway. Suddenly, the field was flooded with players, coaches, managers, and even fans who'd vaulted the fence. Some blows were landed, but no one was hurt. Hawaii's Steve Huntz and Salt Lake City's Julio Cruz and Chuck Dobson were ejected.

As Mike Dupree warmed up for the fourth inning, Julio Cruz, who had been ejected, charged the mound, glancing over his shoulder to make sure teammates were right behind. Again, players raced onto the field, but the umpires quickly stepped in.

In the fourth, Dupree faced PCL batting champ Paul Dade, self-proclaimed "the Executioner," claiming he was death for opposing pitchers. Dade led off with a single and Butch Alberts singled him to third. A sac fly by Mike Miley got Salt Lake City on the board.

Knocking hitters off the plate with fastballs up and in and striking them out with sliders away, Wayne Simpson pitched strongly into the fifth. After Gene Richards singled, Jim Fairey lifted a fly ball to left, an easy chance for Frankie George. But

George dropped the ball, a two-base error. Bobby Valentine was walked intentionally to load the bases. Then Dave Hilton cashed in Richards with a sacrifice fly to tie the score at 1–1.

In the fifth, Simpson's defense betrayed him again. Bill Almon hit a slow bouncer to second baseman Fred Frazier, who sailed his throw over the first baseman's head, putting Almon at second.

Rod Gaspar with champagne (photo by Mel Proctor)

Mike Champion singled in Almon to give the Islanders a 2–1 lead. Later in the inning, Frazier dropped a throw at second on a routine force out. Another error, another run: 3–1 Islanders.

Reliever Chuck Hartenstein retired the Gulls easily in the seventh and eighth, but in the ninth Carlos Lopez led off with a single and Butch Alberts doubled to left center. Lopez rounded third, started back, and then reversed di-

Wayne Simpson (right) congratulates Bobby Valentine (photo by Mel Proctor)

rections again. Gene Richards fired the ball to third baseman Dave Hilton, who relayed to catcher Dave Roberts. Lopez tried to bowl him over, but Roberts tagged him, spinning away to avoid a collision. Lopez's indecisiveness may have cost his team a championship.

Alberts took third on the play and scored on a sacrifice fly, but that was Salt Lake City's last gasp. As Frankie George flied weakly to Richards in left for the final out, on KGMB-TV, I told viewers, "That will do it. Despite incredible adversity, the Islanders have won their second consecutive Pacific Coast League pennant, and all Hawaii can be proud. Final score: Hawaii 3, Salt Lake City 2."

Used with permission of the artist, Corky Trinidad

THE KING WITHOUT A COUNTRY...

The Islanders had done it, just as they knew they would. Again they toasted with the other team's champagne.

"This is the greatest thrill of my baseball life," Rod Gaspar said, champagne dripping into his eyes. "It easily tops last year's win and even the World Series win with the Mets in '69."

In the Islanders' clubhouse, players dowsed each other with champagne and even drank some. Finally, we decided to take the party elsewhere. But where? This was Salt Lake City, Mormon country. As we walked the streets looking for a bar, most of the lights were off. Finally, the team found the perfect place, the No Name Bar.

"Baseball's strange," said Chuck Hartenstein, sipping a beer. "You battle side by side, all year long, and then it's over, and most of these guys will never see each other again. But weeks from now, months from now, even years from now, we'll look back on this season and say, 'I don't believe it.'" Thirty-five years later, I still don't believe it.

A good ole Atlanta boy, Roy Hartsfield had plenty of country sayings, like "The sun doesn't shine on the same dog's ass every day, but when it does, spread your cheeks and let the rays filter in." The sun was about to shine on Roy Hartsfield's ass.

Impressed by how Hartsfield had calmly piloted the Islanders through a maze of adversity to win back-to-back PCL titles, Pat Gillick, general manager of the expansion Toronto Blue Jays, hired Hartsfield as the team's first manager.

New owners cleared up the Islanders' financial obligations, and in 1977, the team was readmitted to the PCL as Fred Whitacre replaced Jack Quinn as GM and Dick Phillips succeeded Roy Hartsfield as manager.

A pregame chat with Jim Fairey (photo by Leonard Nakahashi)

Only Steve Huntz and Jim Fairey remained from the 1976 PCL championship team. One newcomer was Julio Cruz, the cocky second baseman who, playing for Salt Lake City, had ignited two fights in the 1976 title series. "The Cruiser" belonged to the Seattle Mariners but was on loan to the Islanders.

I hated Cruz until I met him. Impossible to ignore, the Cruiser loved baseball and people. He visited with fans, media, grounds crew, and stadium employees and befriended them all.

The Cruiser was a great bunter. I asked him to give me a sign when he was going to bunt for a base hit. He said he would tap the top of his batting helmet before he stepped into the batter's box.

That night Julio Cruz came to bat, glanced at our booth, and tapped his helmet. "It wouldn't surprise me if Julio tried to bunt for a hit here," I boldly predicted. "The Islanders have had trouble scoring runs lately, and he might want to start a rally." The Cruiser laid down a perfect bunt, beat it out, and tipped his cap toward our broadcast booth.

One night, Julio asked for a favor. He said he lived in a boarding house owned by an old woman named Mama Nickerson, who sat in a rocking chair on her porch, listening to our broadcasts. "Please say hello to Mama Nickerson," Cruz said, "and tell her I love her." If I had a dollar for every time we said hello to Mama Nickerson, I'd have a beach house on Maui.

When Cruz reached first base, fans chanted, "Go, Go Julio." The Islanders' stolen-base record was 58, set by Fred Valentine in 1965; the PCL record was 63 by Albuquerque's Glenn Burke in 1976. Julio Cruz was on pace to steal 100 bases. I proposed a "Go, Go Julio" contest to Earl McDaniel. Fans would guess the date he'd break the team's stolen-base record and predict his final number of steals. Earl loved the idea but asked, "What if Julio gets called up before he breaks the record? Talk to the Mariners and find out what their plans are for him."

The Seattle Mariners' farm director assured me Julio Cruz wouldn't be called up. The M's had a second baseman, were in last place, and wanted to keep Cruz in a winning atmosphere.

At considerable expense to KGMB, I ordered life-size cardboard standees of Julio Cruz leading off from first base with the caption "Go, Go Julio." Whoever won the contest would get a new car, a trip to Maui, and $1,000 in cash. We promoted the hell out of the Go, Go Julio contest. He loved it. Fans loved it. Sponsors loved it. I pounded my chest with pride. Fans flocked to Aloha Stadium with "Go, Go Julio" banners, and every time the Cruiser got on base, the "Go, Go Julio" chants got louder.

At 75 games into the season, Julio Cruz had 47 stolen bases. As fans chanted, "Go, Go Julio," suddenly he took off. For Seattle. The Mariners called him up. Furious, I called the M's farm director, who apologized, saying their second baseman had been injured and they wanted to see what Julio could do. When he left the Islanders, Julio Cruz led the Pacific Coast League in hitting (.366), stolen bases (47), triples (9), and runs scored (71).

Before he left, the Cruiser, accompanied by a gorgeous brunette, came to say goodbye. "Guys, I'd like you to meet Mama Nickerson." Mama Nickerson was Becky Nickerson, an Islanders ballgirl who soon became Mrs. Julio Cruz. The Cruiser enjoyed a nine-year major league career with the Seattle Mariners and Chicago White Sox.

Now I had to face Earl McDaniel. Surprisingly, Earl was supportive. He had a framed saying on his wall, "If you don't promote, a funny thing happens, nothing." So we tried again.

We promoted July 4th, featuring fireworks and an automobile giveaway. On Independence Day, I stood with Earl, proudly looking out the back window of our booth, as 33,903 fans snaked their way into Aloha Stadium.

Instead of "Go, Go Julio," we could have promoted a "Where's Luis Alvarado?" contest. Alvarado, a veteran major league infielder, had been released by the Detroit Tigers, and in the midst of a long road trip, the Islanders signed him. In seven games Alvarado hit .462 with 12 hits in 26 at-bats and seemed to drive in every winning run. "Come see the Islanders and Luis Alvarado when the team comes back to Aloha Stadium," we said over and over.

Preparing for a re-creation of the final game of the road trip, we checked the lineups. No Luis Alvarado. Injured? Sick? Why wasn't he in the lineup? The Islanders were usually diligent about calling us with information regarding injuries. They didn't call, and there was no answer when we called the team's offices. We asked our correspondent to find out why the PCL's hottest hitter wasn't in the lineup. He never got an answer.

The next day, we found out that Luis Alvarado had been arrested for having a teenager in his hotel room. Reportedly, the child's mother said she wouldn't press charges if the Islanders released Alvarado. So the team returned home without Alvarado, who never played a home game in Hawaii.

Despite injuries and player recalls, Dick Phillips kept the team in first place, and the Islanders won their third straight PCL Western Division title.

In the playoffs, the Islanders faced the Eastern Division champion Phoenix Giants, who won two of the first three games in Hawaii.

When we arrived in Arizona, the temperature was 101 degrees at sunset. The Islanders' bats were almost as hot. With six-run rallies in the second and fourth innings, Hawaii won 15–4 to even the series at 2–2. Islanders ace Mark Wiley, the winning pitcher, agreed to meet me for a beer.

Arriving early, I sat at the horseshoe-shaped bar and ordered a cold one. Then I noticed the seating arrangement: pretty girl, empty bar stool, hot babe, vacant seat, all the way around the bar. A gorgeous girl sitting next to me explained that these were groupies, holding seats for the players. When I asked her if she was a groupie, she said, "Oh no, I just came with a friend who is." Maybe I had a chance. As I was about to lay my best lines on her, several Islanders walked in, and she turned away, reaching into her purse for a pen and baseball.

Phoenix won the next two games to dethrone the Islanders as PCL champions. They never won another PCL title in Hawaii. As the Islanders' top prospects moved to the major leagues, I wondered if my chance would ever come.

Chapter 6
Big Leagues or Bust

I loved Hawaii, but I wanted a shot at the "Bigs." Did major league teams know who I was? Or did they picture me wearing a grass skirt, running barefoot on the beach and sipping mai tais? They would've been right about the mai tais.

When Roy Hartsfield became the Blue Jays' manager, he tried to help me land the radio play-by-play job, which went to Tom Cheek, who became a legend in Toronto. Then I flew to Houston, met with the Astros, and finished second to another future great, Dewayne Staats.

Dreaming of the big leagues (photo courtesy of KGMB Radio)

During the winter, the Baltimore Orioles called. Legendary announcer Chuck Thompson was thinking about cutting back his schedule, and the Orioles wanted to have a replacement in the bullpen. I flew to Baltimore, 20 degrees. Steam rose from the sidewalk vents. Do people live here? After lunch at Sabatinos in Little Italy, Orioles GM Frank Cashen said they would have me do a West Coast series during the upcoming season. In August, I worked a two-game series in Oakland with Chuck Thompson and Bill O'Donnell. But Chuck decided not to cut back on his schedule and went on for 30 more years.

In the fall of 1977 my girlfriend Julie and I were in San Jose for a UH-San Jose State football game. In the hotel coffee shop, we ran into Jerry Coleman, the San Diego Padres broadcaster.

"We have an opening for an announcer," Coleman said. "You'd be perfect. Go to San Diego." At our own expense, we flew to San Diego, and outside our room in Hotel Circle, Julie and I did a mock interview.

I interviewed with GM Ballard Smith, owner Ray Kroc's son-in-law, and business manager Elton Schiller. I asked if I could meet Ray Kroc but was told he was too busy. But as we left, we walked past Ray Kroc's door. Open. I walked in, introduced myself, and we had a great conversation. Yes!

That night, Jerry Coleman called. I had impressed the Padres and he thought I had the job. I was ecstatic. Until the next day.

"I don't know how to explain this," Coleman said, "but they've decided to hire Dave Campbell." Campbell had been fired as the Padres' AA manager, and the Padres thought it would be great to have two ex-major leaguers in the booth.

KMPC Radio in Los Angeles was going to hire a third announcer to work with legends Dick Enberg and Don Drysdale on California Angels broadcasts. KMPC producer Steve Bailey asked me to send a resume and tape.

When I heard nothing for two weeks, I called Bailey, who said, "We've narrowed the field to 20. Call me next week."

Looking back, I should have said, "No, Steve, you call me when you've made a decision." But like a trained seal, I called every week.

"You're in our top 15. Call next week."

"We've narrowed it to 10. Call me."

"You're in the top five. Let's talk next week."

"It's down to two, Mel baby. You're still in."

"Mel, thanks for calling. You're a great young announcer, but we've decided to go with Al Wisk. Part of this job entails play-by-play for the Los Angeles Rams, and Al has been the Kansas City Chiefs play-by-play man. That was the deciding factor."

"Fuuuuuuuuuuuuuuuck."

I had come close to jobs with the Blue Jays, Astros, Orioles, Padres, and Angels but still, nothing. Fuck it. Julie and I accepted Hawaii as our home and decided to just be happy.

KGMB-TV news staff 1978: from the left, Bart Fredo, Phil Arnone, Joe Moore, Linda Coble; back row, from left: Bob Sevey, Bill Canter, Mel Proctor, Tim Tindall, Bambi Weil, Mickey Gallivan, Jan Anderson; top: Dan Chun (photo courtesy of KGMB-TV)

Come on. This wasn't friggin' Buffalo or Newark. Her family was on Maui and we loved Hawaii. Besides, I thought I had a future in Hawaii TV.

KGMB-TV news director Bob Sevey promised me that if sports director Joe Moore ever left, the job was mine. When Joe took a job at KHON-TV, Sevey hired Jim Leahey. I confronted Sevey, who said he didn't hire me because he knew I'd soon get a major league play-by-play job. Bob, are you a fortune teller?

Like a colony of Honolulu Stadium termites, ambition gnawed at my soul I loved Hawaii but wondered how far my talent could take me. As Oscar Wilde, a former Hawaii Islanders second baseman, said, "The gods have two ways of dealing harshly with us. The first is to deny us our dreams, and the second is to grant them."

On a beautiful Sunday afternoon in August 1978, Julie and I sat on our lanai, drinking wine and watching the sunset. The phone rang.

Talking football with 49'er Russ Francis at the Columbia Inn (photo courtesy of Gene Kaneshiro)

"Mel, Orrin McDaniels, general manager of WTOP Radio in Washington, D.C. We'd like to offer you the job as play-by-play announcer for the Washington Bullets and sports director of WTOP Radio."

After I got up off the floor, I said, "I'll take the job." We agreed on salary, $25,000, the same I was making at KGMB. I was so excited, I didn't even try to get a few more dollars.

"We'd like you to come to D.C. early so you can find out who the sharks are in this market," McDaniels said. I heard the theme from *Jaws*. Sharks? What was I getting into?

As Julie and I celebrated, an hour later, the phone rang again. "Mel, Irv Kaze, general manager of the San Diego Clippers. How'd you like to be our radio play-by-play announcer?" After years of writing letters and mailing countless tapes and resumes that wound up in broadcasting's wasteland, I was offered two big-time jobs in one day.

I told Irv Kaze we would rather live in San Diego, but I'd already accepted the Bullets job. Irv, who became a lifelong friend, told me the Bullets had just won an NBA championship and that Washington, D.C., was a bigger market. He also candidly revealed that the Clippers had an uncertain future in San Diego, and if I backed out of the commitment I'd made to the Bullets, my reputation might be tarnished forever. I respected Irv Kaze's honesty, but whenever we met, over the next 30 years, I'd bust his balls for not hiring me.

Julie and I had lived together for two years and decided to get married. With no time for a conventional ceremony, we planned a baseball-themed wedding at the Columbia Inn, where I hosted a Sunday night talk show. Since corned beef hash was our usual breakfast fare, the wonderful Tosh Kaneshiro, the Columbia Inn's owner, made a huge corned beef hash wedding cake. Islanders team doctor David Eith did the blood tests, and Guido Salmaggi agreed to sing the national anthem, as he did before Islanders games. I bought a cheap ring with my over-the-limit American Express card and, unable to decide on a best man, made Bruce O'Neil and Tim Tindall co–best men.

Bob Jones announced on the Channel 9 news that Muhammad Ali would attend the wedding. Ali wasn't there,

Married at the Columbia Inn (photo courtesy Columbia Inn)

but the Columbia Inn was packed with people we didn't know, looking for the champ.

I gave Julie the ring, we exchanged vows—something about a "no cut contract"—and it was party on. I was excited about my new job, but when the reality of leaving Hawaii set in, I was terrified.

Morning sports at WTOP (photo courtesy of Mel Proctor)

Chapter 7
Swimming with Sharks

After finding an apartment, Julie and I drove to Landover, Maryland, to tour the Capital Centre, home of the NBA champion Washington Bullets. A cavernous venue—partially lit and eerily quiet—with 19,035 empty seats, the enormity of the building scared the hell out of me.

The next day I drove to WTOP. I'd gone from Earl McDaniel to Orrin McDaniels. They definitely weren't related. Orrin McDaniels was a walking pawn shop, with rings, necklaces, earrings, and a gold watch.

"Hey babes," McDaniels said, as I wondered whether to go with the soul shake or a conventional hand shake. McDaniels explained that as WTOP's sports director, my first sportscast each weekday was at 6:00 a.m. I'd come home at 6:00 a.m. a few times but never gotten up that early.

Up at 5:00 a.m., I showered, dressed, and was on the road. Fortified by massive doses of caffeine, I welcomed the rush hour crowd to another wonderful day in the nation's capital. I did two sportscasts an hour until 10:00 a.m., taped afternoon reports, and on game day prepared for a Bullets game. Normally, I reached the Capital Centre by 5:00 p.m. for a 7:30 game. By the time I got home, it was past midnight. I was still wired and couldn't sleep, so I usually read and had a glass of wine. Or maybe two. I crashed around 1:00 a.m. and got up at 5:00 a.m.

"WTOP Sports, Mel Proctor. May I help you?" I said, answering a rare 6:00 a.m. call.

"No honey, but I can help you," said a sultry female voice that would have gotten my attention at any hour. "Honey, you're not making enough money," said Evelyn Freyman, head of the local chapter of AFTRA, the American Federation of Television and Radio Artists. Evelyn explained that because

Bullets games were aired on a network of radio stations, according to AFTRA's contract with WTOP, I was owed an additional $15,000 a year.

"Evelyn, I appreciate what you're trying to do, but this is my first big-time job. I don't want to cause trouble."

"Well honey, it's out of your hands. This is between AFTRA and WTOP. You will soon get a check for $15,000 from Orrin McDaniels."

The next day, Orrin didn't say a word, but one of his gophers handed me a check: $15,000.

Evelyn Freyman called. "Honey, did you get the check?"

"Well, yes," I stammered, "but what if WTOP fires me?"

Evelyn laughed. "Honey, they can't fire you. That would violate the union contract. That's why you belong to AFTRA."

When I traveled, hotel and airfare were prepaid, but I expensed dinners, cab fare, and incidentals and was usually reimbursed within a week. After the AFTRA confrontation, my checks arrived later and later. As I prepared to leave on a two-week West Coast trip, WTOP owed me $3,000.

WTOP's comptroller lived in our apartment complex, and after tennis and a couple of beers, he admitted Orrin McDaniels was screwing me.

"You owe me $3,000," I said, walking into Orrin McDaniel's office. "I have a two-week trip beginning tomorrow. If I don't have the money, I'm not getting on the plane, and you can take that up with the Bullets and AFTRA."

Later that day, I got my check.

Between feuding with my boss, getting lost in D.C.'s traffic circles, and getting four hours of sleep a night, I was a wreck.

One frigid morning after an ice storm, I slipped and slid out to my car at 5:00 a.m. to go to work. I shivered as I tried to put my key in the door lock. It was frozen. I went back to our apartment, boiled water, and carried it outside. As I poured hot water on the lock, I thought, *I am, without a doubt, the dumbest son of a bitch on the face of the earth. A couple of months ago, I was on the beach at Waikiki, enjoying sunshine, blue skies, and women in bikinis. What the hell am I doing here?*

Then, driving to a commercial audition, I got lost in a D.C. ghetto and pulled to the side of the road. I looked at the street sign: Hawaii Avenue. Are you shitting me? Should I laugh or cry? Was this a sign telling me to return to Hawaii? I called Earl McDaniel, who said I could always come back, but he thought I'd be making a career mistake by leaving D.C. Give it a couple of months, he said.

Muhammad Ali didn't come to my wedding, but he came to WTOP. Retired from boxing, Ali represented the American Dental Association and was the good guy, who would knock out "Mr. Tooth Decay" played by Chuck Wepner, Sylvester Stallone's inspiration for the Rocky character.

I interviewed Ali and did blow-by-blow commentary as he and Wepner sparred, with a photographer taking publicity pictures. As Ali was leaving, he looked out the window and pointed to all-black Woodrow Wilson High School. "What's that?" he asked. When I explained, he said, "Let's go," and I joined his entourage as we crossed the street.

Ali pushed opened the school doors and marched down the hallway. When kids saw Ali, they bolted out of their seats, leaving teachers in midsentence. Ali's fan club grew as he walked through the school, sat down outside on the steps, held court, and signed autographs. The kids were spellbound. They would have stayed all day, but Ali told them to go back to school.

1978-79 Washington Bullets
Bottom row, left to right: GM Bob Ferry, Coach Dick Motta, Larry Wright, Charles Johnson, Tom Henderson, Phil Chenier, Owner Abe Pollin, VP Jerry Sachs
Back row, left to right: Assistant Coach Bernie Bickerstaff, Kevin Grevey, Roger Phegley, Greg Ballard, Elvin Hayes, Dave Corzine, Mitch Kupchak, Wes Unseld, Bobby Dandridge, Trainer John Lally (photo courtesy Washington Bullets)

Chapter 8
Washington Bullets

Broadcasting Washington Bullets basketball kept me sane. During my two hours on the air, I was in heaven, totally focused on the action. I got phone calls and letters complimenting me on my work. Bullets general manager Bob Ferry and Coach Dick Motta were especially supportive. Motta missed a game due to illness but listened on WTOP Radio. "You're really good," Dick said. "From your description I knew exactly which plays we were running every time." I was only as good as the team I was covering, and the Bullets were the best team in the NBA.

Center Wes Unseld was the foundation of the defending NBA champion Bullets. Listed at 6'-7", Wes later admitted he was just 6'-5¾", yet every night he'd battled 7-footers like Wilt Chamberlain, Kareem Abdul Jabbar, Nate Thurmond, Bob Lanier, and Moses Malone.

In his first year in the NBA, Wes had been MVP and Rookie of the Year. By the time I started broadcasting Bullets basketball, Wes was a 10-year vet, an old 32 with shot knees playing in pain every night. Because Wes couldn't jump anymore, we kidded him about his "tippy toe" dunk, his feet barely leaving the floor as he managed a weak dunk.

Wes Unseld scores over Dr. J (photo courtesy Washington Bullets)

He still set the best picks in the league and was the best outlet passer of all time. He could stand beneath one basket and fire a two-handed outlet pass that hit the backboard at the other end of the court.

After a Bullets win in Houston, I looked at the stat sheet. "Hey, Wes," I said, looking to the back of the bus where he sat.

"What is it 'Smell'?" he said, using his endearing nickname for me.

"Wes, Moses kicked your butt." Moses Malone had 24 points and 15 rebounds while Wes had 10 points, 10 rebounds, and 8 assists.

"Smell, what'd he do in the fourth quarter?"

I checked the play-by-play sheet. Malone: two points, one rebound. Wes taught me a lesson. Stats often lie. Wes had delivered body blows for three quarters. By the fourth period, Moses Malone was exhausted.

In boxing, they say, "Kill the body and the head will die." That's what Wes did. Forearm shots to the ribs, knees to the back of the legs, and an occasional slap upside the head, especially for players like Rick Barry or Flynn Robinson who wore hairpieces.

Interviewing Elvin Hayes (photo courtesy of Mel Proctor)

Wes was the strongest man in the NBA. One day at practice when I was ragging on him, he picked me up, gave me an airplane spin over his head, and set me back on the floor. I stumbled away, dizzy and flabbergasted.

Elvin Hayes and Bobby Dandridge were the forwards. The 6'-9", 240-pound Hayes, one of the best college players of all time, is remembered for his duels with

UCLA's Lew Alcindor, now Kareem Abdul Jabbar. Fans would chant "Eeeeeee" when the Big E hit one of his patented turnaround jumpers.

Bobby Dandridge had played on an NBA championship team in Milwaukee, with Kareem Abdul Jabbar and Oscar Robertson. "Bobby D" was the missing pane in the Bullets' championship mosaic, acquired to neutralize Philadelphia's "Dr. J" Julius Erving as the Bullets won an NBA title. Dandridge was a tenacious defender who pushed, held, scratched, and clawed, whatever it took to stop his man.

The guards were former University of Hawaii star Tom Henderson and ex-Kentucky great Kevin Grevey. Tom Henderson wasn't a great shooter but did one thing as well as any NBA guard I've seen. Pressured by an opponent, Henderson advanced the ball quickly into the front court and made an accurate first pass to initiate Dick Motta's offense. That may not sound like a big deal, but with only 24 seconds to shoot, the faster the team got into their offense, the more time they had to get good shots.

Kevin Grevey and I became friends and later broadcast partners. I still thought I could play a little so I challenged Grevey to play one-on-one. I knew I'd lose but figured I could at least hit a couple of shots against another slow white guy. Kevin Grevey blocked every damned shot I took.

Grevey's nickname was "Fleetwood" because he drove a Cadillac Fleetwood. When Kevin was recruited out of high school in Hamilton, Ohio, his dad Norm, a prominent lawyer, cautioned Kevin that if schools offered anything unusual or illegal he should call Dad. When Kentucky, coached by Joe B. Hall, asked Kevin what his favorite car was, he said a Cadillac Fleetwood. Dutifully, Kevin called his dad and said Kentucky had offered him his favorite car. "What should I do?"

"Kentucky? Great school, Kevin. Great school. That's where you should go."

With Mitch Kupchak, Greg Ballard, Charles Johnson, and Larry Wright, the Bullets' bench was loaded. I was having so much fun broadcasting Bullets games, I forgot about moving back to Hawaii.

I looked forward to March when the Bullets would play in Kansas City on a Friday night and two days later would play in Denver. With an off day before the Nuggets game, we'd planned a family reunion. My wife Julie was flying in from Maryland, and all the aunts and uncles and cousins I hadn't seen for years would be there. I really wanted to spend time with my dad, who'd been battling depression.

On the night before the Kansas City game, I was about to walk out of my hotel room to join Wes Unseld and trainer John Lally for dinner at Gates Bar-B-Q, when the phone rang.

"Mel?" My sister Anne. Something was wrong.

"Dad is dead."

My dad had shot himself. Crying all the way, I flew to Denver.

I told WTOP general manager Orrin McDaniels that I couldn't possibly fly back to Kansas City for the game the next night. There were alternatives: fly someone in to do the game, hire an announcer in Kansas City, air the Kansas City Kings broadcast, or simulcast with Bullets TV. Later, Orrin McDaniels called. "You're going to have to do the game. We can't find anybody else." Bullshit.

I considered refusing to do the broadcast. Then I thought about how Dad had handled difficult situations. "Keep a poker face, and never let your opponent know how you're feeling," he said, "because he'll use it against you. And never quit."

After grieving with my family and saying goodbye to Dad, I flew back to Kansas City. Before the game, Dick Motta, assistant coach Bernie Bickerstaff, trainer John Lally, and each of the Bullets expressed their condolences. Guys, it's been years, but you have no idea what that meant to me.

Play-by-play demands total attention. You're so focused on the game, you temporarily forget life's problems. I don't remember what I said, but broadcasting that game was two hours of not grieving for Dad.

Sometimes, life cooperates. Before we returned home, Orrin McDaniels was fired.

The Bullets finished the 1978–79 regular season with the NBA's best record, 54–28. In the playoffs, they beat Atlanta in seven games but fell behind 3–1 in the Eastern Conference Finals against San Antonio with "Iceman" George Gervin and "Captain Late" James Silas. No team had ever recovered from a 3–1 deficit to win an NBA playoff series.

After a postgame interview with Elvin Hayes, we walked off the court. "Don't worry," E said, "We've got the Spurs right where we want them."

"E, you're down three games to one."

"I know," he said, "but they know they can't play any better, and we know we can."

He was right. The Bullets won the series 4–3.

I couldn't believe it; I was going to the NBA Finals my first year in the league. Little did I know that it would be the only time.

In the Finals, the Bullets again faced Seattle. In Game 1, Larry Wright hit two free throws with no time remaining to give the Bullets a win. But with starting guards Tom Henderson and Kevin Grevey playing hurt, the Sonics' backcourt of Gus Williams and series MVP Dennis Johnson dominated. Seattle won four in a row to take the series, 4–1.

When a Bullets player appeared on our pregame show, he'd get a free rental car for a weekend. Players loved it; with friends, relatives, or girlfriends in town, they had a car to use. Most players returned the cars when the weekend ended. Except Elvin Hayes.

Our rental car sponsor called me and said the Big E hadn't returned a car after two weeks.

"E," I said, "Where's the rental car?"

In his high-pitched voice, he said, "Well, you know, you know, you know, I'll return the car."

Three weeks passed. A month. The rental car guy called often. Hell, I was the announcer; I wasn't the salesman who cut the deal. Still, no car. Our sponsor canceled his advertising. After retiring, Elvin Hayes owned an automobile dealership in Houston.

Bobby Dandridge wouldn't do interviews. When Bobby D scored his 15,000th point, a significant milestone, I had to get him on the postgame show. Guests received expensive watches from a local jeweler, so I upped the ante, telling Bullets PR director Mark Pray that if Bobby did an interview, I'd give him three watches, one for him, one for his wife, and one for a friend.

Confident my bribe would work, I extolled the virtues of Bobby Dandridge, stalling until he arrived. Finally, Mark Pray returned. "Bobby said to tell you he has enough watches."

In each of the next two years the Bullets had identical 39–43 records. Dick Motta knew the team was getting old, so he left to coach the expansion Dallas Mavericks and was replaced by Gene Shue.

Wes Unseld
Appreciation Day

March 29, 1981

Courtesy of Washington Bullets

In 1980–81, Wes Unseld retired. Starting his final game at home against Cleveland, the Cavs let Wes win the opening tip and score the game's first basket. Then the Bullets called time-out as Wes left to a thunderous ovation, his career over. His replacement and rookie protégé Rick Mahorn scored 28 points in that game.

Soon Elvin Hayes and Bobby Dandridge were gone and so were the Bullets' winning seasons. After losing to Seattle in the Finals in 1978–79, the Bullets spiraled downward. In the next 30 years, they never again won 50 games and never returned to the NBA Finals.

Chapter 9
Two-Stepping to Texas

With help from Washington columnists William Taaffe, Leonard Shapiro, and David Dupree, who praised my work, I was suddenly a hot item. The Washington Diplomats soccer team offered me their radio play-by-play job; the Minnesota Twins wanted me to do TV, and WITS Radio in Boston called. They wanted to hire Jon Miller, the Texas Rangers announcer, but if Miller couldn't leave Texas, I was the second choice. Miller took the Red Sox job, and I replaced him in Texas. Because the broadcast rights were owned by the city of Arlington, with two years left on the contract, the Rangers could only offer a two-year deal. Until they could offer a longer contract, I could continue to do Bullets games.

With the 1979–80 NBA season ending and baseball's spring training beginning, I broadcast a Bullets game on a Friday night and then had to fly to Ft. Myers, Florida, to debut as the Rangers' announcer Saturday afternoon.

With all the travel and lack of sleep, my sinuses were plugged and my voice was fading. The Capital Club bartender concocted an elixir of hot tea with orange juice and honey, fortified by shots of whiskey. I threw back a couple of those and felt no pain in my throat or anywhere else.

Radio Grades Are In; Proctor Makes the Dean's List

Used with the permission of the Washington Post

I conked out on the connecting flight to Atlanta, and when I woke up, I couldn't talk. I guzzled hot tea with lemon, took an oath of silence, and rested my voice on the flight to Florida.

Upon arrival, I asked the cab driver to stop at a local pharmacy and bought every cold medicine known to man. In my hotel room, I took Nyquil, shot Afrin up my nose, chewed Aspergum, stuffed my mouth with Hall's Cough Drops, and slept for an hour, praying God would give me back my voice.

I took a taxi to the ballpark. I hadn't spoken for hours. When I met my partner Eric Nadel in the broadcast booth, he said hello. I tried to answer but had no voice. When Eric introduced me as the new play-by-play announcer for the Texas Rangers, I smiled and waved at the camera. Eric and a Kansas City Royals announcer did the game.

Eddie Chiles, a Texas oilman, owned the Rangers and inherited many veteran players signed by previous owner Brad Corbett. Ferguson Jenkins, Sparky Lyle, Doc Medich, Jon Matlack, Bud Harrelson, Mickey Rivers, Al Oliver, Richie Zisk, Johnny Grubb, and Pepe Frias were all in their 30s. And then there was 41-year-old Gaylord Perry.

At 37, future Hall of Famer Ferguson Jenkins had lost his good fastball but threw slider after slider and won 12 games. A native of Ontario, Fergie was named Canadian Athlete of the Year, and on our first trip to Toronto, he was showered with gifts and accolades. On the next trip to Canada, customs officials found cocaine and marijuana in Fergie's suitcase.

From left to right, Gaylord Perry, Jim Kern, Fergie Jenkins, Sparky Lyle (photo courtesy of Texas Rangers)

Mounties arrived at the SkyDome, arrested Fergie, and took him to jail. Fergie was bailed out but had to return to Canada later for a court appearance.

As a result of Jenkins' arrest, when we left Canada, customs officials busted our balls. I had to take off my cowboy boots and socks for inspection, and they took the toothpaste from my bag and squeezed all of it out. They treated everyone the same way until after three hours, we cleared customs.

Reliever Sparky Lyle, at 36, had some great years with the Boston Red Sox and New York Yankees and still had a wicked slider. After a pregame workout at Arlington Stadium on a 100-degree night, Sparky walked toward the clubhouse to put on a dry uniform. Some Red Sox fan yelled, "Spahky, Spahky, I'm from Woostah and I love you man. Throw me your cap."

Sparky threw his cap to this adoring fan.

"Spahky, Spahky, throw me your glove."

Up went the glove.

"Spahky, Spahky, throw me your uniform."

Playing to the crowd that had assembled near the right-field wall, Sparky took off his uniform top and pants and threw them into the stands, walking into the clubhouse wearing an undershirt, shorts, socks, and spikes.

"Thanks, Spahky. We love you."

Third baseman Buddy Bell was the son of former major league outfielder Gus Bell. Buddy often brought his seven-year-old son David on road trips. I was standing in the Seattle Mariners' dugout with Buddy and David, talking with M's coach Vada Pinson, who'd replaced Gus Bell in the Cincinnati Reds' outfield. Young David studied Pinson, his eyes working up from Pinson's spikes to his face, and

Buddy Bell (photo courtesy Texas Rangers)

"Scoop" Al Oliver (photo courtesy of Texas Rangers)

said, "Dad, he's the guy who took Grandpa's job." David Bell became a third-generation major leaguer, played in the big leagues for 12 years, and then retired. I had broadcast games for father and son. Do I feel old? Don't ask.

Rangers left-fielder Al Oliver played for the "We Are Family" dynasty of the Pittsburgh Pirates. When Kansas City's George Brett flirted with .400 in 1980 and wound up hitting .390, "Scoop" tried to convince everyone that he was a better hitter than Brett because he hit the ball harder and his line drives reached fielders more quickly. Huh?

With the Rangers losing, Eddie Chiles said he might bring in a motivational speaker, like Zig Ziglar, to talk to the team. "Shit," said Scoop, "Eddie can save his money. I'll talk to the team." Based on his stats, it was hard to argue with him. Twelve times Scoop hit over .300 and finished with a lifetime average of .303 with 2,743 career hits.

Mickey Rivers. Just saying his name, I smile. Rivers played on the New York Yankees' World Series championship teams in 1977 and 1978. Mick was 31 when he came to Texas. The leadoff batter, Mick walked gingerly to home plate, like a senior citizen stepping on hot coals, spun his bat like a baton, and once hit himself in the mouth, drawing blood. But in 1980 he hit .333 and set a Rangers

Mickey Rivers (photo courtesy of Texas Rangers)

record with 210 hits. "Too Sweet," Mickey's rapper friend, recorded "Mick the Quick, Bad Man with the Stick" that got some local radio play.

Mickey's brother Willie shined shoes at an Arlington hotel and often worked out at the stadium. He looked exactly like Mickey, and like his brother, Willie was left-handed. The Rangers gave him a jersey with "Rivers" on the back. When Mickey tired of signing autographs, Willie took over, signing "Mickey Rivers." Nobody knew the difference.

Mickey Rivers was always in a good mood. Would you expect anything else from someone whose philosophy was, "Ain't no sense worryin' about the things you got control over, cause if you got control over 'em, ain't no sense worryin'. And ain't no sense worryin' about the things you don't got control over, cause if you don't got control over 'em, ain't no sense worryin'."

Another beauty was 41-year-old Gaylord Perry, who won 314 games, became the first pitcher to win a Cy Young Award in both leagues, and was elected to the Hall of Fame. When Perry, best known for doctoring baseballs with spit, Vaseline, or K-Y Jelly, faced his former team in Cleveland, he convinced a groundskeeper friend to put flour in the resin bag. He then powdered his pitching hand and threw a "puffball" that flew out of a cloud of white powder.

In Seattle, as the pitchers walked to the bullpen, Gaylord spotted a camera on a tripod next to the dugout. He reached over and clicked off several shots. The Mariners photographer shouted at Perry, so he returned and clicked off more photos. The cameraman and Gaylord exchanged obscenities and began to push and shove until Gaylord's teammates pulled him away. The photog wasn't finished. During the game, the press box announcer informed the media that the Seattle Mariners' team photographer had filed assault charges against Gaylord Perry.

It was a getaway day for the Rangers. After the game, as we boarded the team bus, police arrived to arrest Gaylord Perry. They slapped handcuffs on a tall, bald man who fit Perry's description. But it was Rangers coach Fred Koenig, who produced a driver's license and was released. Where was Gaylord Perry?

As we boarded the charter, Gaylord sat, with his feet propped up, enjoying his second beer. During the game, the Rangers had snuck Perry out of the bullpen, into the clubhouse, and then put him on a catering truck to the airport.

In 1982, at age 42, Gaylord Perry won his 300th game, pitching for—can you believe it?—Seattle, where he was known as the "Ancient Mariner."

Mario Mendoza (photo courtesy Texas Rangers)

In 1981, Mario Mendoza became the Rangers' short-stop. Mendoza, a veteran of the Mexican Leagues, had played for Pittsburgh and Seattle. A good fielder but poor hitter, he became part of the baseball lexicon with "the Mendoza line." The Mendoza line is a .200 bat-ting average. Mario Mendoza actually had a lifetime average of .215, but in a normal season, his average would often drop to .170 or .180. In 1979, when Mendoza hit .198, his Seattle Mariners teammates, Bruce Bochte and Tom Paciorek, coined the phrase and then used it to poke fun at Kansas City's George Brett, who was in a rare slump. Brett popularized the term.

Although I was one of the first announcers to use the term "the Mendoza line" on air, I remember Mario more for having the best burro imitation ever. "Heee ... haaaw, heee ... haaaw," came from the back of the bus. I could have sworn there was a jackass there. Actually, there were several.

I broke my wrist playing tennis in Baltimore. "Take a number," said the ER nurse. With a gunshot victim spurting blood, a crackhead doing the OD dance, and auto accident victims being carried in on stretchers, I was a low priority. After listening to moaning and wailing for two hours, I took a cab to Memorial Stadium to see the doctor. Rangers pitcher George "Doc" Medich was completing medical studies at the

University of Pittsburgh, soon to become an orthopedic surgeon. Twice Doc had gone into the stands to assist heart attack victims. Doc wrapped my wrist with an Ace bandage, and the next day a doctor slapped a cast on my arm. I credited Doc with a save.

Broken wrist in Baltimore (photo courtesy of Mel Proctor)

Thirty-six-year-old Rusty Staub was the Rangers' designated hitter. A 6'-3", 220-pounder, Rusty dragged his huge bottle bat to the plate, choked up, and sprayed line drives all over the field. Since Rusty was mainly a DH, he worried about putting on weight. On the road, I usually jogged, and Rusty asked if he could join me. In Cleveland, we ran on a vacant road near the airport as Rusty carried a white hotel towel. Suddenly he stopped.

"I've got to take a shit. I've got the runs," he said.

I started to laugh.

"Keep running," Rusty said, "I'll catch up with you."

A save for Doc Medich (photo courtesy of the Texas Rangers)

Laughing and jogging, I reached the end of the road and turned around as Rusty rejoined me. We ran for a couple of minutes.

"Fuck . . . fuck . . . fuck," Rusty yelled.

Rusty said that when he'd stopped near a fire hydrant to take a dump, he used the hotel towel as toilet paper. For some reason Rusty had $1,000 wrapped up in the towel, which he laid next to the fire hydrant. As Rusty's face turned redder than his hair, I couldn't stop laughing.

"Motherfucker, you can't tell anybody."

Rusty Staub (photo courtesy Texas Rangers)

"Fine," I said, covering my mouth to stifle more laughter.

"Let's go," Rusty said, running faster than he ever did on the bases. When we reached the fire hydrant, the towel and Rusty's money were gone.

"This stays between us," Rusty said sternly.

"You mean I can't tell people about the 'thousand dollar dump'"?

"Motherfucker," Rusty said. "I'm serious."

"Rusty, since you were known as 'La Grande Orange' in Montreal, can we call this 'La Grande Poop'?"

"Don't say a word or I'll kill you."

Years later, in Shea Stadium's press dining room, Rusty told the story. Of course, everybody laughed like hell. "Rusty, now is it okay for me to tell the story of the thousand dollar dump?" I asked.

"Motherfucker, go ahead." And of course, I've gotten some mileage out of that story.

Richie Zisk and the Lone Ranger (photo by Linda Kaye)

On a flight to God knows where, to face God knows who, after God knows how many beers, veteran Richie Zisk and I talked about family. I told Richie that my wife Julie and I wanted to have a child. We'd gone through all the tests, and the doctors determined we were both fine, but there were still no results.

Richie said he and his wife had the same problem, until they tried a teammate's suggestion. "Mel, after you have sex, grab Julie by the ankles and hold her upside down for several minutes. I know you think I'm crazy, but it worked for us."

On November 11, 1981, Julie gave birth to William Paul Keoni Proctor. Thanks, Richie.

In baseball, everybody second-guesses, but you don't expect it from your boss. Roy Parks heard me say, "Pat Putnam might be bunting here." Normally, the power-hitting first baseman would be swinging away, but he was in a slump, and the Rangers were struggling to score runs. Roy ran to Ranger GM Eddie Robinson, who agreed that it was probably not a bunt situation, and Roy couldn't wait to tell me I was wrong. Was he going to nitpick everything I said? With the Rangers playing the California Angels, Roy sat on the stairway behind us, with a steno pad, taking notes.

In the bottom of the ninth, the Rangers trailed by a run. With two outs and a runner at second, the Rangers batter hit a line drive to deep left center. Angels center fielder Fred Lynn raced to the warning track and leaped, extending his glove up and over the fence. Lynn landed on the warning track, head down in dejection. I looked at third base coach Jackie Moore and then at the umpires. Nobody knew whether it was a game-winning homer or an incredible game-ending catch. Lynn continued to walk in and kicked the dirt in disgust. "Home run Rangers!" I shrieked. Then, with a huge smile on his face, Fred Lynn held up the baseball. He had caught it. Game over.

I turned to watch the replay on the monitor and saw Roy Parks write, "Proctor—sight problem."

"Roy, out here, now!" I yelled, ripping off my headset and pushing him into the hallway. "Look, damn it, Roy. You're my boss, and you can critique my work, but I don't have a sight problem. Nobody knew where that ball was. Don Zimmer doesn't pull up a chair behind the mound and critique his pitchers, and you're not going to sit behind me and take notes. If you want to fire me, fine, but don't ever do that again." Sitting down, my face flushed, my hands shaking, I put on my headset, took a deep breath, and calmly said, "Welcome back to Arlington Stadium."

Julie and I lived in Texas during the Rangers' season and returned to Maryland for the Bullets'. The Dallas Mavericks were created in 1980 with my old friend Dick Motta as the head coach. He offered to get me the job as the Mavs' radio announcer. Finally, we could live in one place. I told Dick I'd love to do it, but, as a courtesy, I wanted to run it past the Rangers first.

Definitely not, said Roy Parks. He felt the Rangers and Mavericks would compete for sports dollars in Dallas. Ridiculous. So we had to continue living in two places. In retrospect, instead of trying to be respectful, I should have grabbed the Mavs job and let the Rangers deal with it.

In 1981, Eddie Chiles hired Sam Meason to run the business side of the Rangers. Meason's qualifications? Friend of Chiles, both Oklahoma football boosters, and former CEO of toy company Mattel. Perfect.

The Rangers opened the season in New York, losing the first two games but beating the Yankees in the final game. Sam Meason must have thought Oklahoma had upset Texas in football because he called our booth, telling me to encourage fans to meet the Rangers at the airport, with placards and signs congratulating them on their victory in New York. I explained to Sam that the Rangers had played three games and there were 159 left on the schedule, including nine with the Yankees.

Sam Meason wanted a woman on our broadcast team. "We'll hire the girl and teach her baseball," he said. "I could bring Barbara Walters in here and teach her the game in a month."

I imagined Baba Wawa calling a game. "Mickey Wivers at first base as Wusty Staub steps in. Dave Woberts is on deck. The Wangers and Wed Sox are tied 1–1."

Meason wanted celebrities to join us during road games. Maybe an out-of-work actor in New York or L.A., but what about Seattle? The head fish cutter at Pike Street Market?

"Sam the Sham" thought the Rangers needed a slogan. "Coming Alive," with a theme song and stadium banners, ushered in the 1981 season. When the Rangers were losing, newspaper photographer Linda Kay snapped pictures of

Meason, asleep in his box seat next to the Rangers' dugout. Snoozing Sam was on the front page of the sports section with the headline, "Coming Alive."

Meason's dumbest idea was "Ranger Aide," marketing a drink to compete against Gatorade. Between innings, Rangers ballgirls brought cups of Ranger Aide to the umpires. Linda Kay struck again, snapping a three-photo sequence depicting a ballgirl handing a cup of Ranger Aide to the home plate umpire, the ump trying it, and the ump spitting it out. In 1981, with all of Sam Meason's misguided projects, the Rangers lost a reported 4 million dollars.

Despite the craziness, I concentrated on broadcasting baseball. But one morning, late in the season, wearing my bathrobe and holding a cup of coffee, I walked into the front yard to get the paper. Then I saw my picture, with the headline, "Rangers to Change Announcers."

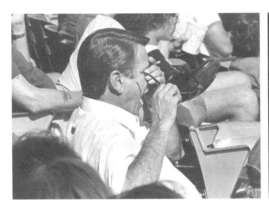 

Rangers' president Sam Meason "Coming Alive!" (photo by Linda Kaye)

Photo courtesy Texas Rangers

Ranger Aide samples — Photo 1: "Thank you young lady." Photo 2: "Ooh, this looks good." Photo 3: "Yuck…what is this stuff?" (photos by Linda Kaye)

"Tell Sam I'm on my way," I told Meason's secretary before I drove to his office.

Meason said the article didn't refer to me but to the other announcers. He liked my work, my enthusiasm had improved, and he wanted me to do TV the next year. The Rangers only televised 35 games, but Sam promised the schedule would increase and asked if I wanted to be part of the Rangers' future.

"Sure, if you'll give me a contract."

"Not right now," he said. "You'll have to trust me." Right.

The story played out in the papers with the media supporting me. I had hoped to stay with Texas, but I wasn't going to compromise my credibility for this moron.

In the final days of the season, Roy Parks said, "Sam Meason wants to know if you want to stay with the Rangers."

"Roy," I said, "please tell Sam to take this job and shove it up his ass." On the Rangers' final road trip to Seattle, my hotel room was so far away from the rest of the team that I had to ask for a bus transfer to get to the lobby. Thanks, Sam.

After the final Rangers game, Julie and I went to a party and sat around the pool, with friends, reminiscing about the good times and sharing our sadness at leaving Arlington. I walked into the kitchen to get a beer. The lights were off, but a flickering TV in the living room sometimes exposed a silhouette sitting in darkness.

"Hi, how are you?" I said.

Our friends' teenaged son said he'd been in an auto accident and was thrown through the windshield, cutting his nose off. Awaiting plastic surgery, he was embarrassed to be seen. I talked him into joining us outside.

Sometimes God sends a message. Why should I worry about having lost a job? It's just a job. There are other jobs. This poor kid faced more serious challenges. I was being told to forget my selfish feelings and do what I could to comfort him. I don't know whatever happened to him, but I hope he's well.

Chapter 10
Back to the Bullets

Since I still had a job with the Bullets, we returned to Maryland. The team had acquired 6'-11", 275-pound bruiser Jeff Ruland from Golden State. Ruland had worked as a bouncer and bartender in his mom's Long Island bar, and his right forearm was bigger than his left because he'd opened so many beer bottles. With the Bullets, Ruland found his tag-team partner. Who knows why Jeff Ruland and Rick Mahorn became best friends. One common interest they shared was knocking the shit out of opposing players.

In a home game against Phoenix, Ruland and Suns center Alvan Adams got into a fight. "I hit him so hard," Ruland said, "that his eyes turned black before he hit the floor." With Adams out cold and lying on the floor, the Suns bench screamed obscenities at Ruland. He walked up to the players and coaches and asked, "Who's next?" There were no takers.

Rick Mahorn's mentor was Wes Unseld, who set the best picks in the NBA. The 6'-10", 260-pound Mahorn planted himself at midcourt. A quick Bullets guard like Frank Johnson dribbled, full speed, up the court. If a defender tried to stay with him, the guard ran his helpless opponent into a blind pick set by Mahorn. As the player crumbled to the floor, the Bullets played five on four and scored. I winced every time I saw Mahorn flatten a player.

Against Philadelphia, Mahorn KO'ed three 76'ers guards in one game. Two of them never returned. Sixers coach Chuck Daly screamed at the officials, but Mahorn's blind screens were legal.

The Bullets were preparing to release a poster of Ruland and Mahorn, who'd become known as "the Beef Brothers." In the team's office, I saw color photos of the two, wearing white meat cutter's jackets, surrounded by slabs of beef, each holding a butcher knife in one hand and a steak in the other, like a scene from *Rocky*. One photo stood out.

THE BEEF BROTHERS

Rick Mahorn (left) and Jeff Ruland (right) (photo courtesy Washington Bullets)

In it, Ruland and Mahorn clenched bloody raw steaks in their teeth, looking fierce and holding butcher knives. The caption read "The Beef Brothers." "You've got to use that one," I suggested. Too violent, said the PR people, who used a tamer picture. I got a copy of the best photo, had it made into a poster, and asked the boys to sign it. It proudly hangs on my office wall.

They were the Beef Brothers in Washington, but in Boston, legendary Celtics announcer Johnny Most called them "McFilthy and McNasty." When we went to the Boston Garden, they asked me to point out Johnny Most.

"Are you Johnny Most?" the boys said in unison.

"Yes," croaked the cigarette-tainted voice.

"My mother listens to our games in her bar on Long Island," said Ruland, "and she doesn't like it when you call us McFilthy and McNasty."

"Knock it off, you old fart," added Mahorn.

Jeff Ruland grew a ponytail and, on the air, I busted his balls, suggesting that he might play women's basketball. One night before a game, Ruland called me over. "Here," he said, handing me a Ziploc bag with something brown inside. "Here's my fucking ponytail. Now get off my ass." Ruland had cut off his ponytail and given it to me. I stuffed the bag in my pants pocket and forgot about it.

"What's this?" screamed my wife Julie, in the laundry room, holding up a plastic bag "Is it alive? Will it bite?" Going through my pockets she had found Ruland's ponytail. I was laughing so hard I couldn't talk. When I explained it was Jeff Ruland's hair, she questioned exactly what we did on road trips.

One night, Jeff Ruland came into our booth in Baltimore during an Orioles telecast. As we broke for a commercial, I said, "Stay with us. When we come back, we'll visit with the star center of the Washington Bullets, Jeff Ruland."

Ruland held his jaw, shaking his head no, and mumbling, "No . . . pain . . . aarh . . . mmph . . . can't talk . . . tooth." The mighty giant had been felled by a toothache and needed a dentist. Our producer Bill Brown remembered that Dr. Charles Steinberg, who worked in the Orioles front office, was also the team dentist. Steinberg took Ruland to his office and pulled the painful tooth.

While losing teams often cut their losses and sink into last place hoping for a franchise-changing lottery pick and rebuilding with young players, the Bullets patched holes, bringing in veterans in their 30s, most on the back nine of their careers. John Williamson, Gus Williams, Spencer Haywood, Dan Roundfield, Tom McMillen, and Mel Turpin were among those who stayed at the Bullets' Golden Age Home.

Adrian Dantley, one of the greatest scorers in NBA history, had played at DeMatha Catholic in Hyattsville, Maryland, was an All-American at Notre Dame, and had won three NBA scoring titles. A. D. wanted to come home.

In what became a running joke, whenever Dantley came to town, he'd lean on the press table and ask my partner Phil Chenier and me, "So are the Bullets ready to bring me home?"

"How old are you A. D.?" I'd ask.

"Twenty-seven."

"Still too young. Come back in a few years."

Dantley played in the NBA for 15 seasons, won two scoring titles, was an All-Star six times, and was elected to the Basketball Hall of Fame. A. D. retired at 35 but never made it home.

Cocaine was a huge problem in the NBA in the 1980s, and the Bullets were not spared. John Lucas, who'd starred at the University of Maryland, joined the team in 1981–82. Lucas missed practices, and even a game, and it was obvious he had a drug problem. In a game at the Capital Centre, Lucas stole a pass, drove the length of the court to score, and kept running, off the court and into the locker room. They say the NBA is a game of "runs."

Luke hired a bodyguard to keep him out of trouble. Bullets trainer John Lally dubbed the bodyguard "Agent Double Oh Nothing" because he spent most of his time hanging out at bars with Luke and his teammates. Fortunately, John Lucas went to rehab and after his career ended, started a substance abuse program that has helped many NBA players.

One of my favorite venues was the creaky old Boston Garden. The wooden firetrap smelled like stale peanuts, spilled beer, and sweat. You could feel the ghostly presence of Celtics past like Bill Russell, Bob Cousy, and John Havlicek.

Two hours before a game, I sat at the press table, filling out my scorebook. Larry Bird walked onto the parquet floor. I

watched him hit a couple of shots and then returned to my work. I kept hearing *swish, swish,* and I laid my pencil down and watched. Bird started off on the right side of the floor, 18 feet away, hitting every shot as he rotated through eight spots he'd designated. Then, retracing his route, he did the same thing again. Finally, he stepped behind the three-point line and went around the world again, hitting every shot. I looked around to see if anyone else was watching. I was the only one. When Bird finished, he turned and winked at me. Talk about a spiritual moment.

Larry Bird (photo by Steve Lipofsky, Basketballphoto.com)

I got to know broadcast legends like Marv Albert of the New York Knicks, Joe Tait of the Cleveland Cavaliers, Bill Schonely of the Portland Trailblazers, Hot Rod Hundley of the Utah Jazz, Bill King of the Golden State Warriors, and legendary Chick Hearn, voice of the Los Angeles Lakers.

Chick Hearn was perfect for the Lakers, flash and dash, bright sweaters, perfectly coiffed hair, and a ready handshake. He was

Interviewing Shaquille O'Neal (photo courtesy of Home Team Sports)

also very nice to me. Hours before a game at the Forum, I walked down to visit with Chick. I heard, "Magic behind the back to Kareem, skyhook good." When I asked him what he was doing, Chick said, "I'm shooting layups getting ready for the game."

We all have a dream job. Mine is play-by-play announcer for the Los Angeles Lakers. When I was a kid, my family spent part of every summer in Southern California. I hitchhiked to Loyola Marymount University, where the Lakers trained, and watched Jerry West, Elgin Baylor, Wilt Chamberlain, and the other Lakers working out. In college, I drove with two friends from Denver to L.A., watched the Lakers beat the Utah Jazz, and can still remember Wilt Chamberlain dunking with two defenders hanging from his arms. I still have the program from that game.

In 1980, the NBA All-Star Game was played in D.C. My wife Julie and I went to a dinner the night before the game. Julie knew about my dream job, and when I pointed out Dr. Jerry Buss, my lovely wife, fortified by several glasses of wine, walked up to the Lakers owner. "Dr. Buss, my husband Mel Proctor is the play-by-play announcer for the Washington Bullets and one of the best young announcers in the NBA. His dream is to do play-by-play for the Lakers. I know Chick Hearn is getting old, and if you're thinking about replacing him, you should hire my husband." Oh shit.

I apologized to Dr. Buss, who thought it was hilarious, and said, "I think Chick has a few years left." Chick was 64 at the time. He did Lakers play-by-play until he was 86.

John Chanin, executive producer of the Mutual Radio Network, wanted me to do NFL broadcasts. TVS and NBC called asking if I could do college basketball. I was able to work a few network events around my Bullets schedule, but WTOP GM Michael Douglas wouldn't allow me to miss a single Bullets game for a network assignment. I was making little money and was frustrated that I couldn't expand my career.

New Jersey Nets on WNBC Radio, 1982 (photo courtesy of the New Jersey Nets)

Chapter 11
North to New Jersey

The New Jersey Nets offered me their radio play-by-play job on WNBC Radio in New York. I didn't want to move, but WNBC offered more flexibility and more money. I said yes. Since I had a year left on my contract, both WTOP and the Bullets threatened legal action. When they accused Nets GM Lewis Schaffel of tampering, he wanted to withdraw the offer. I begged him to give me a week to straighten things out.

I filled in for Mutual's sports director Tony Roberts, doing morning sports. Larry King was Mutual's overnight talk show host and network star. Larry knew about the New Jersey Nets job. I asked him not to say anything since I was in the midst of delicate negotiations.

"Now with sports," said Larry King, "here's Mel Proctor, the new radio play-by-play voice of the New Jersey Nets." Damn it, Larry.

As the sportscast ended, I confronted Larry. "That was good radio, good radio," he said, walking away.

With Larry King (photo courtesy Home Team Sports)

One of Larry's producers suggested payback. By the end of Larry's overnight show, he was exhausted and tried to catnap during sportscasts. As long as Larry heard a voice, he'd nap.

"And once again with sports, Mel Proctor."

"Thanks Larry," I said, watching his eyes close. "In NBA action last night the New York Knicks beat the Chicago Bulls, 98–94." Larry was asleep.

"And in Philadelphia . . ." I paused. Larry's eyes jerked open. "The 76'ers edged the Utah Jazz, 98–85, as Doctor J, Julius Erving, scored 35 points," I said, as Larry's eyes closed again. "In other games, the Denver Nuggets . . ." Another pause. Again Larry's eyes flew open. I tried to keep from laughing as this continued for five minutes. "And that's sports," I said. "Larry, back to you." As we walked off the set, Larry glared at me.

"Larry, now that's good radio," I said.

"We're moving heeeeere?" whined my bride Julie as we drove through the Meadowlands on a hot, humid, gray day in scenic New Jersey. I tried the historical perspective. "You know honey, Jimmy Hoffa might be buried in that swamp."

"Who'd he play for?" she asked.

After I was released from the Bullets contract, I went to New York to meet WNBC GM Randy Bongarten, who introduced me to the station's stars, Don Imus of *Imus in the Morning,* and Howard Stern, the afternoon shock jock. Since Howard Stern's show aired before the Nets' pregame show, Randy asked me to "banter" with Howard to make a smooth transition from his show to mine.

"It's time now for New Jersey Nets basketball on WNBC," Howard said. "Let's go out to the Meadowlands and the new radio voice of the Nets, Mel Proctor."

"Hi, Howard, how are you tonight?"

"I'm great, but Mel, I need to ask you something. There's a rumor that one of the Nets cheerleaders isn't wearing panties. Is that true?"

The next morning, Nets GM Lewis Schaffel called me into his office. He was understandably pissed. I agreed that Howard Stern's topics didn't jibe with the Nets' wholesome image, but I worked for WNBC, they paid me, and Randy Bongarten wanted Howard and me to chat. Some fans loved our conversation, others loathed it, but they all talked about it.

Then Howard Stern hit me with another knee-buckler. "Once again, we go to the Meadowlands and Mel Proctor. Mel, I actually went to a Nets game Sunday."

"Really, Howard?" I said, cautiously. "Did you enjoy the game?"

"Sure did, great game, but Mel, I went into the Nets' locker room. Darryl Dawkins is hung like a horse. I asked him if I could borrow that thing for a week." When Lewis Schaffel saw me, he shook his head and kept walking. Something had to give.

Howard Stern was funny and popular but crude. Randy Bongarten was one of Howard's targets. Howard often called Randy's wife and on the air, asked, "Well, Mrs. B, how was Randy in the sack last night?" Hilarious.

When Bongarten was promoted by NBC, a new GM took over, didn't like Howard's shenanigans, and fired him. After Stern was canned, he went to an FM station and then into syndication en route to superstardom.

On the Nets' first trip to Landover to play the Bullets, as we walked into the Capital Centre, a crew was setting up musical instruments for a postgame concert. I asked one of the roadies who was performing. "Frankie Valli and the Four Seasons," he said.

Are you shitting me? My all-time favorite group. I knew the lyrics to all their songs. Then a short, weathered Italian guy bounded on stage. Frankie "Fucking" Valli. I tried to be cool. "Frankie, hi, I'm Mel Proctor, play-by-play announcer for the New Jersey Nets, one of your biggest fans."

As we shook hands, Frankie said, "Mel, I'm a Jersey guy. I love the Nets. I listen to the games. Can you introduce me to the players?"

I took Frankie Valli, who is maybe 5'-6", into the Nets' locker room, where he reached up to shake hands with giants like Darryl Dawkins, Mike Gminski, and Buck Williams. Frankie was jazzed.

"Frankie, would you be my halftime guest on radio?" I asked.

"Mel baby, whatever you want. You introduced me to the Nets." Frankie Valli promised to join me at halftime.

I promoted the hell out of Frankie Valli and the Four Seasons and even mixed lyrics into my play-by-play. "Darryl Dawkins, 'the big man in town,' scores. Remember, Frankie Valli at halftime."

"Buck Williams twisted his ankle. Hey Buck, 'Walk like a man, fast as you can.'"

"Stan Albeck doesn't like that call. Remember Stan, 'Silence is golden, golden.' Coming up, an exclusive interview with Frankie Valli."

As the first half ended, no Frankie. I read some meaningless stats while waving frantically at Bullets PR director Mark Pray. I took another commercial break. "Mark, where the hell is Frankie Valli?" Mark went to find him.

I stalled, and we ran PSAs for everything from athlete's foot to halitosis. "I can't find Frankie," Mark Pray said. "There's so much smoke in his dressing room that I couldn't see two feet in front of me."

New Jersey Nets with Mike DiTomasso (photo courtesy Mel Proctor)

As the second half began, I said, "The hell with Frankie Valli and the Four Seasons. My new favorite group is the Four Tops."

One of Stan Albeck's first moves as Nets coach was to compile a tape of Darryl Dawkins' fouls, hoping to convince NBA officials that DD didn't commit nearly as many fouls as he was called for. Since Dawkins was always in foul trouble, he couldn't get into the flow of a game. Albeck's tactic worked. Dawkins still fouled out more than any player in the NBA, but he played longer stretches and had his best year, averaging 16.8 ppg and 6.7 rebounds.

Besides Dawkins, the Nets also had talented players like Buck Williams, Albert King, Mike O'Koren, Mike Gminski, and Otis Birdsong. All they needed was some sugar. In the second half of the season, the Nets added Michael Ray Richardson, who'd been suspended for drug use. The

Michael Ray Richardson (photo courtesy of the Nets)

Knicks' first pick in the 1978 draft, "Sugar" flourished in New York but developed a sweet tooth for cocaine. In 1983, after bouncing from the Knicks to the Golden State Warriors to the Nets, and going to three rehab clinics in five weeks, Richardson was waived by the Nets.

In 1984, the Nets gave Sugar another chance. Rusty at first, Richardson hit his stride late in the season and transformed the Nets into a winner. A long-armed 6'-5" guard, Sugar played three different positions, controlled the game with his passing, and often dominated with his scoring. Defensively, he made steals and deflected passes that became easy fast-break baskets.

Before a game at the Meadowlands, my wife Julie sat in the stands watching the Nets warm up. Suddenly a Nets ball boy appeared. "Michael Ray wants to know if he can have your phone number."

"Who the hell is Michael Ray?" she asked.

"Michael Ray Richardson," the ball boy said as he pointed to Richardson on the floor, jumping up and down and waving wildly.

"You tell Michael Ray that I'm Mel Proctor's wife," she said. She watched the ball boy return to the floor and deliver the message to Richardson. Buck Williams, Albert King, and Darryl Dawkins heard the conversation. They were merciless, pointing at Richardson and laughing hysterically.

Michael Ray Richardson was naïve and also stuttered. As we boarded the bus to Philadelphia the next morning, when Sugar arrived, I stepped in front of him. "Michael Ray, you motherfucker, I heard you tried to pick up my wife last night."

"Well, well, well . . . wh . . . wh . . . wait a minute," he managed to spit out. I could hear his teammates, inside the bus, snickering as they listened.

"Le . . . le . . . let . . . me . . . ex . . . explain," he pleaded.

I stuck my finger in his face. "If you ever try to hit on my wife again, Michael Ray, I'll kill you."

I tried to hit Michael Ray with one more blast, but the players were laughing so hard and pounding on the bus windows that I started to laugh. "Oh shit, Sugar, don't worry. I'm just kidding."

His teammates were in tears as he got on the bus. "You . . . . m . . . mm . . . moth . . . mother . . . motherfuckers," he stammered. With Richardson, the Nets went 19–6 down the stretch and grabbed the final playoff spot in the East. Nobody gave them a chance against the defending NBA champion Philadelphia 76'ers, but Stan Albeck boldly predicted the Nets would win their first-ever playoff game.

Besides Julius Erving, the Sixers had Maurice Cheeks, Moses Malone, Andrew Toney, and Bobby Jones. But the Nets had a secret weapon—Mitch Kaufman, the team's director of video—who put together individual video profiles of each Philadelphia player. If Michael Ray Richardson had to face Maurice Cheeks, he found, in his locker, an edited montage of every move Cheeks had. So did every Nets player.

The cocky young Nets didn't care who they played and shocked the champions, winning the first two games in Philadelphia. Ahead 2–0 in the best-of-five series, on the bus to New Jersey, players celebrated like they'd already won the series. Players danced in the aisles to "No Parking on the Dance Floor," a hit song by Midnight Star, which blared over and over from a boom box. Stan Albeck and his staff cautioned the players that the series wasn't over, but the Nets knew they only had to win one more game, and with two at the Meadowlands, how could they lose?

Despite their coach's warnings, the Nets lost the next two in New Jersey, to even the series at 2–2.

Philadelphia had regained momentum and Game 5 was at the Spectrum. None of that mattered to Michael Ray Richardson, who scored 24 points and had 6 steals as the Nets won 101–98 to win the series three games to two, their first-ever playoff series

Photo by Don Grayson

win. But then in the Eastern Conference Semifinals the Nets were eliminated by Milwaukee, 4–2.

The San Diego Chicken performed when the Nets played the Detroit Pistons at the Pontiac Silverdome. As part of his act, he'd placed a telephone on the edge of the press table, dangerously close to WNBC's telephone, our broadcast line. During a commercial break, the Chicken picked up the wrong phone, ours. Afraid he was going to knock us off the air, I grabbed the phone. He held on. "Damn it, let go of the phone!" I yelled as we played tug of war. Finally I jerked the phone away from him.

As we came back on the air, I looked at the Nets' bench, next to us. Everyone was laughing so hard that Coach Stan Albeck didn't even try to talk to his team during the timeout. Tears rolled down the cheeks of Nets TV announcers Steve Albert and Bill Raftery.

Bernard King (photo by George Kalinsky for Madison Square Garden)

"What a wonderful business," I explained to listeners as we came back on the air, "where a grown man in a three-piece suit can play tug of war with a chicken."

Christmas Day, 1984, Madison Square Garden. The Nets against the Knicks. Nets assistant coach John Killilea joined me on the drive into Manhattan. "Killer" was a Boston Irishman who'd spent many years with the Celtics. "Fahk . . . I'm worried," he said in Bostonian.

"What's the matter, Killer?"

"Buh-nahd fuckin' King, that's what's the mattah. We've got nobahdy to gahd him."

Bernard King scored from everywhere. Post-up turnaround jumpers, fast-break dunks, perimeter shots, it didn't matter. The Nets put everybody on him, including his brother Albert, Kevin McKenna, Jeff Turner, and Michael Ray Richardson. Bernard had 40 points by halftime, but with Michael Ray Richardson having a great all-around game, the Nets stayed close. With King still scoring from everywhere, out of desperation, in the finals seconds of the game, Stan Albeck put 7-foot shot blocker George Johnson in. When King tried a baseline jumper, Johnson flew from 10 feet away to block the shot. Despite an incredible 60-point game by Bernard King, the Nets won, 120–114. "What the fahk," muttered John Killilea, studying the stat sheet, on the drive home.

I hosted the Nets' season-ending luncheon. I was rolling. People laughed at my jokes and clapped when appropriate. I got serious as I prepared to hand the Most Inspirational Player Award to Kevin McKenna.

As I described McKenna's dedication, work ethic, and character, fans started to laugh. This wasn't funny. Soon, they were howling. A fan pointed to a corner of the stage. Four-year-old Billy Proctor had pulled a coat rack down to his level, and using it as a microphone, the little ham sang Bruce Springsteen's hit "Born in the USA." Cradling Billy in my armpit, I handed the award to Kevin McKenna, who laughed harder than anyone.

As my contract ran out, so did the Nets' contract with WNBC. The Nets had to find a new radio station, which left me in limbo. I waited all summer and didn't hear a word from the Nets. I was worried.

Chapter 12
Home Team Sports

Fortunately, Jody Shapiro, executive producer of the new Home Team Sports cable network, offered me a three-year deal to do the Bullets, Orioles, and local sports. I said yes. I knew Julie would be happy to return to the Baltimore-Washington area, but what was I getting into? A start-up network with no viewers? Several times a week I ran to sales manager Jeff Wagner's office and frantically asked, "Did we get any subscribers today?"

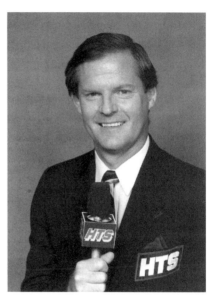

Mel Proctor—Home Team Sports (photo courtesy Home Team Sports)

Besides the Bullets, Capitals, and Orioles, HTS acquired quality college events like the Cotton States Classic, a college basketball tournament in Atlanta featuring Georgia Tech, DePaul, Texas, and Navy. HTS hired ESPN analyst Larry Conley to work with me.

Our producer was there only because his dad had a connection to HTS. The kid was young, inexperienced, and had a drug problem. I've heard he's straightened out so, instead of using his real name, I'll call him "Boy Wonder" or variations thereof.

Five minutes into our first telecast, I realized Boy Wonder didn't have a clue. During commercial breaks, producers, directors, and announcers talk. A producer might say, "Mel, we've got a shot of Lakers general manager Jerry West coming out of break," and I'd think about what I would say.

Boy Wonder? Silence. Then, "3-2-1, Mel, you're on."

Larry and I looked at each other; we were in a video shooting gallery, firing at whatever popped up on our monitor. As the game neared the end of the first half, I asked B.W. what he'd planned for halftime.

Silence.

I told him DePaul coach Joey Meyer was nearby and said he'd be glad to do an interview.

Instead, our coke-numbed producer showed a Special Olympics basketball game. God knows, I love these kids, and we were right in giving them airtime, but not the whole halftime. Since we had no information about the game, teams, or players, Larry and I tap danced. Sammy Davis Jr. would have been proud. We got through two games because of our production crew. With our producer clueless, there were enough old pros to keep the ship from hitting an iceberg.

The telecast ended. Exhausted, mentally and physically, Larry and I walked to the production truck just as our boy, like Tommy Tune in a Broadway show, danced down the steps, singing, "I thought things went pretty well tonight."

"Cocktails," I yelled. Our crew set a record for tequila shots consumed in one night.

As the second night began, after a minute of the first game, nothing had changed. I told Larry Conley, "I've never done this before, and I hope I never have to do it again, but this is a mutiny. We're taking over the ship."

Somehow, we announced, directed, and produced the games. Is that a triple double? If Boy Wonder said, "Let's show the Georgia Tech band," I'd say, "No, coming out of commercial, give us a shot of Bullets general manager Bob Ferry at courtside," and our crew gave it to us. If B.W. said do this, we'd do that. Larry Conley just looked at me and shook his head. Somehow, we survived two more games. When we finished the telecast, I threw down my headset and angrily walked to the production truck.

"Well, guys, I thought everything was much smoother tonight," said Boy Wonder.

"You dumb son of a bitch," I yelled, foaming at the mouth. "This was a fucking disaster. If it hadn't been for our crew, it would have been the worst train wreck in broadcast history. I don't know what the fuck your problem is, but I promise you, I'll never work with you again." I figured I was fired but was so pissed off I didn't care. After last call, I went to my room. My telephone message light flashed red.

"Mel this is Jody Shapiro," said the message. "I promise you'll never have to work with Boy Wonder again. I've gotten calls from the crew explaining what happened. Thanks to all of you for pulling us through."

HTS televised *A Night of Boxing,* a black-tie fundraiser at the Washington Hilton Hotel. Tickets went for $500 each, and the ballroom was filled with high rollers. Muhammad Ali, Joe Frazier, Floyd Patterson, George Chuvalo, Gene Fullmer, Sugar Ray Leonard, and others were flown in. The organizers brought in two boxers for the main event, and an auction raised thousands of dollars for charity.

Two hours before the event, I sat down in an empty seat in the ballroom where the bouts would be held. I thought I was the only person there until I spotted a regal, white-haired man in a tuxedo. Jake LaMotta. I introduced myself and said I was a big fan and had just watched *Raging Bull.* Jake LaMotta took a huge drag on his cigar, blew smoke into my face, and asked, "Where the fuck is my seat?"

HTS broadcast Navy basketball during the David Robinson era. "The Admiral" entered Navy as a 6'-4" freshman but stretched to 7'-1" as a senior. A center, he was faster than any guard in the league. In gymnastics class, the instructor used David to demonstrate the exercises. When the players went to McDonalds for lunch after practice, the 7-footer walked, on his hands, out of Mickey Dees, holding a bag of food in his mouth, as jaws dropped in the parking lot. I told my NBA colleagues that David Robinson was a monster in waiting. They argued that he played in the soft Colonial League, didn't love basketball, and wasn't aggressive enough. When he lit up Kentucky for 50 in an NCAA playoff game, everybody wanted him. He was the No. 1 draft pick in the 1987 NBA Draft.

After David Robinson graduated, Navy basketball sunk to normality. One year, the Middies were shooting 50 percent from the free throw line. Working with Kevin Grevey, I said, "I could go to the free throw line right now, wearing a coat and tie, and hit seven out of ten free throws. There's no excuse for a college team shooting free throws so poorly. Just learn proper technique, concentrate, repeat over and over, and you'll make a decent percentage."

"OK, big talker, prove it," said Grevey.

So, not having shot a free throw in 10 years, before the next Navy game, with the HTS cameras on me, I made seven out of ten.

Although I'd done well at the free throw line, I missed a layup that has haunted me forever. Standing with Bullets GM John Nash as the Bullets shot layups before a game, I said, "John, I've always had this perverse desire to jump into the layup line wearing my coat and tie. Would you mind?"

He laughed. "Go ahead."

As I approached the basket, my best friend on the team, Harvey Grant, howled with laughter as he passed the ball to me. It's hard to shoot wearing a sport coat, and I missed the layup. I grabbed the ball on the other side and missed a reverse layup. Shit. The players laughed their asses off, and so did everyone else who saw it on *SportsCenter* that night.

Kevin Grevey interviews my kids, Maile and Billy (photo courtesy of Home Team Sports)

In 1985, the Bullets and New York Knicks played a preseason game at George Mason College in Virginia, Patrick Ewing's pro debut. As I looked around, I did a double take. Jack Nicholson? I walked into the stands, and when I saw his devilish smile, I knew it was him.

"Jack," I said.

"How ya doin'?" he said, sitting with some hot babe.

Jack said he was shooting a movie in Virginia and came to see Ewing's first NBA game. When I asked him to be my halftime guest, he said, "I don't do TV." Think about it. Have you ever seen him with Johnny Carson, Jay Leno, or David Letterman?

Hangin' with Jack (photo courtesy of Los Angeles Lakers)

I told Jack I was his biggest fan and had seen all his movies and even did a passable Jack Nicholson imitation. "Well then," Jack said, "why don't you interview yourself?"

So I did. On camera, I said, "Our halftime guest is Jack Nicholson. After some basketball small talk, I said, "Jack, my favorite is the diner scene in *Five Easy Pieces*. Could you do that for us? So with Nicholson shown on camera, I voiced the scene, ending with, "And now all you have to do is hold the chicken between your knees."

When the Bullets played in Los Angeles, Nicholson, the Lakers' biggest fan, was at the Forum, early, watching two rookies go one-on-one. I said hello and reminded him about the interview in Virginia. We laughed, and Jack agreed to have a photo taken with me and my partner Phil Chenier.

In 1985 the Bullets drafted Manute Bol, at 7'-7" the tallest player in NBA history. A Dinka tribesman from the Sudan, he'd reportedly killed a lion with a spear, although nobody knew whether the lion had been awake, asleep, or drunk. One night, Manute took calls on our HTS phone-in show.

"Hi, you're on the air on HTS' *Sportstalk*," I said.

"My name is Brenda and my question is for Manute Bol."

"Shoot," said Manute, using one of the 10 words in his English vocabulary.

"Manute, I know you killed a lion, but I want to know, how long is your spear?"

"Long enough," Manute answered.

With tribal markings across his forehead and gnarled fingers, Bol wasn't a scorer, but he blocked shots like nobody I've ever seen.

Because his legs were so long, Manute was uncomfortable on airplanes. One frigid morning we boarded a commercial flight in Cleveland. When the passenger in front of Manute reclined his seat, Manute was scrunched up like a spring waiting to explode.

"Fuck this," Manute said. "Let me off."

The flight crew warned him there wouldn't be another flight to D.C. for hours. As we were about to take off, somebody banged on the door. The stewardess opened it, and as Manute returned, we all started laughing. Manute tried to give us the finger but messed that up too. He pulled a glove off of his hand and gave us the one-finger salute, with his ring finger. We laughed even harder.

In 1987, the tallest player in NBA history was joined with the shortest player in league annals, 5'-3" Tyrone "Muggsy" Bogues of Wake Forest. The Bullets' first-round pick, Bogues had played at Dunbar High School in Baltimore with future NBA players David Wingate, Reggie Lewis, and Reggie Williams. Muggsy viewed his lack of height as an advantage. Already at floor level, he got to loose balls quicker than bigger players, kept his dribble low to avoid turnovers, and with his quickness, pressured opponents like a pit bull snapping at a mailman's heels.

After seven straight losing seasons, Bullets GM Bob Ferry thought he'd struck gold when the team selected LSU's John Williams as the Bullets' first pick in the 1986 NBA Draft. Williams, a 6'-9", 225-pound forward, had been the Los Angeles City High School Player of the Year before being lured to LSU. Williams could score, rebound, handle the ball, and was a great passer. His future seemed unlimited.

Williams averaged nine points and five rebounds as a rookie, but over the next two seasons, he improved so quickly, we were all excited about the Bullets' future. In a home game against Utah, Williams chased a loose ball right in front of us at press row. Hitting a slick spot on the court, he lost his balance, did the splits, and then writhed in agony. He had torn the ACL (anterior cruciate ligament) in his right knee and after surgery was never the same. Rehab and John Williams didn't agree. Sometimes he'd show up, sometimes he wouldn't. As he got increasingly fatter, he was nicknamed "Hot Plate" Williams to distinguish him from Cleveland's John "Hot Rod" Williams.

On the road, Dennis Householder, the Bullets' strength and conditioning coach, took Williams to every meal, making sure he ate the right food. One night Dennis had to meet a friend for dinner. He told John Williams that he'd checked the hotel restaurant's menu—which offered chicken, fish, or pasta—and told John any one of those was fine. When Dennis returned to the hotel, he asked John what he'd had for dinner.

"Chicken, fish, and pasta," answered Williams.

Williams' increasing weight put pressure on his gimpy knee. Over the next five years, he bounced to the Indiana Pacers, Los Angeles Clippers, to Spain, to Magic Johnson's All-Stars, and then to obscurity.

After his 60-point game in 1984, Bernard King tore the ACL in his right knee, usually a career ender. The injury was so severe that the ACL was removed and replaced by ligaments from his upper thigh. King missed the entire 1985–86 season and all but six games the next year. The Knicks released him, and desperate for scoring, the Bullets signed him in 1987. Bernard King averaged 17 points a game in his comeback season, and his numbers increased until 1990–91, when he averaged 28 points per game, third best in the NBA.

I've never seen a player completely rebuild his game like Bernard King did. Before his injury, King would post up and use his strength, either shooting bump-and-fade jumpers or skying over opponents for dunks. King's knee injury stole his explosiveness. So, he faced up, slashed to the basket, filled lanes on fast breaks, developed a midrange jumper, and learned to draw fouls.

Bernard King was a chameleon. Usually jovial and friendly, by tipoff, his smile had disappeared as the "Bernard King Game Face" emerged. That, in itself, was worth 10 points.

Bernard was a loner and was well, different. Having battled addiction problems early in his career, he didn't hit the bars with his teammates. Who knows where he went? He was articulate and a great interview, when in the mood. After one of his great games, I walked up to Bernard, standing half dressed at his locker, put a microphone in his face, and asked a question. He held up his hands to block the camera and said, "Wait a minute, I'm not ready yet."

"What?"

"Look, I make a lot of money and buy expensive clothes, and that's how I want to look on camera."

So the media waited while Bernard put on his dress shirt, cuff links, vest, and sport coat.

"OK, I'm ready," he said.

I had called Bernard King's 60-point game, but his performance on January 31, 1991, was the most emotional I've seen. That day, King had been selected for the All-Star team, the first player ever to appear in the game without an ACL. Although he was now a Bullet, Madison Square Garden fans still loved "the King." His parents, surgeon, and rehab therapist all attended the game. Bernard King scored from everywhere. The New York Knicks crowd, the most demanding of all fans, stood and cheered Bernard King. When Bernard left the game with 49 points, having assured a Bullets win, he was given a five-minute standing ovation. I had tears in my eyes. My goodness, to be a part of moments like that.

Bernard gave game balls to his doctor and therapist. New York papers headlined Bernard King's comeback. Since the Bullets had a couple days off before playing in Miami, Coach Wes Unseld told Bernard he could spend the day with his family and fly to Florida later.

When we prepared to fly to Miami the next morning, a stewardess said that Richard Nixon, former president of the United States, would be joining us in first class.

As Nixon boarded, I saw why he'd been a master politician, as he stopped at each player's seat and introduced himself. When Mark Alarie said he went to Duke, Nixon said, "I went to law school there." With each player, he found common ground.

As we took off, the players fell asleep, and after Nixon finished talking to Bullets coach Wes Unseld, I introduced myself, telling Nixon I'd spent a year at his alma mater, Whittier College. "Welllllll . . . sit down . . ." he said.

Nixon was headed to Florida to go fishing with his friend Bebe Rebozo. He said that most former presidents have six or seven Secret Service men, but he kept only one retired agent, which allowed him to sit in the stands at New York Giants games and talk football with fans.

Having seen Bernard King's incredible performance the night before, Nixon looked around the plane, whipped his head toward me, jowls shaking like Jell-O, and asked, "Whaaaaaaair's Mister King?" I turned away and looked out the window, fighting off laughter. Every time I think of Tricky Dick, I hear him saying, "Where's Mr. King?"

On an off night in Minneapolis, Harvey Grant, Dave Feitl, rookie Ledell Eackles, and I met for dinner. Eackles was a great kid from New Orleans, but man was he naïve. As we stood at the bar, I said, "Ledell, I'm going to give you a geography lesson. Right now we're in Minneapolis. The city next to Minny is St. Paul. They're known as the 'Twin Cities.'"

"Boolshit," Ledell said, "I'm not falling for that."

The other players laughed so hard they were spitting up beer. "No, really Ledell," said Harvey Grant, "Mel's telling you the truth, he's trying to teach you something."

"No, no, boolshit." We never could convince him.

The next night as the Bullets warmed up, I sat at courtside, filling out my scorebook. Harvey Grant walked up. "Yo, Mel, ask Ledell what the Twin Cities are."

"Ledell," I yelled. He walked over to me. "Ledell, what are the Twin Cities?"

"Your mamma and your sister," he said, his face breaking into a proud grin.

I believe NBA officials have the toughest job in sports. They're in constant motion, trying to keep up with younger, faster players, watching for hand checking, holding, and pushing, and trying to control the physicality without ruining the game's flow. Officials can affect the outcome of games as much as players or coaches.

In a 1991 game between the Bullets and Portland Trailblazers at the Capital Centre, young NBA official Steve Javie threw Bullets guard Darrell Walker out of the game in the fourth quarter. Javie had also ejected Walker from a game three years earlier. "Javie doesn't like me," Walker said later. "I was mad about what he was doing to our team. Harvey Grant and Jerome Kersey were having a great battle. John Williams and Buck Williams were knocking heads. It was a helluva game. We just wanted a fair shake." Bullets center Pervis Ellison was next. Upset by a foul called by official Don Vaden, Ellison threw the ball fairly hard to another ref, Bill Spooner, who caught it. Neither Spooner nor Vaden had any problem with Ellison, but Steve Javie stormed into the situation, giving Ellison a technical and throwing him out of the game.

"Oh, no, Steve Javie is going crazy," I told viewers. "He's just teed up Ellison. What's Javie doing? He doesn't belong in the NBA; he's incompetent and has had it in for the Bullets for years."

Upset about the ejections of Walker and Ellison and a 40–11 difference in fouls called, Coach Wes Unseld ran onto the floor, yelling at Javie, who threw him out of the game.

Fans charged the court, screaming obscenities. First Walker, then Ellison, and now Unseld. Who's next? When the team's mascot, "Hoops," ran onto the floor, I thought, no, he wouldn't, would he?

Oh yes he would. Steve Javie threw the mascot out of the game as the crowd howled even louder. "I know officials get upset," I continued, "and sometimes make mistakes, but how can a guy like Steve Javie singlehandedly destroy a game? Gee whiz, I know a guy's gotta make a living, but isn't there something else Javie can do? Pathetic." When the Bullets lost, fans booed and threw objects onto the floor. Our cameraman followed Steve Javie walking off the court, the loneliest man on earth.

"Boy, oh boy, this is the worst officiating I've seen in 13 years in this league." As Javie disappeared into the locker room, I added, "Thanks, Steve, terrific job. Boy was he awful."

The next day, the *Washington Post*'s sports headline was "Proctor: Broadcast Views," followed by all of my comments, which you've just read.

I expected to hear from the NBA, but Bullets owner Abe Pollin complained so vehemently that the NBA interviewed those involved and quietly gave Steve Javie an unpaid vacation.

Years later, after an Orioles game in Chicago, I walked into the Lodge, a sports bar on Rush Street. Steve Javie sat at the bar. We stared at each other, both uncomfortable. Then we shook hands, drank beer, and reminisced about "the Night." I discovered Steve Javie is a nice guy, and he became one of the top officials in the NBA.

Karma. A charity game, the media all-stars against some former Bullets. Since all that was left of my game was my shot, I quickly lost interest as former Redskins quarterback Joe Theisman hogged the ball and fired like a man with a machine gun. While the ex-pros were knocking the crap out of us aging sportswriters and broadcasters, I was called for a foul. I raised hell with the rent-a-referee, who gave me a technical foul. "You can't do that, this is a fundraiser. You're not even a real official."

"Shut up," yelled the zebra, "or you're out of the game."

Since I still had work to do before the telecast, I said, "Fine, throw me out. I've got stuff to do." Our statistician Marty Aronoff, who's worked every event from the NBA Finals to the Super Bowl, said I had just made history, the first person ever ejected from a charity game. Somewhere, Steve Javie was smiling.

My daughter Maile with Gheorghe Muresan (photo by Mel Proctor)

In 1993 Gheorghe Muresan arrived. At 7'-7", Muresan was the same height as Manute Bol, so the Bullets had the distinction of having the two tallest players in NBA history. Unlike the skinny Bol, Muresan weighed over 300 pounds, wore size 19 shoes, and had a wingspan of 7'-10". Unlike many big men who are self-conscious about their size, Gheorghe loved being a giant. When we walked through airports, people stopped, gawked, and asked stupid questions like, "How's the weather up there?" With his lopsided grin, broken English, and warm personality, Gheorghe answered every question. Fans loved him.

Although incredibly slow and mechanical, through hard work, Muresan made himself into a decent NBA player. In 1995–96, Muresan averaged 14.5 points, 9.6 rebounds, 2.3 blocks; made a league-leading 58 percent of his field-goal attempts; and was named the NBA's Most Improved Player for the 1995–96 season.

Gheorghe Muresan didn't know most people's real names so he created nicknames. Since I was the television announcer, Gheorghe called me "Tee Vee."

I learned that Muresan was from Transylvania, a historical region in the central part of Romania. I had watched enough Bela Lugosi movies to know that Transylvania was home to vampires, and I couldn't wait to ask Gheorghe about Count Dracula.

On a bus one night, I snuck up behind Gheorghe and whispered in his ear, "Gheorghe, my name is Count Alucard, *Dracula* spelled backward. I vant to suck your blood."

He whipped around and shook an enormous finger in my face. "No joke, Tee Vee. There are vampires in Transylvania."

"Sure Gheorghe."

"Tee Vee, not funny. My father knows vampire." Gheorghe was serious.

"Tee Vee, you tink eez funny? You vant to meet vampire?"

"Sure."

Gheorghe leaned closer and explained how to attract a vampire. He said that when I got to my hotel room, I should rub cream all over my face, make a slight cut on my neck, turn off the lights, light a candle, and look into a mirror. We were probably in Cleveland or Indianapolis, and I'd had several glasses of red wine, so I had nothing else to do.

When I told Gheorghe that when I woke up, my face was covered with cream, there was a cut on my neck, but there were no vampire footprints, Gheorghe said, "Tee Vee, you did something wrong. It vill verk, try again."

Billy Crystal thought so highly of Muresan's size, personality, and acting potential that he cast him in a 1998 movie, *My Giant.* Gheorghe drove us nuts on team flights, constantly reading from the film's script and practicing his lines.

Ben Wallace was a rookie free agent from Division II Virginia Union who'd played a year in Italy and signed with the Bullets in 1996. Raw and strong, Ben couldn't shoot and was atrocious at the foul line. But boy could he rebound and block shots. On road trips, Ben carried his huge boom box on his shoulder, hip hop music blaring.

One night on a bus ride, with my ear drums pulsating, I turned around and said, "Ben, why don't you put some real music on that thing?"

"Like what?" he asked.

"How about Frank Sinatra?" I suggested.

"Who?"

"Well, then how about the Beatles? Surely, you must have heard of them."

"Man, them nigguhs been dead for years," Ben said, maxing the volume and shaking his head to the beat.

Ben Wallace played on the Detroit Pistons' NBA championship team in 2004 and four times was named NBA Defensive Player of the Year.

Bullets' Plane Makes Forced Landing

Happy landings are no joke for Bullets in Denver

Plane Trouble Fouls Bullets' Trip to Utah

WES UNSELD: Airplane engine problem 'frightening.'

Chapter 13
Fear of Flying

For many frequent flyers, fear is a constant traveling companion. As former Orioles manager Earl Weaver put it so eloquently, as he retired, "I was afraid I might wake up dead in the Oakland Hyatt House." Baseball announcers Don Drysdale and Harry Kalas and NBA broadcaster Don Poier all died on the road. I think all of us who've spent thousands of nights on the road share the same fear.

On January 13, 1982, as the Bullets readied to fly to Atlanta, a snowstorm blanketed Washington, D.C. We met at the Capital Centre to board a team bus to Washington National Airport when we were told a plane had crashed near the airport and all flights were canceled.

Since the Washington Capitals were hosting the Edmonton Eskimos, we all went to the hockey game, the only time I've seen the great Wayne Gretzky in person. When the game ended, we bussed to the Marriott Hotel near Washington National and listened to WTOP News Radio: "Air Florida Flight 90 has crashed into the 14th Street Bridge, ripping off guardrails and shearing off tops of cars on the bridge before sinking into the Potomac River. A total of 78 people, including four motorists, have been killed."

As we checked into our hotel, the lobby was packed with media from all over the world who'd arrived to cover the disaster. We went to the bar and watched the news. It was hard to believe we were in the middle of the story. We were also on the first flight the next morning.

Nobody slept. Most of us tossed and turned and then gave up and watched CNN until the sun came up. In the morning, we silently boarded the bus to the airport. As we crossed the 14th Street Bridge, we saw topless cars, and in the Potomac River, rescue workers searched for survivors. Nobody said a word as we took off for Atlanta.

On December 3, 1990, the Bullets flew on United Airlines Flight 417 to Salt Lake City, with a stop in Denver. As we took off from Denver's Stapleton Airport, with 105 passengers aboard, I sat in an aisle seat, the middle seat vacant and a woman by the window. We were both reading books. It was a smooth flight until we heard several loud pops and the plane shook.

"Ladies and gentlemen," the pilot said in a soothing voice, "we've encountered a situation and we'll have to return to Denver. Let's stay calm. I don't think it's anything serious."

An eerie silence settled over the plane. Then, with more strain in his voice, the pilot said, "We've blown our number-two engine." The University of Utah basketball team sat in the rear of the plane, and several players screamed after seeing sparks flying from an engine.

Frightened flight attendants, clutching purple emergency booklets, ran up and down the aisles, trying to calm passengers. One flight attendant sat next to Bullets coach Wes Unseld, asking for his help if the plane crashed and passengers had to slide down an emergency ramp. As the plane turned and headed back to Denver, it lost altitude. As we got a much closer look at the Rocky Mountains than we'd anticipated, I looked into first class and my eyes met Darrell Walker's. On the court a fearless player, he closed his eyes and shook his head. No words necessary.

"As we approach Denver," said the pilot, "I want everybody to practice the emergency drill. That doesn't mean we'll have to use it, but I want everyone prepared. Take off all eyeglasses, remove all sharp objects, bend forward, and hold your knees." As passengers complied, the pilot said, "OK, that's fine. We hope we don't have to use emergency tactics, but in the event we do, you are prepared." Our plane dropped lower as we cleared the mountaintops and approached Denver.

"All right," said the captain, "assume the emergency position." This was the real deal. As I grabbed my knees, I bargained with God. I promised to stop drinking, cussing, looking at other women, and smoking. Wait a minute. I didn't smoke. I prayed for my wife and kids. I knew I could be dead within minutes. Suddenly, serenity, unlike any I'd ever experienced, settled over me. As we began our final descent into Denver, fire trucks and ambulances rimmed the runway. The airport had been completely shut down to accommodate our emergency landing.

The woman next to me, who hadn't said a word the entire flight, suddenly slid into the middle seat, grabbed my hand, and screamed, "I have two kids!"

"I do too!" I screamed back, squeezing her hand.

As the plane was about to touch down, we heard a *whoosh* as the plane shook and then static as the pilot opened his microphone. "Well, we got real lucky," he said, "That number-two engine came back on." As we landed, people cheered and gave thanks.

When the door opened, we raced off the plane, sprinted to the airport bar, and threw downs shots of tequila as fast as we could. Even the nondrinkers drank. Trainer John Lally gulped a shot and said, "You motherfuckers stay here. I'm going to straighten this shit out." I sensed an Oscar-winning performance coming and followed Lally to the ticket counter.

"OK, Mr. Lally," the attendant said, "we'll get your team on the next available United flight."

"No, look, motherfucker," John said, spit flying out of his mouth, "your airline took our high-priced, gifted athletes up in the air, spun them around, and scared the living shit out of them. Here's what you're going to do." As Lally fanned out the United tickets in front of the agent, he said, "There's a Delta flight to Salt Lake City in an hour. You take these tickets to Delta, exchange them, and get us on that flight. Then you bring the tickets to me in the bar. You understand?"

WTOP Radio, 1978 (photo courtesy WTOP Radio)

When the United attendant came into the bar and handed the Delta tickets to

Lally, he held them aloft. We gave him a standing ovation and lifted our glasses to the "Great One," John Lally.

Doing the Bullets, NFL football, and boxing, I was stressed to the max. On a Bullets flight to Houston, my stomach was rocking and rolling, and I hadn't even eaten the airline meal. I was convinced I had cancer. I tried to sleep but was suddenly overwhelmed by thoughts about Ray Hester, a former Hawaiians linebacker who'd died of cancer. What the hell was going on? Why did I think of Ray Hester? I barely knew him. I'd never thought of him. He was just one of thousands of names on countless team rosters I'd seen. I was losing my fucking mind.

"Which team is this?" asked an attractive blonde, standing next to me at the baggage claim.

"The Washington Bullets."

"My husband was a pro athlete."

"Really, what sport?"

"Football."

"Would I know his name?"

"Ray Hester."

The blood drained from my face, my body went numb, and I thought I was going to pass out.

"Are you OK?" she asked.

"I have to sit down before I fall down. When I come back, I'll explain."

I sat down and took deep breaths. What the hell was going on? This was more than coincidence. For this meeting to occur, the two of us had to be in the same city at the same spot in the same airport at the same time on the same date and in the same year. Impossible.

After I explained, she offered me a ride to my hotel. During the drive, she said that she'd married Ray Hester, they had children, and while playing for the Hawaiians, he developed stomach cancer. She said that in his final days, Ray was sedated, wasn't in pain, and spent most of the day on the couch, curled up with their kids, watching TV.

She dropped me off and gave me her card. She owned a hair salon. Several times, while in Houston, I looked at her phone number, dialed a few digits, and hung up. I was terrified of calling her. When I finally summoned up the courage, the number had been disconnected.

If the Bullets played a game and had to fly to another city for a game the next night, an NBA rule said the team had to take the first available flight in the morning. My body recoils at the memory of 4:00 a.m. wake-up calls in Cleveland and Detroit. I was always half asleep as I struggled onto the team bus to the airport.

"My man, what color do you want?" asked an old black man, as I sat down at his airport shoe shine stand.

"What do you mean?"

"Well, you're wearing one cordovan shoe and one brown shoe."

I tried to be cool. "Well, shine the brown shoe brown and the cordovan shoe cordovan."

As I paid and walked away, I heard the man laughing and telling everyone, "The dude had one cordovan shoe and one brown shoe."

On a flight, a stewardess asked, "Sir, do you know you have your sweater on backward?"

"Yes, I do," I answered. "It's a new European style."

One frigid morning, I pulled my red, white, and blue Bullets stocking cap over my ears, reclined the seat, and tried to sleep.

"I love that cap," said a woman with a lovely English accent. I looked up. Oh my, Audrey Hepburn.

"Thank you," I said.

In her fifties, she was still beautiful.

"We live in Switzerland, and my son could use a warm cap like that. How could I get one?"

I thought about asking for her address and having the Bullets send her a box of stocking caps or personally delivering them. Instead, I acted like Cary Grant and said, "Miss Hepburn, I'll give you this one. I've only worn it a couple of times. Wash it and it'll be as good as new." I couldn't believe I was handing my dirty stocking cap to Audrey Hepburn.

Clowning around with TNT's Ron Kramer (photo courtesy of Turner Sports)

Chapter 14
Network High Jinks

While calling Bullets games, I sent a VHS tape of my work to the TVS Network. TVS exec Rich Hussey said he'd use me on some college games but asked about the other voice on the demo. I told him it was James Brown, a D.C. high school legend and great player at Harvard who was drafted and cut by the Atlanta Hawks and was now trying to transition from computer sales to broadcasting. Hussey hired both of us, took us with him to NBC, and for J. B. it began his rapid climb to a network career.

Since WTOP wouldn't let me miss any Bullets games, it was often a tight squeeze getting from a Friday night NBA game to a Saturday afternoon TVS telecast. If my college assignment was in Boston or New York, Hussey told me to just use an air charter service, to the tune of $2,000 a trip. I felt like a big wheel, by myself, drinking fine wine, in a Learjet to my next game.

If my TVS game was reasonably close, say in West Virginia, I rented a limo, drank a few beers, and fell asleep, arriving early in the morning. After a day game in Morgantown, I told the limo driver to stop at a 7-11 so I could grab some snacks for the road. As I got out of the car, someone asked who was in the limo.

"Elvis," I said, entering the store.

When I came back, loaded down with Pringles, beef jerky, and red licorice, a crowd surrounded the limo, faces pressed against the windows, trying to spot Elvis. As I got in, I didn't have the heart to tell them Elvis had died two years earlier.

In 1982, promoter Shelly Saltman, whom I'd known since the WFL days in Hawaii, called me. Saltman is best known as daredevil Evel Knievel's manager, the guy Knievel tried to beat to death with a baseball bat because Knievel didn't like Saltman's book, *Evel Knievel on Tour*. With NFL players on strike, Saltman was promoting two NFLPA All-Star games in Washington and Los Angeles, to be televised by Ted Turner's superstation WTBS. Saltman had hired Lakers announcer Chick Hearn to do the L.A. game and Chargers play-by-play man Tom Kelly for the D.C. game, but Chargers owner Gene Klein threatened to fire Kelly if he did the game. In a panic, the day before kickoff, Saltman asked me to do play-by-play. I explained that there was no way I could prepare in 24 hours—the rosters weren't even set, and nobody knew who was playing. "I'll give you $1,000," Saltman said.

"I'll do it."

John Riggins, Mark Moseley, and Lee Roy Selmon were among the few recognizable names in the game. The rest were no-names, hoping to pick up a $3,000 winners' check or $2,500 for the losers. Hell, I should have volunteered to be a long snapper.

Knowing I was worried about damaging my career by doing this fiasco, my partner, Alex Hawkins, said, "I pissed away my career at CBS. You might as well ruin yours today." During a CBS telecast, when Hawk saw a player wearing a cast, he said, "I played once with two broken wrists and two casts. You find out who your friends are when you go to the men's room." And as Dallas Cowboy quarterback Roger Staubach jogged off the field, Hawk said, "He runs like a sissy." CBS said bye-bye to Hawkins.

Near the end of the first half, I saw someone crawling on his hands and knees toward the interview position. Ted Turner, my halftime guest—shitfaced. When the camera's red light went on, Turner faked sobriety. When the interview ended, he stumbled out of the booth. Fortunately, few people watched the game, in person or on TBS.

Apparently Turner execs liked the way I'd handled a difficult situation. I started doing NBA games for TNT/TBS. My partners included Rick Barry, Bill Russell, and Red Auerbach. I respected Bill Russell's accomplishments with the Boston Celtics, but as a broadcast partner, he was aloof, unprepared, and didn't seem to give a shit. Since he didn't know players' names, it was "Big Guy" or "Little Man." I'm sure he never knew my name. When kids approached for an autograph, Russell said, "I don't sign, but I'll be glad to shake your hand." Wonderful. Now that autograph prices have soared, he's signing.

I loved working with Red Auerbach. He wasn't a TV guy; he tried to coach on the air, just as he had from the bench. His analysis was, "Come on, set a damn pick," or "Can you guys play some defense?" In the cab to the hotel, I asked Red why, when the Bullets came to Boston, there was always a bomb scare or fire drill at the hotel or the locker room heat was stifling and the showers spewed ice water. Red puffed his cigar, blew smoke rings, smiled, and said, "It's called home court advantage."

In 1986 Turner Broadcasting offered me the play-by-play job for the World Basketball Championships, part of the initial Goodwill Games. The Games were held in Russia, but some guy in Spain had retained the basketball rights. Let's see now, tapas and fine wine or gruel and vodka?

My partner was Atlanta Hawks coach Mike Fratello, making his broadcast debut under the most difficult circumstances. Our makeshift studio was the basement of a television station in Madrid. Game tapes were delivered to the station, and we did voiceovers as if these were live games. We rarely had accurate names or numbers of players, and when we called venues for information, nobody spoke English.

Squinting at a borrowed television set, our monitor, we worked all night and by sunrise were exhausted but wired. The station's vending machines sold beer, so we pooled our quarters and carried cans of beer to the hotel to wind down.

Mike Fratello introduced me to Victor de la Serna, a basketball junkie who spoke five languages and was also food and beverage editor for *El Pais,* the national newspaper. After hearing Victor talk hoops, I pulled Fratello aside. "Mike, if we have to pay him ourselves, we need Victor." Victor was a godsend, getting lineups and pronunciations and passing us priceless information on the air. Thanks to Victor's restaurant recommendations, we all packed on 20 pounds.

Mike Fratello's TV exposure opened up a new career for him. Every time he got fired as an NBA coach, he went back to TNT to broadcast NBA games and became "the Czar of the Telestrator." Every time I got fired, I went home and picked up dog poop.

After the first round, we broadcast games live. There was political unrest in Spain, and Basque terrorists had just blown up a busload of Spanish police trainees. So, armed guards with machine guns searched our briefcases as we entered the gyms in Madrid, Barcelona, Zaragoza, and Malaga.

In Barcelona I watched the best young center I'd ever seen. Twenty-two-year-old Arvydas Sabonis was 7'-3". An incredible passer, he could also run the floor and hit hook shots with either hand.

The cold war was still on, and Soviet security guards prevented any chance to get to know the players. But one late night, I walked down to the hotel bar, where Sabonis and his teammates relaxed at a table, throwing down shots of vodka. When I sat down at the empty bar, they asked me to join them. I spoke no Russian, and they spoke little English, but somehow we managed to drink vodka and talk basketball.

Despite the presence of future NBA players Arvydas Sabonis, Alexander "Sasha" Volkov, and Sarunas Marciulionis, the Soviets lost the championship game, 87–85, to the U.S. team, which included David Robinson, Kenny Smith, Muggsy Bogues, and Steve Kerr. The USSR avenged the loss, beating the Americans for the gold medal in the 1988 Olympics.

By the time Arvydas Sabonis reached the NBA, he was 31, his knees were shot, he'd torn an Achilles tendon, and was overweight. Still, he managed to have a productive seven-year NBA career with the Portland Trailblazers. A Blazers assistant coach once told me that in his prime, Arvydas Sabonis was the greatest center who ever played.

I did play-by-play for the 1987 McDonald's Open, a three-team round-robin affair in Milwaukee featuring the Milwaukee Bucks, the Soviet National Team, and Tracer Milan, the European champions. The night before the tournament, I joined TNT's Kim Bohuny, who spoke Russian and English, and Soviet assistant coach Ivan Edeshko in a Hyatt Regency hotel room, sipping Russian vodka with a legend.

In the gold medal game in the 1972 Olympics, Ivan Edeshko had thrown a court-length pass to Alexander Belov, who scored the game-winning basket as time ran out in the Soviets' controversial 51–50 win over the United States. The American players were so upset that they refused to accept their silver medals.

"Ivan, the U.S. won that game," I said. "Three times the U.S. got screwed by . . ."

"Nyet. Mel, understand your pride and love for country," Edeshko said, "but vee von."

"Bullshit. Doug Collins made two free throws with three seconds left. Game over."

"No, we had called timeout."

As our voices rose, Ivan gave the international sign for a timeout and walked away. Our personal cold war ended when Ivan returned with tins of Beluga caviar he'd brought from Russia. We clinked glasses, hugged, drank ice-cold Russian vodka, ate the world's best caviar, and talked basketball deep into the night.

TNT exec Rex Lardner offered me the play-by-play job for the network's prime-time Saturday night college football telecasts, replacing the legendary Lindsey Nelson. My partner was "the Golden Boy," Paul Hornung, the former Heisman Trophy winner at Notre Dame.

We stayed in the same hotel as the teams, so that on Saturday mornings we could have breakfast with the coaches. I learned to expect a call from Paul about 7:00 a.m. "Pardner, I stayed out too late last night," he said,

College football on TNT (photo courtesy of Turner Sports)

a female giggling in the background. "Could you possibly take notes for me?"

"Sure Paul."

As players, Paul Hornung and Alex Karras had been suspended by NFL commissioner Pete Rozelle for betting on NFL games. Paul suggested that he and I should be billed as "Proctor and Gamble."

CBS analyst John Madden used a telestrator to diagram plays and, adding a few *booms* and *pows,* became a star. I convinced Paul to do a low-budget takeoff on Madden, called "Paul's Blackboard." He stood in front of an old chalkboard as I asked, "Paul, explain how USC's offense plans to attack Cal today. Paul rambled aimlessly, speaking nonsense, as he used a stick of chalk to draw zigs and zags, dots and dashes, and arrows. None of it made sense, but man it was funny.

Most broadcasters prepare before a game, but Paul showed up, an hour before kickoff, with a blank sheet of poster board and started making his spotting charts. Then he would jump up to make one of many phone calls and never finish his homework. If Paul heard of a last-minute injury, he was on the phone to Las Vegas. The Golden Boy. One of a kind.

In 1985, I began doing NFL games for the NBC Radio Network, and my partner was Dave Rowe, former defensive lineman with the Oakland Raiders. After a Bullets telecast in Chicago, the next morning I met Dave at O'Hare Airport for a 7:00 a.m. flight to Seattle for a 4:00 p.m. game between the Seahawks and Denver Broncos. All flights to Seattle were canceled because of fog. Portland was the nearest city to Seattle, but those flights were booked. We tried to buy tickets from passengers but found no sellers. We were screwed.

Then a guardian angel appeared, a sympathetic American Airlines exec, who agreed that it would be tragic if we didn't make it to our national broadcast. With the packed plane about to depart, he pulled two passengers off the flight as Dave and I took their seats.

We landed in Portland, but Seattle was still 200 miles away. Rental cars were gone.

"What are we going to do?" Dave asked.

"Taxi," I yelled, and a cab pulled up.

"Wait, do you know what that'll cost?"

"No," I said, as we got into a taxi.

"Where to?" asked the driver.

"Seattle."

"You're kidding. I can't drive that far."

"How much money will you make today?" I asked.

"Maybe a hundred dollars."

"I'll tell you what," I said, "We'll give you two hundred and a one hundred dollar bonus if you get us to the Kingdome before kickoff."

He turned the meter off, called in sick, and floored it, the speedometer hitting 100 miles per hour as Dave and I stuck our heads out the window, watching for cops. In Seattle, we hit bumper-to-bumper traffic six blocks from the Kingdome. We gave our driver $300, grabbed our bags, and ran, shouting, "NBC Radio!" as we blew past security.

In our booth, minutes before kickoff, two replacement announcers were primed for their network debuts. "Out," we said as Dave and I confiscated their headsets. "Amazing," said NBC executive producer Jack O'Rourke.

One of the replacements asked if he could be my spotter. Sure. Early in the game, "Elway to pass, it's intercepted by the Seahawks . . ." *Boom!* My spotter, a Seattle fan, got so excited he hit me in the head, knocking my headset off and depriving our national audience of the greatest touchdown call in NFL history.

We stayed in Seattle that night, but fog was predicted for three days. All flights were canceled, every rental car gone. If four of us had to stay in Seattle, with hotel, meals, and other expenses, NBC would take a financial hit.

I called private airlines. Nobody would fly in this fog. Finally, one charter service said they'd get us out of

The $2,500 charter from Seattle. Notice that the pilot (far right) is smiling. Little did we know we were risking our lives. (photo courtesy Mel Proctor)

Me (L), Dave Rowe, and Henry Makrin (R) (photo courtesy Mel Proctor)

Seattle for $2,500. The owner-pilot said he could fly to San Francisco, where we could connect with flights to our destinations. Reluctantly, NBC approved the expense.

So, producer Rich Bonn, engineer Henry Makrin, Dave Rowe, and I boarded the small plane. Nobody said a word as the pilot taxied down the runway and lifted into the air. We flew, engulfed by whiteness, for miles but finally popped through the fog into a blue sky and landed in San Francisco.

A year later in Seattle, during an NBC-TV game, the Kingdome scoreboard flashed, "Welcome to NBC announcers Mel Proctor and Merlin Olsen." After the game, an attractive blonde waited for me. I recognized her, the girl from the air charter service. Over cocktails, she admitted that our flight out of Seattle had been illegal, against FAA rules, and life threatening. She said her boss needed the money to avoid bankruptcy.

The highlight of my three-year stint on NBC was the 1987 AFC title game between the Cleveland Browns and Denver Broncos. Cleveland Stadium shook as 79,953 Browns fans stomped on their seats. At one end of the field, in "the Dog Pound," thousands of Browns fans, dressed like dogs, howled and barked and threw dog bones into the end zone.

Trailing 20–13, with the ball at their own 2-yard line, Broncos quarterback John Elway began what has become known as "the Drive." In five minutes, Elway drove the Broncos 98 yards for a touchdown. Here's how I called it on NBC Radio:

"Third-and-1 at the 5, Elway from the shotgun, backpedals, fires into the end zone . . . caught for a touchdown by Mark Jackson. I smell overtime."

The score was tied 20–20 as we went to overtime. After Cleveland failed to score on their first possession, the Broncos moved into field-goal range:

"The Denver Broncos will try to win it in overtime. A 33-yard attempt by Rich Karlis, the barefoot kicker from the University of Cincinnati, trying to break a 20-all tie. The ball is spotted down. The kick is on the way. It is G-O-O-D. The Denver Broncos have won, and the Dog Pound is silent."

The 1987 Fiesta Bowl was a classic: No. 1 Miami vs. No. 2 Penn State. When I arrived in Tempe, Arizona, two days before the game, I couldn't talk. I had laryngitis but told Jack O'Rourke that with rest, I'd be fine. I wasn't going to miss "the Duel in the Desert" for the national championship.

For two days, I left my room only to get a massage. I slept all day, overdosed on hot tea with lemon, and took decongestants and an oath of silence. I could hear everyone else celebrating the new year, but I pulled a pillow over my head and slept. By game day, I hadn't spoken a word. My broadcast partner Dave Rowe drove to the stadium as I sat silently. Finally, I quietly said a few words as a test. Not bad, but I wasn't going to force it. I didn't know if I could get through the game, but I was going to try.

As producer Rich Bonn pointed to me and said go, I let it fly. "Hello everybody and welcome to the 1987 Fiesta Bowl." It was a great broadcast and terrific game as Penn State won, 14–10.

In 1988, Don McGuire, TNT's executive producer, asked me to do boxing. I'd never done boxing, but McGuire, one of the best I've ever worked for, was confident I could handle it.

The athletes we covered were members of the U.S. Olympic Boxing program. Mostly inner-city kids from 18 to 21 years old, many became the nucleus of the 1992 Olympic boxing team including Oscar De La Hoya, Eric Griffin, Sergio Reyes, Raul Marquez, Tim Austin, Vernon Forrest, Montell Griffin, and Chris Byrd.

Kevin Kiley wound up as my boxing partner, but the path to picking Kiley was like navigating the Hana Highway. Analysts included SEC commissioner Dr. Harvey Schiller, who often brought heavyweight champ Evander Holyfield with him;

Kevin Kiley (L), Evander Holyfield, and me (R) (photo courtesy Turner Sports)

Olympic high jumper Dwight Stones; and New York boxing writer Mike Marley, who joined me for the United States vs. Italy bouts in Reno, Nevada.

Joe Conforte was one of the event promoters. Conforte owned the infamous Mustang Ranch, the first legal brothel in Nevada, where in 1976, heavyweight boxer Oscar Bonavena had been killed. Reportedly, Joe found out his wife Sally was fooling around with Bonavena, and Conforte's bodyguard put a bullet through the boxer's heart.

Conforte waved us over to his table. Short, jowly, with a thin black mustache and salt-and-pepper hair, Conforte asked us to say hello to his brother in Italy. "Yes sir," we said, not knowing if the bouts would even be televised in Italy.

After the telecast, thanking us for shouting out to his brother, Conforte invited Mike Marley and me to join him, two stars from the ranch, and his bodyguard to the bar of our hotel, which Conforte owned. As we cocktailed and talked boxing, many of the U.S. boxers stopped by to say hello. Joe Conforte started handing them passes for free admission to the Mustang Ranch. Wonderful.

Joe Conforte's limo took us to the Mustang Ranch and we sat at the bar. When customers entered, a bell rang, Joe's girls lined up for inspection, and patrons selected their dates, heading to a bedroom. I did my journalistic duty, sitting at the bar with an attractive black girl, who was working her way through college. That's my story and I'm sticking to it. Sipping a drink, I noticed some U.S. boxers, half clad, running through the halls. Oh shit! Time to go. I said goodbye and found a giddy Mike Marley in the parking lot, clutching a fistful of Mustang passes. Although the sun was coming up, he was staying. I took a taxi. Marley might still be running around the Mustang Ranch in his underwear.

As TNT assignments increased, HTS executive producer Jody Shapiro proposed a trade. I could continue to do boxing and other events, and in return, TNT would provide HTS with free Southeast Conference football telecasts. Jody, brilliant.

I was doing 220 events a year. I did three different sports in three days in different cities: an NBA game in Milwaukee, boxing in Colorado Springs, and NFL football in Chicago. In one day, I broadcast an Orioles day game and a Bullets night game. I loved it.

The morning after a TNT boxing telecast in Biloxi, Mississippi, I drove to New Orleans, flew to New Jersey, stayed in a hotel overnight, and the next day went to the Newark Airport to catch a 6:00 a.m. flight to Baltimore for an 1:00 p.m. Orioles game.

My flight was supposed to go to Baltimore and then Atlanta, but since I was the only Baltimore passenger, the airline canceled that leg of the flight. I did my best John Lally imitation and managed to get a free ticket and a first class seat on a 10:00 a.m. flight. I tried to read but exhausted, fell asleep as my glasses slid down my nose. As we approached BWI Airport, I woke up.

Tony Bennett's sketch of me (photo courtesy Mel Proctor)

"I hope you don't mind," said the man next to me, "I was drawing you while you slept." I recognized Tony Bennett. We talked baseball and show biz, and as we landed, he handed me the signed drawing. Knowing the Orioles were playing his Yankees, Tony asked me to say hi to Yankee broadcaster Phil Rizzuto.

"Holy cow, Tony Bennett," said Scooter when I showed him the signed drawing.

We were packing for a Hawaii vacation when my agent called to say that Ted Shaker, executive producer of CBS Sports, wanted to have lunch with me. Flying to Hawaii without me, my family wasn't happy. I took the train to New York, found the restaurant where Ted Shaker and I were to meet, and waited. And waited. The only shakers there were filled with salt and pepper. Finally, Chuck Milton of CBS arrived and said that Ted Shaker apologized for the no-show but was home packing for his vacation. Are you shitting me?

Although fuming, I maintained my composure, and over lunch, Milton and I found common ground. I'm from Colorado and Milton lived in Telluride. We talked skiing, sports, and television. I felt good about the meeting.

When I heard nothing from CBS, I called my agent who said Chuck Milton didn't think I was CBS's kind of guy. What the hell is a CBS kind of guy?

Months later, in Las Vegas for a boxing telecast, I heard that Ted Shaker was also staying at Caesar's Palace. I called him and we met in the lobby. Later, Shaker offered me a couple of NCAA regular-season basketball games plus the first round of the NCAA tournament. I did the nationally televised Duke-LSU game, Christian Laettner vs. Shaquille O'Neal, and worked with CBS's top analyst, Billy Packer.

Billy and I met with LSU coach Dale Brown and wound up talking about LSU legend Pete Maravich. When I mentioned that my seven-year-old daughter Maile loved the movie *The Pistol* and knew every line in the film, Brown said the film's producer lived in Baton Rouge and that he and Maravich had produced an outstanding series of instructional tapes. When we returned to our hotel, *Pistol Pete's Homework Basketball* videos were waiting for me, with a picture of Maravich and a *Pistol* movie poster. Thank you, Dale Brown.

Maile religiously watched the tapes and learned to dribble through her legs, throw behind-the-back passes, and spin the ball on every finger. She became such a good ball handler that despite being only 5'-2", she was the starting point guard for three years on her high school team and often performed before Bullets games.

In the three years I did the NCAA tournament, I worked with Jack "Goose" Givens and Dan Bonner. At the Eastern Regionals in Syracuse, Bonner and I were joined by sideline reporter Lesley Visser, who wanted to interview cheerleaders. As a lead-in, I said, "Lesley Visser was a cheerleader at Boston College. She's over there among the pom poms. Lesley, are you feeling nostalgic?"

Early the next morning I got a phone call from a furious Ted Shaker, ripping into me, saying my comments were chauvinistic and inappropriate. I was speechless. Then he said, "It was all over the radio this morning."

"Huh?"

He told me Don Imus had vilified me on his radio show, *Imus in the Morning,* and that Imus carried enormous power. I figured I was a goner. I called Bob Dekas, our CBS producer, and as I told him the story, he started laughing. He said that Ted Shaker regularly listened to Imus, who had a crush on Lesley Visser, who was married to sportscaster Dick Stockton. I apologized profusely to Shaker, although I'd done nothing wrong.

In Greensboro, North Carolina, Dan Bonner and I called an NCAA tournament game between West Virginia and Missouri when lightning struck the Greensboro Coliseum and a tornado touched down nearby, causing power blackouts and delays totaling 40 minutes in the first half. Communication between us and our producer and director was knocked out, so I held a telephone to my ear, getting instructions from the truck as I continued to broadcast.

"Play-by-play man Mel Proctor had the unenviable task of filling time there," wrote *Washington Post* columnist Leonard Shapiro. "As the longtime voice of the Washington Bullets, a team that's been getting blown out of games on a regular basis over the last few years, Proctor has lots of practice filling dead air."

My old friend Irv Kaze, the CBA's commissioner, asked me to do the league's All-Star game on ESPN and emcee the banquet the night before in Quad Cities, Iowa. Here was the plan: with lights off in the hotel ballroom, I would introduce the All-Stars; as I announced a player's name, there would be a puff of smoke and a spotlight would follow each All-Star to the stage. After player introductions, I would bring out featured speaker Johnny "Red" Kerr, former NBA player and coach and the Chicago Bulls' TV analyst, followed by CBA commissioner Irv Kaze, who would deliver a "State of the CBA" speech. Finally, I would introduce the entertainment, "the Blues Brothers."

The room was dark, the players black, and I had little light as I tried to read the list of All-Stars. "From the Albany Patrons, Vincent Askew," I said. Several puffs of smoke made visibility worse, and the spotlight operator must have hit happy hour, because the light bounced off the walls instead of following the All-Stars. Finally, the players assembled on stage, the lights came on, and I introduced Johnny Kerr, who delivered a joke-filled speech.

All of a sudden, music blared as the Blues Brothers theme played and the crowd went wild. What the hell? The Blues Brothers weren't supposed to appear until later, but since their intro music played, I assumed they were ready to rock and roll, so I said, "Ladies and gentlemen, it's my pleasure to introduce the Blues Brothers."

The curtains opened. No Blues Brothers. I explained that the Blues Brothers were running late and introduced a bewildered Irv Kaze, who delivered an inspiring speech about the CBA. In the midst of his speech, music rang out again, the curtains parted, and the well-oiled Blues Brothers stumbled on stage. Irv Kaze and I looked at each other, shrugged, and sat down. I was never asked to host another CBA banquet.

When Fox Sports began, I called executive producer Ed Goren, whom I'd known at CBS, and told him I'd love to do football and baseball for Fox.

"Mel, we know each other so I'll be honest. Unless your last name is Albert, Caray, Brennaman, or Buck, forget it."

"Ed, what am I, chopped liver?"

"No, you're a talented, experienced announcer."

Sure enough, Fox hired Marv Albert's son Kenny, Skip Caray's son and Harry Caray's grandson Chip, Marty Brennaman's son Thom, and Jack Buck's son, Joe, who became Fox's main play-by-play man for the NFL and MLB.

Several years later, my old friend Bill Brown, now at Fox, called and offered a West Coast baseball package. "I thought my last name had to be Albert, Caray, Brennaman, or Buck?"

"I convinced Ed Goren that being good is as important as having the right last name." I did Fox baseball for seven years, and Bill Brown said, "You have my word. As long as I'm at Fox, you'll be doing baseball." He's still at Fox, and I'm not doing baseball.

Cal Ripken (photo courtesy Baltimore Orioles)

Chapter 15
Baltimore Orioles

In 1982, the Baltimore Orioles asked me to fill in, on radio, for a series in Chicago. After checking in at the hotel, I went to the bar, where manager Earl Weaver and his coaches were drinking. I'd met Weaver once but doubted he'd remember me.

"Hi Earl, Mel Proctor," I said, resting my hand on his shoulder.

"Motherfucker, cocksucker, get your damned hands off of me," he yelled.

"Earl, I'm sorry I . . ."

Ray Miller, the pitching coach, pulled me away and said, "Mel, don't worry, you didn't do anything wrong. When Earl is smoked he has a phobia about being touched. By tomorrow, he'll have forgotten all about it."

At Comiskey Park, you had to walk past the manager's office to get to the visiting clubhouse, where I needed to go to get lineups and talk to players. The door was wide open, and I could hear Earl Weaver's gravelly voice on the phone.

I tried to tip toe past Weaver's door. "Hey, damn it, get in here," he yelled. "Sorry about last night. When I've had a few drinks, I've got this thing about being touched." Spreading his arms wide and smiling, he asked, "What can I tell you about the ballclub?"

Earl Weaver retired after the 1982 season. Joe Altobelli replaced him, kept Weaver's lineup intact, and the Orioles won the 1983 World Series.

In 1984, Home Team Sports cable network hired me to broadcast 75 Orioles games. With leadoff hitter Al Bumbry injured, Altobelli auditioned replacements. As I looked at the lineup, rookie Mike Young seemed an unlikely choice to lead off, a power hitter en route to 100-plus strikeouts. "Joe, why is Mike Young in the leadoff spot?" I asked.

Altobelli stared at me. "If you're so fucking smart, you figure it out," he said, before walking down the dugout steps into the clubhouse. Joe Altobelli never spoke to me again.

I love baseball, but sometimes games get boring. When your team is out of contention by May, it's only the fifth inning, and your heroes are down 10–1, you search for things to talk about. While the Orioles were getting their butts kicked by Oakland one night, I mentioned the Jose Canseco hotline. If you called 1-900-JOSE, paid $2 for the first minute and $1 for each additional minute, you could hear the latest "State of Jose" spiel. Our gifted young producer Chris Glass dialed the hotline and put it on the air. "Hi, I'm Jose Canseco of the Oakland A's, and thanks for calling. Yes, I've had some problems lately, speeding tickets, an arrest for domestic abuse, and that thing with the gun, but let me explain." We sat back and listened for five minutes. That was the kind of thing HTS let us do. Beautiful.

As I boarded the team bus after another loss, I saw a sign on the windshield, above the driver's seat: "Bill Wheedle, the Singing Bus Driver." "Dear Bill," I wrote, "the Orioles have had a tough weekend. Can you cheer them up? Please sing 'Take Me Out to the Ballgame.'" I passed the note forward. Static, as the driver's microphone was switched on, and then, "Take me out to the ballgame, take me out with the crowd. Buy me some peanuts and . . ."

"What the fuck?" yelled Joe Altobelli.

"I don't care if I ever come back," sang the bus driver.

"Shut the fuck up," shouted the coaches. "What are you doing?"

I was laughing so hard I had to slump down in my seat to avoid being seen. Nobody ever found out who sent the note.

Rex Barney was my first broadcast partner on HTS. A former Brooklyn Dodgers pitcher best known for no-hitting the New York Giants, Rex was also the Orioles' PA announcer. Larry King, Mutual Radio's talk show host, joined us occasionally. He could drop names faster than anyone I'd ever met, going from Tommy Lasorda to Angie Dickinson to Henry

With Rex Barney (photo courtesy Home Team Sports)

Kissinger in one sentence. King, a Brooklynite, and Barney, a former Dodger, argued about subjects like who was the best center fielder of their era: Mays, Snider, or Mantle. I often thought they were going to end up in a fist fight and often had to steer them back to the game we were broadcasting.

As Rex missed games because of recurring health problems, HTS used fill-ins and looked for an eventual replacement. "How about Pat Dobson?" asked Jody Shapiro. Dobson was one of four pitchers who won 20 games for the Orioles in 1971. "Dobber" was a good friend and one of the funniest human beings ever, but I'd never heard him complete a sentence without an F-bomb.

Dobber joined us in Kansas City, and we agreed to meet in the coffee shop at the Adams Mark Hotel. I sat down at a table next to pitcher Scott McGregor.

"Scotty, you old cocksucker, how the fuck are you?" Dobber asked as he sat down. "Have you been getting any lately?" I kicked Dobber in the shin. He obviously hadn't met the new Scott McGregor, who'd stopped cussing, smoking, and drinking and was a minister at the Rock Church. After McGregor left, Dobber and I had breakfast and talked about his broadcast debut the next night in Anaheim.

Before his interview with Ray Miller, the Orioles' pitching coach, Dobber wanted to have some fun. At Anaheim Stadium, Dobber and Miller sat in folding chairs in front of our TV camera. "I'm Pat Dobson, and our pregame guest tonight is pitching coach Ray Miller." Dobson asked a couple of baseball questions and then, "What's it like being the only homosexual pitching coach in the American League?"

"Well Dobber, I'm proud of our pitchers' staffs, I mean our staff," Miller said. "We have well-endowed pitchers who can work deep into games."

As we cracked up, an angry Angels employee vaulted the fence. "What the fuck are you idiots doing?" he yelled. "Don't you know your audio is being piped into the Executive Dining Room where our owner Gene Autry is hosting a luncheon for the board of directors?" Oops.

With Rex Barney returning from foot surgery, John Lowenstein joined us in Detroit. Brother Low's pinch-hit three-run homer won Game 1 of the 1979 World Series. He hit .308 in 10 World Series games with the Orioles and teamed with Gary Roenicke to form one of the best platoons in history. But he is best remembered as one of baseball's all-time screwballs. Pretending to be a Samurai warrior, he often took a bat to birthday cakes in the clubhouse, and when asked how, as a part-time player, he stayed ready, he said, "I flush the toilets between innings to keep my wrists strong."

At Tiger Stadium, ready to do a live on-camera open, I stood in the middle holding the microphone, with John on my left and Rex, wearing a heavy protective boot to protect his surgically repaired foot, on my right.

I was going to ask Rex a question and then turn to John for his comments. I asked. Rex answered. He went on and on. We only had two minutes. As Rex rambled, I saw my microphone cord trapped under Rex's combat boot. Sensing my dilemma, John began to snicker. I kicked Rex's foot twice, hoping he'd lift his boot and free the cord. John snorted.

As Rex continued his filibuster, I kicked him harder and jerked the microphone just as he lifted his foot. The mike flew out of my hand, and I caught it in midair. John was laughing so hard, I didn't bother to ask him a question. Live TV. No do-overs. An Orioles TV classic.

In 1985 John Lowenstein became my full-time partner. Brother Low had become a cult hero in 1980. In a game at Memorial Stadium, Baltimore trailed the Oakland A's, 3–2, but had two men on with two outs in the bottom of the seventh. Lowenstein, a pinch hitter, singled to right to drive in the tying run, and Al Bumbry raced from first to third. On the throw to the plate, Lowenstein tried to take second, but the A's first baseman cut off the throw and fired to second, hitting Brother Low in the neck as Bumbry scored what proved to be the winning run.

Brother Low becomes a cult hero (photo courtesy of Baltimore Orioles)

Lowenstein was hurt, the crowd silent as he was carried off the field. John realized he wouldn't have many opportunities like this, so as the stretcher reached the Orioles' dugout, he sat up and raised both fists, as the crowd went nuts. With that kind of improv ability, I figured he'd be perfect as a broadcaster.

We made our season debut during spring training in Ft. Myers, where the broadcast booth was elevated high above the field. I was in the midst of award-winning play-by-play when John tapped me on the shoulder. "Are you hungry?" he asked, on the air.

Fighting laughter, I said, "Boddicker gets the changeup over for a strike. Well, yes John, now that you mention it, I am hungry."

"I'm getting a ham sandwich with cheese," he said calmly. "What do you want?"

"The same."

As the broadcast continued, John leaned out of the booth, with his headset on. "Hey, up here," he yelled to a vendor below, who looked everywhere, trying to figure out who was calling him. Finally, he looked up. "Two ham sandwiches with cheese," yelled John.

He turned to me and politely asked, "Do you want mustard?"

Between attacks of laughter, I said yes.

"And don't forget the mustard," he shouted.

Our bosses, Bill Aber, Jody Shapiro, and Bill Brown realized a loose cannon like Brother Low was perfect for a fledgling cable network. Anywhere else, we would have been fired, arrested, and institutionalized.

As Orioles second baseman Lenn Sakata came to the plate in New York, John reminisced about the team's trip to Japan after the 1983 World Series. "When we went to Japan, Lenny got lost in a crowd and we couldn't find him for two weeks."

After the Yankees won, most of the crowd was gone except for a pocket of fans in the right-field bleachers. "John, what's going on?" I asked. "The game has been over for 20 minutes. Why don't they go home?"

"Mel, that area is known as Peso Park," John explained. "It takes them two hours to clear immigration after a game."

John pushed his creativity, and fans loved him. In a boring game, our cameras searched for anything we could talk about besides another walk or pitching change. Our cameraman found a huge man, maybe 400 pounds, draped over empty seats on either side of him. He was eating peanuts, peanuts, and more peanuts. I'm sure the peanut vendor retired off what he made from that guy. Our camera zoomed in on the mountain of peanut shells beneath our hero's seat.

"Good Lord," John said, "That man has eaten enough peanuts to feed third-world countries forever."

The "Peanut Man" called HTS, threatening to sue. For what? HTS asked John to apologize on the air. We should have settled with this guy for a year's supply of peanuts.

On Seat Cushion Night every fan who came to the game at Memorial Stadium got a black and orange Orioles seat cushion. "Hold up your seat cushions," instructed the PA announcer. "Let's do some tricks like they do at the Rose Bowl."

On camera, John and I held up our seat cushions, and then John said, "Not only are these seat cushions, they also make great Frisbees." He sailed his seat cushion out of our booth. When fans saw Brother Low, they started throwing their seat cushions. Soon, thousands of seat cushions rained down on the field, as the announcer said, "OK, that's enough."

The game was stopped. Both Orioles and A's players helped the grounds crew pick up the seat cushions that littered the field. Seat Cushion Night was removed from future Orioles promotional schedules.

In Milwaukee, the Orioles stayed at the Pfister Hotel, which had a five-star restaurant where John and I met for dinner. After cocktails, we looked at the menu. Beluga caviar? I told John how my Russian basketball friend, Ivan Edeshko, had introduced me to this delicacy. John agreed that we owed it to ourselves to share a tin of the world's finest caviar accompanied by ice-cold Russian vodka. John loved it. Waiter, more caviar and vodka.

After shrimp cocktails and salads, we ordered the thickest steaks on the menu with sides of mushrooms, asparagus, and baked potatoes. John knew wines so he ordered an expensive cabernet. We liked it so much, we had a second bottle. To top off this exquisite meal, we ordered crème brûlée for desert. We were stuffed and happy. Until the bill arrived.

Shit, $400. For two people. Home Team Sports was reasonable, but this wouldn't get past the comptroller.

"John, let's put down dinner with the coaches," I suggested.

"No, how about dinner with the infield?"

"How about dinner with the pitching staff?"

"Dinner with the farm system?"

We finally settled on dinner with the coaches, turned in the expense report, and were reimbursed without question. What wonderful people to work for.

On an off night in Detroit, John and I drove to Windsor, Ontario, to Jason's, where sexy half-naked French-Canadian women danced. Holding a fistful of five dollar bills, John tucked them in the girls' garters as they performed. Hey, it was better than watching *SportsCenter* for the 14th time. At the border, an agent asked, "Do you have anything to declare?"

"Just an erection." John said.

Everybody loved Brother Low. Well, almost everybody. In Chicago at the Smith & Wollensky Steak House, I ran into the umpiring crew for the Orioles-White Sox series. I said hello to crew chief Don Denkinger and bought the guys drinks.

Me, my son Billy, and John Lowenstein (photo courtesy Mel Proctor)

"Don't you work with John Lowenstein?" asked crusty John Shulock.

"Yes."

"Give him a message for me."

"Sure John."

"Tell him to go fuck himself," Shulock said. Apparently he didn't agree with John's commentary.

With John Lowenstein's star rising, NBC asked him to do their *Game of the Week,* with play-by-play announcer Ted Robinson. John wore sunglasses, day or night. As John and Ted set up for their pregame open, the producer told Ted, "Tell John to take off his shades."

When John refused, the producer asked Ted to have John explain why he was wearing sunglasses.

Ted asked, "John, why are you wearing sunglasses?"

"I think it was that third cocktail that got me last night." NBC never asked John to return.

As John's teammates retired, he became distanced from the players. When an Orioles opponent made a pitching change, John's standard scouting report was "Good live arm, decent heater, a little breaking ball, changes speeds, and throws strikes." John used this so often that I knew it by heart.

As a new pitcher came in, I said, "Here's so and so. John, he's got a live arm, a decent heater, a little breaking ball, changes speeds, and throws strikes. What else can you tell us about him?" John was laughing so hard he couldn't talk.

In 1989, the Boston Red Sox came to Baltimore shortly after Wade Boggs' affair with Margo Adams became public. As Boggs came up, Orioles fans serenaded him with "Margo-rita-ville," a parody of Jimmy Buffet's "Margaritaville."

When I told John that Wade Boggs was superstitious and his wife prepared a chicken dish before every game, John said, "Really, I wonder who's cooking his chicken now?"

"I don't know," I said, "but we know who cooked his goose."

Two minutes of dead air. We were laughing so hard we couldn't speak.

John and I worked together for 12 years and became good friends. We spent three hours together in the booth, enjoyed postgame cocktails and dinners together, and spent more time with each other than with our families.

Broadcasting baseball is a joy, but being on the road half the time gets boring. Three days in Cleveland? Four days in Detroit? John and I began to pass the time by buying baseball ties. "Look at this baby," John crowed, showing up in the broadcast booth wearing a Nicole Miller tie. "It has all of the 500 home run hitters on it."

"Nothing but baseballs," I said, showing off my newest tie the next day. The competition became insane and expensive as we tried to outdo each other. Nicole Miller ties go for $40, but I took pride in buying cheaper ones from street vendors and kiosks. It became a sickness. My wife went crazy when I'd return home from a trip with seven new ties. Fans began to send me ties. Hall of Fame announcer Ernie Harwell presented me with a bat-shaped tie. As my tie count climbed to 150 I was featured in *USA Today* as "the Prince

"Prince of Ties" (photo courtesy USA Today)

of Ties." In Minnesota, when I showed off seven new ties from the Mall of America, John said, "No Mas."

That night as we began our telecast, our booth cameraman at the Metro-dome said, "When you finish the on-camera open, be careful when you stand up." "There's a low ceiling here," he said, pointing to a cement abutment above our heads. Was the booth built for Mini-Me?

We finished our opening, and with little time to get back to the broadcast position, I stood up quickly. *Boom!* I dropped to my knees, my vision blurred, and crawled toward my chair. Instead of coming to the aid of his fallen partner, John laughed hysterically. Hand over hand, I pulled myself into the chair, put on my headset, and heard our producer, "3-2-1, go Mel." I hoped my partner would save me, welcome the viewers back, and stall until I stopped seeing the Fourth of July fireworks show in my head, but all viewers heard was John, laughing. Finally, I mumbled, "Welcome back to the Metrodome." I could have killed Brother Low.

When he wasn't calling network games for ABC, Hall of Fame pitcher Jim Palmer frequently joined us in the HTS booth.

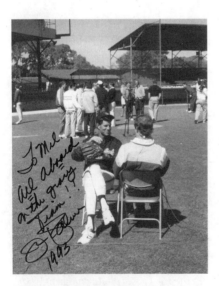

On the gravy train with Jim Palmer (photo courtesy Jim Palmer)

Nicknamed "Cakes" because he ate pancakes before he pitched, Palmer had the best memory of anybody I've known. He could remember a 3-2 slider he'd thrown to a hitter in the eighth inning of a game 20 years ago. Thanks to his Jockey underwear ads, Palmer was well known to the ladies, a good-looking guy who attracted attention. I loved to go to dinner with Cakes because he knew his wines and picked up the tab. I kidded Palmer about riding the gravy train, living half the year in Palm Beach, Florida, playing golf and tennis, making lucrative appearances, and then spending the summer broadcasting baseball.

Although he was 45 and hadn't played in a big-league game in seven years, Cakes thought he could still pitch and in 1991 attempted a comeback. Encouraged by workouts with a University of Miami assistant coach, by throwing batting practice, and pitching well in an Orioles intrasquad game, Cakes was ready.

McKechnie Field in Bradenton was sold out. HTS taped the game against the Boston Red Sox. As Palmer warmed up, he looked the same: smooth windup, high leg kick, and fluid delivery.

Wade Boggs lined a bullet to right for a single. Jody Reed, a "Punch & Judy" hitter, rocked shortstop Cal Ripken back on his heels with a line drive. Mike Greenwell sent a tracer to right for a hit. Jack Clark and Ellis Burks launched missiles that nearly tore fielders' gloves off. In two innings, Palmer allowed two runs on five hits, with an 80 mph fastball.

Producer Bill Brown said there were technical problems and HTS couldn't air the tape. I think they were protecting Jim, who'd finally realized his playing days were over.

During a telecast, we talked about Sabatino's, a Little Italy restaurant we both loved. "Let's test the power of television," I suggested. "We'd like to make reservations at Sabatino's, party of four, the Proctors and Palmers, for tomorrow night at 7:00 p.m."

Twenty minutes later, press box attendant Fred Trautman announced, "Gentlemen, your reservations have been confirmed." The next night, fans packed Sabatino's to see that we'd actually shown up. Bon appétit.

One night, Cakes and I sat in the booth preparing. I reached into my briefcase for a pen and instead grabbed a snake. "Oh, shit!" I screamed as fear sent me three rows back. A rubber snake. Just a little trick from Cakes.

The Detroit Tigers' 35–5 start in 1984 knocked every team out of contention. The Orioles finished fifth, going 85–77, but two future Hall of Famers, Cal Ripken Jr. and Eddie Murray, were just entering their prime years.

Cal Ripken Jr. was born to be an Oriole. His father, Cal Sr., had managed for 13 years in Baltimore's minor league system, and Junior spent summers in Aberdeen, South Dakota; Elmira, New York; Rochester, New York; Ashville, North Carolina, or wherever Dad was managing.

Cal Ripken Sr. often said, "I wish baseball was played 365 days a year. God, I love this game." He passed along his passion to his son. There had never been a shortstop like Cal Jr., who at 6'-4" could leap to snag a line drive, was agile enough to glide into the hole to make a backhand stop, and had a bazooka for a throwing arm. His mind was a computer that processed the game situation, hitters' strengths and weaknesses, and where the pitcher would deliver what pitch. The ball always seemed to find Cal Jr. He also hit .304 with 37 doubles, 27 home runs, and 86 RBIs in 1984.

Cal Ripken Jr. was also a perfect role model for kids. I enlisted Cal's help when my son Billy said he was going to get an earring. Cal pulled Billy aside one night before a game. "Billy, I know you want to be a baseball player, right?"

"Yes," said Billy.

"Well, you know real ballplayers don't wear earrings." I never heard my son mention another word about an earring.

Eddie Murray hit .306 with 29 homers and 110 RBI in 1984. Murray was a fearsome presence, hovering over the plate,

Eddie Murray (photo courtesy Baltimore Orioles)

batting left-handed or right-handed, as fans chanted, "Eddie . . . Eddie." My four-year-old son Billy even wore an "Eddie, Eddie" T-shirt.

In 1985, the Orioles set a record that may never be broken. Three managers in three days. After a five-game losing streak in June, Joe Altobelli was fired and replaced by Cal Ripken Sr. With Rip Sr. managing, the

Orioles won a home game, but owner Edward Bennett Williams, working behind the scenes, coaxed Earl Weaver out of retirement, offering him $500,000 a year.

Earl Weaver's philosophy was "pitching, defense, and three-run homers." In 1985, the Orioles set club records with 214 home runs and 818 runs scored, but their pitching was poor, and the defense, once a trademark of Orioles teams, was even worse. The team committed 129 errors, most by an Orioles team in 26 years. The O's finished 83–78, in fourth place.

Waging a courageous battle with cancer, Orioles owner Edward Bennett Williams craved a World Series championship. Forget rebuilding with young players. The Orioles signed free agents Fred Lynn, Lee Lacy, and Don Aase and acquired Alan Wiggins from San Diego.

In 1984, as the Padres' leadoff hitter, Wiggins stole 70 bases and scored 106 runs as San Diego won their first National League title. The Orioles hoped Wiggins would be the same kind of catalyst for them, but he was addicted to cocaine. He was terrible on the bases and brutal in the field. Earl Weaver said Wiggins was the worst player he'd ever seen and suggested that he might play better if he sniffed the foul lines before every game.

The Detroit Tigers pulled the hidden-ball trick on Wiggins. When the Tigers' pitcher threw to first base, first baseman Dave Bergman faked a return throw and kept the ball. As Wiggins danced off the bag, Bergman tagged him. When I interviewed Bergman the next day, he admitted he'd pulled the trick one other time, in the National League. When I asked for the name of his victim, he wouldn't tell me. Guess who?

"Yo man," Alan Wiggins said, pointing at my briefcase, as I walked into the clubhouse. "Is that where you carry your knives?"

"What?"

"What are you talking about?" I asked.

"My spies tell me you've been cutting me up on the air. I figure that's where you keep your knives."

I shook my head and walked out of the clubhouse.

The next day, Wiggins said, "Yo, man, I guess it wasn't you cutting me up on the air. My spies tell me it was that big-nosed fucker on Channel 2." This was his apology.

Wiggins and teammate Jim Dwyer got into a fistfight around the batting cage, and Wiggins was involved in another altercation in the clubhouse.

Alan Wiggins was suspended indefinitely, was in rehab three times, and tragically died of AIDS in 1991 at the age of 32. At least there is a heartwarming twist to the story.

Wiggins' daughter Candice was born in Baltimore when her dad played for the Orioles. She was a high school All-American basketball player in San Diego, and my daughter Maile played against her. Candice became Stanford's all-time leading scorer, the top scorer in Pac 10 history, and now stars for the Minnesota Lynx of the WNBA.

Earl Weaver called the 1986 Orioles "the worst team he'd ever managed." It was sad watching this great manger try to wring wins out of this club. For the first time in 19 years, the Orioles finished with a losing record, 73–89, and in seventh place in the AL East.

Before games, Earl Weaver loved to sit around the dugout and talk baseball. Only 55, Earl announced that he would retire when the season ended. "Earl, how can you retire?" I asked. "You're young and managing is what you do best. If you get some players, you'll be back on top."

He took a drag on his cigarette, exhaled, and said, "Mel, if you've got all the fuckin' money you'll ever need and you can get up every fuckin' day and do any fuckin' thing you want, what the fuck you would do?" Well, now that you put it like that Earl. So, Earl and his family moved to Florida, where he played golf, went to the race track, and drank gin and tonics. While on an Orioles cruise in January 2013, he suffered a heart attack and died. Earl Weaver was 82.

A Hall of Fame player, Eddie Murray was also a Hall of Fame pain in the ass. Murray's hatred of the media reportedly began in 1979 after a story by Dick Young, a jaded *New York Daily News* columnist. Based on a conversation with the Orioles scout who signed Murray, Young wrote that during negotiations the scout had been rudely treated by the Murray family. Eddie decided that not only was Dick Young a racist, so were most of the media.

I praised Eddie when he played well, which was most of the time, and if he slumped, I mentioned it, as I would with any player. As my comments were passed from Eddie's friends to wives to girlfriends to relatives and finally back to Eddie, they became distorted. When Eddie thought I had badmouthed him, I offered to let him watch the videotape of the telecasts. He never did.

Occasionally, I'd ask Eddie to do an interview, just to see if his attitude had changed. He would either ignore me or shake his head no.

After a game in Kansas City, we sat at the bar at the Adam's Mark Hotel, and I actually had a civil conversation with Eddie about his relationship with the media. We even bought each other a drink. As I went to bed, I hoped I'd convinced Eddie that I respected him and that we could build a cordial relationship.

That lasted a week. Honest to God, I went out of my way to avoid saying anything about Eddie Murray other than the facts, just to avoid his bullshit. When he complained again, I said, "Eddie, I feel sorry for you. You're a great player and deep down inside probably a good person, but you won't let us in. Someday, I picture you sitting at a table in your L.A. mansion, with stacks of money piled in front of you, but the phone never rings."

In 1986 Orioles fans ended their love affair with Murray. In June, Murray pulled a hamstring and went on the disabled list for the first time in his career. Murray was stung by Edward Bennett Williams' criticism about Murray's lack of conditioning and motivation. Williams' comments coincided with an Orioles slump, and Murray felt that fans were blaming him for the club's demise. The chants of "Eddie . . . Eddie" faded, and for the first time, Murray was booed.

Now, Eddie Murray wanted to talk. After years of blowing us off, Murray suddenly wanted to use HTS to vent and say he wanted to be traded. My boss Jody Shapiro asked me to interview Murray. No. I wanted no part of it.

So Rex Barney interviewed Eddie Murray, who lambasted the Orioles and their fans, saying Memorial Stadium had become an "ugly place" to play and it was time to move on. On December 4, 1988, Murray was traded to the Los Angeles Dodgers.

In 1996, the Orioles brought Eddie Murray back. I guess they thought it would be good PR. Now 40 years old, Murray was closing in on 500 career home runs. I went to Eddie in the dugout, offered my hand, and said welcome back. My hand hung in midair. With several people watching, Eddie reluctantly shook my hand. As Murray neared his 500th home run, I mentioned that Camden Yards was wired with stacks of fireworks, readying for the celebration. Owner Peter Angelos' wife called, saying we had spoiled the surprise for Eddie.

On September 6, 1996, batting left-handed, Eddie Murray hit Detroit starter Felipe Lira's first pitch over the right-field wall at Camden Yards. Fans gave Eddie a nine-minute standing ovation, the fireworks exploded, and a banner was lowered over the center-field wall reading, "Congratulations Eddie. 500." I guess the surprise wasn't spoiled.

In 1987, Cal Ripken Sr. became the Orioles' skipper, becoming the first to manage two sons, Cal and Billy. But the O's sunk even further, finishing 67–95. It would get worse.

In 1988, actor Tom Selleck, star of *Magnum, P.I.*, was in town to plug his movie, *Her Alibi*. It was a hellish day in Baltimore, 103 degrees and humidity off the charts, but Selleck wanted to take batting practice.

It was so hot, players on both teams let Selleck take all the swings he wanted. Wearing "Selleck" on the back of his Orioles uniform, he hacked away. Finally Al Newman of the Minnesota Twins ran up to Selleck, handing him a towel. How thoughtful. "This is a gift from Cal Ripken Jr.," said Newman, scurrying out of sight. Falling for one of the oldest tricks in baseball, Selleck buried his face into a towel full of shaving cream.

Selleck joined us in the booth during the game. Dehydrated and exhausted, he could barely talk but plugged his movie *Her Alibi*. I tried to steer him to his athletic career at USC where he'd played basketball and volleyball, but he kept going back to the film. The interview bombed and so did *Her Alibi*.

Five years later, Selleck showed up again to plug *Mr. Baseball*, a movie about an aging major leaguer who goes to Japan. Selleck took BP again and joined us in the booth, but this time he wanted to show off his baseball knowledge, to give the movie credibility.

On Opening Day 1988, the Orioles lost their home opener to Milwaukee and dove straight to the bottom of the Chesapeake Bay. The Orioles lost their first six games, fired manager Cal Ripken Sr., and replaced him with Frank Robinson.

After the Orioles lost their 14th straight game, in the hotel bar, Brother Low philosophized, "If the Orioles were just bad they wouldn't attract much attention, but since they might be the worst team in history, the media will be all over this team."

John was right. Noah's ark docked at the Inner Harbor with two of every media animal aboard: national baseball writers, columnists, beat writers, radio talk show hosts, and network TV crews. Fans mailed rabbit's feet and lucky charms, and children knelt by their beds, praying the Orioles would win.

When the Orioles lost in Milwaukee 7–1, they broke their 34-year-old club record with 15 straight losses. Describing the carnage, I felt like the obits writer for the *Baltimore Sun.* Flying to Kansas City, I asked our producer if he could chromatically remove our heads for the on-camera open.

Headless, I said, "Hello everybody. I'm Mel Proctor with John Lowenstein in Kansas City. Tonight the Orioles will try to end their 15-game losing streak. John, when I put my suitcase in the car to drive to the airport, my neighbor asked, 'Hey Mel, where are you going?'"

"To Kansas City, for an Orioles game," I answered.

He said, "Why? Have you lost your head?"

"The players think you're kicking sand in their faces," said Frank Robinson after a 13–1 loss, the Orioles 16th straight defeat.

"Frank, try broadcasting for an 0–16 team," I said.

"Try managing one," he countered.

Media coverage increased as the Orioles made losing an art form, not only losing 12–0 and 13–1 but also 1–0 and 4–3. They lost because of botched bunt attempts, costly errors, bonehead plays, wind-blown home runs, and sun in an outfielder's eyes.

Bill Cosby offered support; the Orioles office was filled with four-leaf clovers, Buddhas, crosses, bouquets of flowers, plates full of cookies and cakes, anything to help the team.

The Royals won 4–3, the O's 17th straight loss.

Then the Royals' Bret Saberhagen "stuffed the Orioles' bats up their pants," said Brother Low in a 3–1 loss to drop their record to 0–18.

Before the 19th game, President Ronald Reagan called Frank Robinson. "Frank, I know what you must be going through."

"With all due respect Mr. President, no you don't." The Orioles lost to Minnesota, 4–2, for 19 straight losses.

A 7–6 loss to the Twins the next night, the Orioles' 20th straight loss, tied the 1906 Boston Red Sox and the 1916 and 1943 Philadelphia Athletics for the American League's longest losing streak.

The Chicago White Sox had won the 1983 AL pennant with Roland Hemond as general manager. Chisox owners Jerry Reinsdorf and Eddie Einhorn sent the O's GM the rumpled suit he'd worn that day. Roland wore the suit, but the Orioles lost to Minnesota, 4–2, to break the major league record with 21 consecutive losses to start a season.

God finally smiled. The next night, the Orioles shut out the White Sox, 9–0. Finally, mercifully, the nightmare ended, at least for a night. The Orioles lost their next two games and limped home with a 1–23 record.

On May 2, 50,402 fans packed Memorial Stadium. Before the first pitch, Governor William Donald Schaefer announced that the Orioles and the State of Maryland had agreed that the state would build a new ballpark to be completed for Opening Day 1992. And the Orioles agreed to a 15-year lease at the new park, squelching rumors that owner Edward Bennett Williams would move the team to Washington, D.C. What great theater.

Williams, taking cancer into extra innings, watched from the press box, too ill to join Schaefer on the field. It was the last time EBW saw his team play in person. He passed away two and a half months later.

In 1989 financier Eli Jacobs bought the Orioles. Wearing a suit and tie and thick glasses, Jacobs looked out of place standing behind the batting cage. John and I introduced ourselves and shook hands with Jacobs. Five minutes later, we got on the elevator with Jacobs and said hello. He had no idea who we were.

Jacobs knew little about baseball but wisely let President Larry Lucchino, GM Roland Hemond, and assistant Doug Melvin run the team. Hemond made 17 trades before the 1989 season started, dumping over-the-hill veterans and adding prospects.

Opening Day 1989, Memorial Stadium. The Orioles vs. the Boston Red Sox. In the first inning Boston's Nick Esasky lifted a drive to deep right field. Rookie outfielder Steve Finley made an incredible catch, slamming into the wall. Center fielder Brady Anderson raised his hand to high-five Finley, who couldn't lift his arm. Separated shoulder. Out six weeks.

Steve Finley's play was a precursor to the Orioles' incredible defense. Finley, Brady Anderson, and Mike Devereaux, all rookies and all true center fielders, caught every ball that didn't leave the state.

The Orioles played .500 ball until May and then caught fire with a five-game win streak, an eight-game streak, and in June, a seven-gamer, putting them in first place with a 41–28 record.

The Orioles got brilliant pitching from unknowns like Bob Milacki, Dave Schmidt, and left-hander Jeff Ballard, who went 18–8. When I think of Ballard, I remember him facing Kansas City's Bo Jackson in Baltimore. As Ballard began his windup, Bo held up his left hand, requesting a timeout. The umpire said no, so Bo wrapped his hand around the bat handle and hit one of the longest home runs I've ever seen.

Rookie closer Greg Olson had 27 saves and in Oakland, with the game on the line, faced Murderer's Row—Dave Parker, Dave Henderson, and Mark McGwire. He struck out all three with his hellacious curveball.

In two months, the Orioles went 38–19, and on July 18, they were 53–38 with a 7½ game lead. Fans began to chant "Why Not?"

The Orioles' signature game was July 15 at Memorial Stadium against the California Angels. With the score tied 9–9 in the bottom of the ninth, Mike Deveraux hammered left-hander Bob McClure's pitch down the left-field line. The ball hooked toward the foul line and disappeared next to the foul pole. But which side of the foul pole? Fair or foul? Third-base umpire Jim Joyce called it a home run and the Orioles won, 11–9. Angels manager Doug Rader and pitching coach Marcel Lachemann went nuts arguing with Joyce near third base. Then Rader and catcher Lance Parrish surrounded crew chief Ken Kaiser, a former pro wrestler, near home plate. During the argument, Rader bumped Kaiser, was ejected, and teammates rushed to home plate to restrain Rader and Kaiser.

Before the game the next day, Rader went to home plate to exchange lineup cards. He handed Kaiser not only the Angels' lineup card but also an Orioles lineup card with four names left blank. "This is where you guys fit in," Rader said. Kaiser ejected him again. The Orioles won in 11 innings as Mickey Tettleton bounced a double over the first baseman's head for a 3–2 win.

The Orioles led their division for 116 days, including 98 in a row. In late August, Toronto began an 11–1 stretch to take over first place. On the final weekend of the season, the O's went to Toronto for a three-game series, with the first-place Blue Jays leading by a game. The Orioles needed two wins to tie and a sweep to win the AL East.

In each of the first two games in Toronto, the Orioles led by one run in the eighth but couldn't hold the lead. Two one-run losses in those games crushed the Orioles' dream.

In 1990 after a game at Fenway Park, producer Bill Bell and I jumped into a taxi, with 30 minutes to make our flight. As we drove through downtown Boston, a roadblock of humanity stopped us. More than 300,000 people waited for South African president Nelson Mandela to deliver his first U.S. speech since being released from prison. We told our driver we'd tip him $200 if he got us to Logan Airport in time to catch our flight. He turned off his meter, spun the steering wheel to the right, jumped the curb onto a sidewalk, honked his horn, and zigzagged for blocks as people scattered. We got to the airport in time to have a beer before takeoff.

That year, the Orioles finished fifth with a 76–85 record and in 1991, their final year at Memorial Stadium, 67–95, for sixth. Frank Robinson was fired and replaced by Johnny Oates.

Goodbye old friend, I said, as the Orioles left Memorial Stadium for Camden Yards. My new friend was a pristine ballpark, with green grass, the feel of an old stadium, a warehouse beyond the right-field wall, and a walkway behind the outfield wall, where a must-stop was Boog's Barbecue.

Fans lined up to say hi to former Orioles slugger Boog Powell, get an autograph, have a picture taken with Boog, and enjoy great barbecue. Often, Boog sent plates of his barbecued best to our booth, and we plugged his business. One night, Boog hand-delivered the food and joined us on air.

"Boog, your barbecue is incredible," I said. "Is there something special you do to treat the meat?"

"Yes, Mel, we bring in Pee Wee Herman once a month to beat our meat." Actor Paul Reubens, aka Pee Wee Herman, had been arrested for masturbating in a porn theater.

OK, Boog, thanks for being with us. Goodbye and good luck.

Rick Sutcliffe started the first game at Camden Yards in 1992, and the bearded red-haired giant threw a shutout. How would I know that the Red Baron would become my broadcast partner?

The Orioles went 10–1 at home to open the season, and remained in contention for most of the year, but struggled to score and wound up 3rd with an 89–73 record. The Orioles set a club record with an average attendance of 48,079.

In 1993, Baltimore attorney Peter Angelos and his minority partners bought the Orioles for a record $173 million. Angelos had made millions in class action lawsuits.

Peter Angelos scared people. On Orioles charters, the four or five smokers on the team cowered in the back of the plane, puffing cigarettes. They were afraid of being fired because Angelos was suing the tobacco industry.

I told Peter that he should visit the clubhouse and get to know his players. He declined, explaining that players were employees, just like lawyers in his firm. He didn't want to get close to them because he might have to fire them.

Walking through the Pfister Hotel in Milwaukee after another loss, I saw the boss. "Let's have a drink," Peter Angelos suggested. We found a long table in the lobby bar. Angelos sat at one end, his back to the hotel entrance. John arrived, and we ordered drinks and began to analyze the struggling Orioles.

As the team bus arrived, players headed for the elevator, but pitching coach Dick Bosman joined us. Where was Orioles manager Johnny Oates?

Soaring marble columns lined the hotel's lobby, from the entrance to the elevator. As we talked with Peter Angelos, I saw Johnny Oates hiding behind a column. Since Angelos' back was to the entrance, he couldn't see his manager slinking, column to column, trying to reach the elevator unseen. But the rest of us saw him and tried to keep from choking on our drinks. Johnny Oates, a grown man, a big league manager, was hiding from his boss.

When I asked Oates why he'd hidden from Peter Angelos, Johnny said he was worried Angelos would fire him, which eventually happened.

A beautiful Sunday afternoon, 1993. While I went to Camden Yards, Julie and the kids walked around the Inner Harbor, went to Phillips Seafood for crabs, and then came to the ballpark.

Baltimore hosted Seattle. The pitching matchup, O's phenom Mike Mussina against Mariners vet Chris Bosio.

With mediocre stuff, Bosio had to pitch inside to keep hitters honest. He buzzed Orioles hitters Mark McLemore and Harold Reynolds with fastballs at their heads.

Retaliating, Mussina planted a fastball squarely in the back of Mariners catcher Bill Haselman, who charged the mound. He and Mussina exchanged punches. Dugouts and bullpens emptied. I figured this would be a typical baseball fight, a lot of pushing and shoving, obscenities exchanged, and then a peaceful ending. But no.

While the blaze was on the mound, brushfires flared up whenever Seattle's Norm Charlton, once a Cincinnati Reds "Nasty Boy," punched an Oriole in the face. A comical sidebar was 6'-6" Rick Sutcliffe, standing in front of the Mariners' dugout, trying to coax 6'-10" Randy Johnson to come out and fight. This fight, the worst I've seen in baseball, lasted 20 minutes. Eight players were ejected and there were plenty of ripped uniforms, black eyes, and bloody noses.

Mike Mussina injured his shoulder and missed two starts. Cal Ripken, at the bottom of the pile, wrenched his knee and was helped off the field. The Streak was in jeopardy. Trainer Richie Bancells did everything: painkillers, heat, ice, ultrasound, and rehab. After more treatment the next morning, Cal limped out of the training room and played the whole game.

Driving home after the game, my wife Julie said, "I guess I'll have to go to Camden Yards more often. That was the best baseball game I've ever seen."

Plowing through another ho-hum game, I was handed a note. "I love the work you guys do on HTS," it read, "I watch all the games on my dish in L.A. All the best. Barry Levinson."

Barry Levinson was Baltimore's favorite son, who'd directed *Diner, Tin Men, Good Morning Vietnam, Rain Man, Avalon,* and one of the best baseball movies ever, *The Natural.*

"Jeez, I wish Barry would have stopped by," I said.

Five minutes later Barry Levinson joined us.

Grant Besser, an obnoxious reporter on Homicide *(photo courtesy Mel Procter)*

Barry was producing *Homicide: Life on the Street,* an NBC television show based in Baltimore. When I told Barry I had my SAG card, he said to call him. He didn't just hand me a part. I had to audition for the role of Grant Besser, an obnoxious newspaper reporter. That came natural. I ended up appearing in eight episodes of the award-winning show.

My friend Taylor Lumia owned Orso, a five-star Beverly Hills restaurant frequented by many celebrities. If I had an off night while in L.A., I'd join him for dinner. There were always stars there, but one Friday night was exceptional. Jerry Seinfeld and his girlfriend dined inside. Christian Slater was there, and "the White Shadow," Ken Howard, joined us for a drink. Sharon Stone and Steve Martin sat at the table next to us.

I asked Taylor why so many stars came to Orso.

"Because they can be themselves here," he explained. "There are no paparazzi, and we don't fawn over them. We don't pick up dinner tabs or send them free drinks. They know they can just come here, relax, and be real people."

As Taylor and I worked on a second bottle of wine, I remembered that an Orioles pitcher, Roger McDowell, had appeared on *Seinfeld.* I excused myself and told Taylor I just wanted to say hello to Seinfeld and mention McDowell.

I introduced myself to Jerry and his girl and we talked baseball as patrons gawked. I said goodbye to Jerry, and as I returned to my table, people asked, "Who are you? How do you know Seinfeld?"

I couldn't resist. "Oh, Jerry and I are old friends."

Back at our table, Taylor looked at me but said nothing. Our conversation resumed and so did the wine consumption. Glancing at Sharon Stone and Steve Martin, I started to tell a story about John Lowenstein.

"Brother Low walked into a shoe store, and there was Michele Pfeiffer, trying on shoes. John walked up to her but got tongue-tied. All he managed to do was extend his hand and say, 'Michele, John Lowenstein, Baltimore Orioles.'" I laughed at how uncool he'd been.

Just then Sharon Stone and Steve Martin stood up to leave. Feeling no pain, I stepped in front of them, choked, and managed to say only, "Sharon, Steve. Hi, I'm Mel Proctor, Baltimore Orioles."

"That's nice," said Sharon.

"Great," added Steve, as they walked away.

"Damn it, Mel," said Taylor, "I told you why Orso is successful, because we don't bother celebrities in here. In about two minutes, you have set my business back five years."

I was devastated. How could I have been so stupid? "Taylor, I apologize. You and I are friends. How can I make it up to you?"

"Take me into the Orioles' clubhouse and introduce me to Cal Ripken and Brady Anderson," he said, laughing. "And we'll call it even." So, the next day, Taylor met Cal and Brady and got a couple of autographs, and as far as I know there was no drop-off in Orso's business.

In 1994 the Orioles signed Chris Sabo, a three-time All-Star and popular player in Cincinnati. A pit bull with goggles, Sabo spent one unhappy, injury-plagued year in Baltimore. Frustrated by lack of playing time, Sabo told the Orioles to trade him or play him. During a boring game in Milwaukee, I noticed Sabo at the end of the dugout, playing in the sand. He was building something. For several innings, we cut back to Sabo, who'd been joined by pitcher Jamie Moyer, who was sticking miniature flags into what looked like an elaborate sand castle. I asked our dugout camera man to ask Sabo what he was building. "I'm building my own ballpark, so I'll have a place to play," he said. Orioles assistant general manager Frank Robinson found no humor in Sabo's comments and phoned the dugout, telling him to destroy his creation.

In 1995, closing in on Lou Gehrig's record of 2,130 consecutive games, Cal Ripken didn't shy away from any streak-breaking activities. On the road, he and Brady Anderson snuck out to play hoops at local YMCAs, and there were off-season roughhouse games in Cal's gym, sometimes involving former NBA players. Before games, Cal hid, waiting for unsuspecting teammates like Floyd "Sugar Bear" Rayford, whom he'd tackle and pin to the floor. Cal took infield every day, something teams don't do today. He lifted weights. He ran. He could've been hurt on a takeout slide, been hit by a pitch, collided with an outfielder, or had the flu.

In Minnesota, a celebrity softball game featured my *Homicide* friends Daniel Baldwin and Isabella Hoffmann, plus Meat Loaf and Dennis Haysbert. They'd had a few beverages when they joined me in the booth.

Baldwin talked about *Homicide,* Meat Loaf discussed his career as a little league coach, and Dennis Haysbert, who played Pedro Serrano in *Major League,* did his "Hats for bats. Keep bats warm" lines.

As we yukked it up, Cal Ripken fouled a ball of his shin. "Ooh, that hurt," said Daniel Baldwin, as we resumed our *Homicide* conversation.

"Get those fucking people off the air, now," demanded our producer. "Cal could have been seriously injured."

One more to go (photo by Mel Proctor)

Interviewing Cal Ripken before the record breaker (photo courtesy Home Team Sports)

The Orioles did a masterful job promoting Cal Ripken's pursuit of Gehrig's record. Four huge white banners, each with a single digit, hung from the warehouse, behind the right-field wall. As each game became official, the numbers were peeled off, counting toward 2,130, as ovations got louder.

On September 5, one of Cal's favorite rockers, Joan Jett, sang the national anthem and Earl Weaver threw out the first pitch. When the game became official and Cal tied Lou Gehrig's record, 2,129 was pulled off the warehouse, revealing 2,130.

Cal Ripken needed just one game to set a new major league record for consecutive games played. Cal had agreed to do a one-on-one interview with me the next day, before the record-breaking game. I was more anxious than Cal. What if I got caught in a traffic jam? What if I got into an accident? What if I suddenly developed laryngitis? What if I was kidnapped by Martians? As my worries grew increasingly irrational, I left for the park two hours earlier than normal. When I arrived at Camden Yards at 3:30, I was the only person there. I went to our booth and prepared for the game, knowing that activity would get hectic before the first pitch.

September 6, 1995. Cal arrived at 4:45 p.m. Since he'd been asked every question imaginable, his answers were as expected. But when I asked him about the Iron Horse, Lou Gehrig, I was surprised that he'd read little about the Yankees star. Cal said he didn't really want to know about Gehrig until he broke his streak. He said when he retired, he'd research Gehrig.

Bradford Marsalis and Bruce Hornsby combined to perform the national anthem. President Bill Clinton and Vice President Al Gore were there. Orioles players recorded the event with minicams. With help from Cal's wife Kelly, the Ripken's children, five-year-old Rachel and two-year-old Ryan, threw out the first balls.

California's Tim Salmon hit a long drive to center field. Brady Anderson leaped and reached over the wall, as his glove appeared to swallow the baseball. The crowd went nuts as Brady hit the warning track and looked into an empty glove. The ball had fallen out on the other side of the fence for a home run: 1–0, Angels.

Rafael Palmeiro's home run tied the score, 1–1.

Bobby Bonilla and Cal both homered to give the Orioles a 3–1 lead. Cal took the first of many curtain calls as we showed the Ripkens: brothers Billy and Fred, his sister Ellen, mother Vi, and Cal Sr.

Also watching was Orioles legend Frank Robinson, sitting with the Yankee Clipper, Joe DiMaggio, Lou Gehrig's teammate.

As the top of the fifth was completed, the white sheets were pulled off the warehouse wall, leaving 2,131. Cal had done it. He had broken Lou Gehrig's seemingly unbreakable record. Cal stepped out of the Orioles' dugout and waved to

Mike Flanagan (L), me, and Jim Palmer (R) (photo courtesy of Home Team Sports)

the crowd. The fans refused to stop cheering. Cal came out a second time. We timed the standing ovations. Six minutes and counting.

Cal came back out two more times, patted his heart, and pointed to the crowd. Eight and a half minutes of nonstop applause.

"We want Cal, we want Cal," chanted the insatiable crowd.

When Cal stepped out for the fifth time, we showed the stadium policemen clapping and cheering. The crowd would not stop.

After 10 minutes of continuous applause, Cal stepped out of the dugout for the sixth time and finally for a seventh encore, bowing and trying to tell the crowd "that's enough." The crowd continued to roar, a standing ovation that had reached 18½ minutes.

Bobby Bonilla and Rafael Palmeiro pushed Cal out of the dugout, and he began an impromptu victory lap. Cal ran down the right-field line, high-fiving fans and the grounds crew, then ran to the left-field line, slapping more hands, stopping occasionally for someone he knew. As he passed in front of the California dugout, the Angels stood, clapping and cheering. He hugged shortstop Gary DiSarcina, who had idolized Cal as a kid. The ovation finally subsided after 22½ minutes. It was magical.

"I have to fire John Lowenstein," HTS producer Bill Brown told me in January 1996.

"Are you crazy? The ratings are great. Fans love him. You and I love him. Why would you even think about firing him?"

Brown said Peter Angelos thought John was a wiseass and wanted to move Mike Flanagan into the job.

John was devastated. "I can't believe it," he said, when I called him. "Nobody could possibly have made more of a commitment to a job than I have for 11 years, and this is the reward?" John never made any effort to find another broadcasting job. He'd invested his money wisely and had no financial worries. We got together a number of times over the years, but John moved on with life, sadly cutting off all relations with the Orioles.

On an airplane, with a beer in one hand and a cigarette in the other, Mike Flanagan was Rodney Dangerfield. We hoped his deadpan New England humor would transfer to television. Flanny prepared, worked hard, and became a competent analyst, but John Lowenstein was a tough act to follow. After a game in Toronto, Flanny and I agreed to meet in the hotel bar. Walking through the lobby, I saw Rick Pitino and asked him to join us for a drink. Before I could introduce them, Pitino and Flanny were hugging. Huh? They had been basketball teammates at the University of Massachusetts.

Then coaching at Kentucky, Pitino said he wanted to go back to Boston, where he'd coached at Boston University. Shortly after that, Pitino became coach, general manager, and team president of the Boston Celtics.

Despite Cal Ripken's record breaker, the Orioles finished a disappointing 71–73 in 1995 and Orioles owner Peter Angelos fired manager Phil Regan and hired Davey Johnson.

Davey Johnson had interviewed for the manager's job the year before but was bypassed for Phil Regan. Johnson spent seven and a half years as an Oriole, played on World Series championship teams in 1966 and 1970, and as a manager had guided the New York Mets to a world championship in 1986.

At the general manager meetings, Davey Johnson tried to convince Pat Gillick, his old minor league teammate, to accept Peter Angelos' offer to become the Orioles' GM. Gillick had retired after winning five division championships and two World Series titles in Toronto.

Gillick was reluctant because he'd heard Peter Angelos was a meddling owner, but Johnson convinced him Angelos just wanted to win. Gillick signed a three-year contract to become GM. The hiring of Pat Gillick and Davey Johnson should have been the best moves Peter Angelos ever made.

In Toronto, Gillick was called "Stand Pat" because of his reluctance to make trades. With the Orioles, he assessed the talent and concluded that the core of the team was solid. He just needed to add some key veterans. Over a two-week stretch Gillick transformed the Orioles from one of the worst teams into a legitimate contender. He strengthened the pitching staff, trading for 16-game winner David Wells, Kent Mercker, Roger

Talking strategy with President Bill Clinton (photo courtesy Home Team Sports)

McDowell, and Randy Myers, who had led the majors in saves the previous four years. He bolstered the offense, adding .320 hitter B. J. Surhoff and second baseman Roberto Alomar, one of the best all-around players in baseball.

The player Gillick really wanted was free agent pitcher David Cone, who had helped Toronto win a world championship in 1992. Peter Angelos wouldn't approve the proposed Orioles' offer to Cone, so he signed a three-year, $19.5 million deal with the Yankees.

On Opening Day 1996, the president of the United States, Bill Clinton, joined Jim Palmer, Mike Flanagan, and me in the booth during the game. Clinton was accompanied by his daughter Chelsea, Vice President Al Gore's wife Tipper, and Leon Panetta, President Clinton's chief of staff. My 15-year-old son Billy was there, wearing his Orioles uniform. He got to meet them all and shook hands with the president.

"Welcome back to Camden Yards," I said. "President Bill Clinton joins us in the booth." During the interview, we talked about Cal Ripken breaking Lou Gehrig's consecutive-games streak. The president had been there that night, and I asked him what that event meant to him.

"I think it meant a lot to me not only as a baseball fan but as a citizen and as the president now, as someone who really wants his country to work well. The idea that a man could show that kind of discipline and devotion to his work and stay with one team for a career in a time and age when a lot of people don't last very long because they don't have the discipline to do it and just go for the big-time bucks in the short run and float around from team to team, or in the case of nonathletes from company to company. I think it is really sort of reassuring, not only to me but to the American people, to see that kind of record set and to see that kind of discipline and loyalty. I liked it a lot."

"You can certainly identify with pressure in your office. What do you see about the way Cal handled the pressure?" I asked.

"I think he did what I try to do; he didn't vary his routine," said the president. "He just focused on the day that was before him. And I think that he must have had the record in mind, but it didn't paralyze his play. Even the night he was here, the night he broke the record, he hit a home run on a 3–0 pitch. So he still had enough presence of mind not to even just take the walk, you know? He was there, ready. He was playing. He was alive to every moment, and I think that's what you have to do. When you're under a lot of pressure, you have to just take a deep breath and do what you know how to do."

I was impressed by how down to earth Bill Clinton was. He even tried to set up a golf date with Jim Palmer before he left. On the drive home, I said to my son, "Billy, do you know how lucky you are? You got to shake hands with the president of the United States."

"Dad," Billy said, "I'd rather shake hands with Bobby Bonilla."

The 1996 Orioles improved to 88–74, finished second in the AL East, and won the wild-card. The Birds blasted a major league record 257 home runs. Brady Anderson hit a career-high 50 home runs, and Rafael Palmeiro hit 39 and drove in 142 runs.

On September 27, in Toronto, Roberto Alomar was called out on strikes by plate umpire John Hirschbeck. Alomar got in the umpire's face and the two engaged in a heated argument. Alomar was ejected, and Orioles manager Davey Johnson had to restrain him. As we took a commercial break, Orioles beat writer Buster Olney ran into our booth. "Do you have a replay of the argument?" he asked excitedly. "I think Alomar spit in Hirschbeck's face."

Before we came back on air, I asked our producer to roll video, and we all crowded around a TV monitor. We had to look closely and viewed the incident several times, but Alomar had clearly spit in John Hirschbeck's face. As we came back on, we showed the replay. "It looks like Alomar spit in John Hirschbeck's face," I said.

After the game, Alomar said Hirschbeck missed the call and after ejecting him, had used a racial slur. But then Alomar fanned the flames. "He (Hirschbeck) had a problem with his family when his son died—I know that's something real tough in life—but he just changed, personality-wise. He just got real bitter." When told of Alomar's comments the next day, Hirschbeck had to be restrained from going after him.

That morning, AL president Gene Budig issued a five-game suspension that wouldn't begin until the start of the 1997 season. Alomar appealed and was in the lineup that day, hitting a tenth-inning home run that clinched the wild-card spot.

I didn't know it at the time, but 1996 would be my last year broadcasting Orioles baseball. Since I left right after Peter Angelos fired Jon Miller, the Orioles' radio voice, people assumed I'd been canned. Nothing could have been further from the truth. Peter Angelos and I had a good relationship, had many sincere conversations, and I'm sorry he hasn't had more success with the ballclub.

In 1996, the Orioles made the playoffs for the first time in 12 years. After winning the wild-card, they beat Cleveland in the ALDS and then lost to the Yankees in the ALCS. In 1997, after I left, the O's went 98–64, won the AL East, beat Seattle in the ALDS, and then lost to Cleveland in the ALCS.

After feuding with Peter Angelos, Johnson resigned as Orioles manager, the same day he was named American League Manager of the Year. Pat Gillick left when his contract expired in 1998. If Peter Angelos had kept Pat Gillick and Davey Johnson and allowed them to do their jobs, the Orioles might have stockpiled World Series championships. After leaving the Orioles, Gillick turned the Seattle Mariners into a playoff team and then won his third World Series championship with the Philadelphia Phillies in 2008. In 2011, Pat Gillick was voted into the Baseball Hall of Fame.

San Diego Padres, 1997 (photo courtesy of the San Diego Union Tribune)

Chapter 16
Goodbye O's, Hello Pads

As Bill Brown and I relaxed on my sailboat in the Chesapeake Bay, storm clouds suddenly appeared. "Get out of HTS," Bill said as we headed into port. "The ship is sinking." Bill said Westinghouse was going to sell HTS, most likely to Fox.

"We love you and want you back, but we can't pay you the kind of money you've been making," said Jody Shapiro. I'd been at HTS for 12 years and had contributed to the network's success, so why should I take a pay cut?

Ken Nigro, a former beat writer for the Orioles, had just been named public relations director for the San Diego Padres. When I called Nigro to congratulate him, he asked, "Have you applied for the TV job here?"

I said I'd sent a resume and tape to team president Larry Lucchino but was told they wanted an announcer known in San Diego. Nigro said Lucchino wasn't happy with the hundreds of candidates for the Padres TV job and asked, "Are you still interested?"

"Yes, I love San Diego, and it would be fun to work with you guys again."

"I'll call you back."

He called within an hour. "How soon can you get out here?"

"How's tomorrow?"

I flew to San Diego, lunched with executives from the Padres and Channel 4, which would televise the games, and flew back to Washington that night. The next day, the Padres offered me the job. Yes, I said, assuming my family would love to move to one of America's favorite cities.

That didn't register with my teenaged kids Billy and Maile, who were playing sports, laughing with friends, and enjoying life. I figured my Hawaiian-born wife Julie would be thrilled to move closer to her family on Maui, but nobody wanted to leave Maryland. Give San Diego six months, I pleaded. If you're not happy, we'll go back.

"Peter wants to know what he can do to get you to stay," said one of Angelos' guys on the phone. I told him that if Peter had approached me earlier, I would have stayed, but I'd given my word to Larry Lucchino.

For two straight days, I was on conference calls with my attorney Lon Babby, Home Team Sports, and the Padres, trying to amicably leave HTS for San Diego. Finally, after arm wrestling over dollars and spending thousands in legal expenses, I became the TV voice of the San Diego Padres.

I had uprooted my family, risked my reputation in a new market, and was working with new partners. Before I'd even broadcast a game, a *San Diego Union Tribune* poll asked, "Who would you rather have as the Padres' TV announcer, Mel Proctor or Jerry Coleman?" Coleman had broadcast Padres games on radio for 30 years. I had yet to say a word on Channel 4. Of course, I got my ass kicked in the poll.

I moved to San Diego because I believed in Larry Lucchino and his staff. With Lucchino as team president, the Padres' attendance had increased every year, the team was improving, and there was talk of a new ballpark. Plus, there was the joy of living in San Diego, where skies are blue, the temperature is perfect, and the beaches are beautiful. It had taken me 24 years to get there, but I felt like we'd be in San Diego forever.

My broadcast partners Rick Sutcliffe and Mark Grant were both former major league pitchers. Sutcliffe was a Cy Young Award winner with the Cubs in 1984, and Grant was a journeyman who'd played with six teams, including the Padres.

At 6'-6" and 240 pounds with a red beard, the Red Baron took over a room. Sut knew everybody. At any time, Bill Murray, Mark Harmon, Charles Barkley, or Brooks and Dunn might show up in the booth.

Sut asked me to help him. Over postgame beers, we'd review telecasts and go over situations. I've never seen an athlete-turned-analyst improve so quickly. I told Channel 4's general manager Dan Novak that he'd better sign Sutcliffe to a long-term deal before someone else grabbed him.

Talkin' ball with Brooks Robinson, Mike Dee, and Rick Sutcliffe (photo courtesy Mel Proctor)

Sut knew he was progressing fast. He was getting a little cocky and asked if he could do his first interview, with Padres reliever Doug Bochtler. I knew Bochtler had a sense of humor; when a Padres charter landed, an apple rolled from the back of the plane to the front, compliments of Bochtler. Stupid but funny. I told Bochtler, "When Sut asks a question, give him a one-word answer like yes, no, or maybe."

Sut prepared like he was cramming for a bar exam; he knew more about Doug Bochtler than Bochtler did. Sitting in front of a Channel 4 camera, Sut said, "My pregame guest is Padres reliever Doug Bochtler." Putting the microphone in Bochtler's face, Sut said, "Doug, you're off to a great start."

"Yes."

"How do you account for your early success?"

"Hard work."

"Are you excited about the Padres' fast start?"

"Yes."

Listening in the booth, we started to laugh, feeling Sut's pain.

"Doug, I know your mother was a big influence on you getting started in baseball."

"Yes."

By then we were howling in the broadcast booth. Sut's microphone looked like a short-circuited metronome, bouncing back and forth from Sut to Bochtler.

"Well . . . well . . . what do you look for in this series?"

"A game every day," Bochtler said as he lost it. Sut knew he'd been had, looked at our booth, and gave us the finger. Beautiful.

While Rick Sutcliffe educated fans, Mark "Mud" Grant, as in former big league pitcher Jim "Mudcat" Grant, entertained. At Coors Field in Denver, Harold Reynolds, a former player and ESPN analyst, joined us. Mud and I had just ordered a mile-high delicacy, Rocky Mountain oysters. When our order arrived, we told Harold to help himself.

"This is great," said Reynolds, munching on an oyster.

"Harold, have you ever eaten Rocky Mountain oysters?"

"No, but this is so good. Tastes like chicken."

"Harold, do you know what Rocky Mountain oysters are?"

"No, but pass me another one."

"Harold, rocky mountain oysters are fried bull testicles."

It was the first time I'd seen a black man turn green. Harold headed for the rest room. Every time I saw him after that, I offered to buy him Rocky Mountain oysters.

In Milwaukee, when a Brewer homered, Bernie the Brewer, a German brewmaster lookalike, slid into a vat of beer, soaking his lederhosen as the crowd went wild. Batting for the Padres, former Brewer Greg Vaughn lifted "a high fly ball to deep left field," I yelled, "way back, gone. Home run!" As Vaughn circled the bases, Bernie the Brewer schussed down the slide. What? Mark Grant and I exchanged puzzled looks.

Had Milwaukee forgotten Vaughn was a Padre, or was this a classy salute to a former Brewers star? As Bernie the Brewer touched down, he pulled the head off of his costume. A beaming Mark Grant threw his arms in the air. Got you.

Mark sat next to me, laughing his ass off. He and our producer Scott Hecht had conspired to tape this comedy bit and had rolled it in at the right time.

Everybody in baseball does a Harry Caray impersonation, but Mark Grant's is one of the best. Shortly after Caray died, Mark, fortified by a few beers at the Lodge, a Chicago sports bar, grabbed the PA microphone. "Hellooo everybody . . . this is Haaary Caray at Wrigley Field." Oh man.

The bar became church quiet. Cubs fans weren't going to tolerate some asshole making fun of their beloved announcer. We were going to have to fight our way out of there.

"Flyyyy baaall to left field. Dropped by Jorge Orta. Howww does a guy from Mexico lose the ball in the sun?"

I said my prayers.

Silence.

Then the bar exploded with applause. Fans knew Mark wasn't mocking Harry Caray, he was saluting him. Free beer all night.

In Philadelphia, Mark's former Padres teammate John Kruk joined us. I'd called Kruk's final game, with the White Sox in 1995 against the Orioles. Kruk had singled and was lifted for a pinch runner. When the inning ended, the press box announcer informed the media that "John Kruk has announced his retirement from baseball." Kruk had figured out that with one hit he could retire with a lifetime batting average of .300.

The former teammates reminisced about the Padres days and talked about their families.

Mark said, "Mary and I have two boys."

"Really," said Kruk. "How many of them look like me?"

"Get him off," yelled our producer.

"And our thanks to John Kruk for stopping by," I said.

Julie and I had dinner with Channel 4 execs Bill Geppert, Art Reynolds, and Dan Novak. Reynolds seemed genuine, Geppert was slick, and Novak, Channel 4's general manager, a little over the top, saying, "We're a team," and shaking his fist like a cheerleader. My wife Julie, the best judge of character I know, said, "Watch out for him." I'm so naïve, I trusted him. We played golf, had lunch, and talked about the vision for

Channel 4. He was an adversary wearing a friend's clothing. When Padres execs Larry Lucchino and Charles Steinberg dubbed Novak "Dr. No," because he was so negative, I should have known.

In April 1997, the Padres and St. Louis Cardinals played the first regular-season major league series in Hawaii. I'd spent five years in Honolulu, married a Maui girl, and visited Hawaii every year. As I welcomed our Channel 4 viewers to Aloha Stadium on this historic night, I said, "When we arrived at the Royal Hawaiian Hotel, Polynesian beauties wearing grass skirts placed flower leis around our necks. Everyone got lei'ed."

"You can't say that," said Dr. No.

Loosen up, Dan.

"Don't mention Pac Bell," said Dr. No as the Padres and Giants met at Pac Bell Park in San Francisco. Cox Communications, which owned Channel 4, and Pac Bell were involved in a lawsuit.

"Dan, everyone knows it's Pac Bell Park," I said. "It's inscribed on the entrance to the ballpark, printed on game tickets, and mentioned on *SportsCenter* every night. How many people are going to the game saying, "What a great park. I think I'll let Pac Bell handle my communication needs rather than Cox." Ridiculous.

I thought I'd learned how to deal with the numbskulls in this business, and there was no point in arguing, so I accepted the challenge. During the three-game series, I referred to Pac Bell Park like this:

"Welcome back to the Giants' new home."

"Back at the ballpark by the bay."

"Welcome back. Isn't the Giants' new home spectacular?"

"That's McCovey Cove in right field, one of the many features of the Giants' new home."

"A beautiful day in San Francisco as we make our first visit to the Giants' new home."

"San Francisco, one of America's most beautiful cities, and this new ballpark is the crown jewel."

By the final innings of the last game, I was a marathoner stumbling toward the finish line. Our crew bet there was no way I could finish without saying "Pac Bell." Finally, I said, "Final score, Padres 6, Giants 2. So long from San Francisco."

Now that I don't work for Dr. No, take this: "Pac Bell, Pac Bell, Pac Bell, Pac Bell, Pac Bell, Pac Bell, Pac Bell, and finally PAC FUCKING BELL."

The Giants' home is now known as AT&T Park. Go figure.

Before the Padres' home opener in 1997, my son Billy and I sat in the Padres' dugout. When Padres star Tony Gwynn said, "Hi, Billy," my son was speechless. "Come on Billy, relax," said Tony. "This isn't Baltimore, this is San Diego." Then the infectious Tony Gwynn cackle cracked us all up.

Playing high school baseball, Billy was in a slump. Padres hitting coach Merv Rettenmund said to bring him in around 10:00 a.m. on Sunday. When we arrived, Merv was in the batting cage with Tony Gwynn. Sweat pouring off of him, Tony had obviously been there awhile. While teammates slept in after a night game, Tony was trying to find a way to hit Seattle's Randy Johnson, the Padres' mound opponent that night.

I loved standing behind the batting cage with Merv Rettenmund, watching Tony take batting practice. It was like watching Picasso paint. Line drives to left, hard ground balls between third and short—the 5.5 hole, he called it—bullets up the middle, and rockets to right, several landing in the bleachers. "The best hitter I've ever seen," Merv said.

Hall of Famer Ted Williams had told Gwynn to look for pitches on the inner half of the plate and pull them to right field. Heeding Williams' advice, Tony hit three homers in four games in June. When pitchers realized he could hit the ball out, they stopped pitching Gwynn inside. In 1997, Gwynn set career highs with 17 home runs, 49 doubles, 220 hits, and 119 RBIs and hit .372 to win his eighth batting title.

Early in his career, in a slump, Tony asked his wife Alicia to videotape his at-bats. Gwynn became Captain Video. On plane trips, while teammates watched movies, Tony studied his swing. Tony suggested that the Padres buy video equipment to help the whole team, but when they wouldn't, Gwynn paid for it himself. Thanks to Tony Gwynn, every major league team now relies on video.

On August 5, 1999, at Busch Stadium in St. Louis, it was possible that Mark McGwire could hit his 500th home run and Tony Gwynn could get his 3,000th hit on the same night. Tony Gwynn needed two hits to reach 3,000. Mark McGwire needed one home run to reach 500. In the third inning, McGwire hovered over the plate as Andy Ashby threw a curveball that hung like a piñata. With his bulging forearms and uppercut swing, McGwire launched a 451-foot bomb over the center-field fence for his 500th home run. McGwire added an eighth-inning home run off Ashby, but Tony Gwynn went 1–4, falling one hit short of 3,000 as the Padres left for Montreal.

Tony Gwynn had played his entire career in San Diego, away from the media spotlight. Maybe it was appropriate that he got his milestone hit in a half-empty ballpark, off a no-name pitcher in a foreign country. Here's how I called it for Channel 4 San Diego on August 6, 1999:

"Gwynn facing Dan Smith . . . a drive to center field . . . there it is! Number 3,000 for Tony Gwynn! In his first at-bat of the night, in a foreign country, in Canada and Olympic Stadium, Tony Gwynn has done it."

As Tony Gwynn aged and became less productive, so did the Padres. Injuries limited Gwynn to 36 games in 2000 and 71 games in 2001. He was 40 years old, overweight, battling bad knees, and couldn't play the outfield—but he could still rake. He hit .323 and .324 his last two years.

The legend of Ken Caminiti began in 1996 when the Padres played the Mets in Monterey, Mexico. Before the final game of the series, Caminiti lay on the floor in manager Bruce Bochy's office, suffering from food poisoning. Bochy told Cammy to take the day off, but he said no. As the Padres took the field, Caminiti was given intravenous fluids, ate a candy bar, stretched, ran a couple of halfhearted sprints, and told Bochy he was ready. In his first at-bat, Caminiti homered and staggered around the bases. Then, after hitting a three-run homer, he left the game. When the players came into the clubhouse to celebrate the win, Caminiti, in his underwear, was in the trainer's room. Caminiti played the entire year with a torn rotator cuff in his left shoulder but won the National League MVP award. He hit .326 with 40 homers and 130 RBIs and also won a Gold Glove.

In a spring training game in Peoria, Arizona, Cammy struck out his first time up. "Caminiti, you stink," yelled some guy. This clown was on Cammy's back for five innings. After Cammy left the game and showered, he went into the stands. "Hi, I'm Ken Caminiti. I don't come to your place of work and criticize you. Why are you doing it to me? This is only spring training." Soon, Cammy and the heckler were sitting together talking baseball.

In 1997, the Padres played the Mets in the Hall of Fame Game in Cooperstown. In a memorabilia shop, I spotted an old friend, Clete Boyer, autographing pictures. Clete had played on five pennant winners and two World Series champions with the New York Yankees. Boyer was one of the best-fielding third basemen of all time, overshadowed only by the Baltimore Orioles' Brooks Robinson.

"Mel, your guy Caminiti is the best third baseman I've ever seen," Clete said.

"Clete, what about Brooks, what about you?"

"First of all, he's a better hitter than either of us, and he's got a better arm," said Boyer. "And he's fearless. He thinks he can get to any ball, and he'll sacrifice his body to prove it. Do you think he'd mind if I autographed a picture for him?"

Mind? I told Clete that Cammy would be overwhelmed by any comparison to him and Brooks. He signed his picture like this: "Ken, you are a better third baseman than Brooks or I ever was. All the best. Clete Boyer."When I handed the signed photo to Cammy, he held it as if it was the *Mona Lisa.* Finally, choked with emotion, he whispered, "Thank you, and please thank Clete."

Before the first game of the 1998 NLCS series in Atlanta, I was on the field interviewing Ken Caminiti.

"Get off the grass," yelled a Braves employee.

"Hey, you just messed up our interview," I yelled back.

"I don't care. Stay off the grass."

As I resumed the interview, the Grass Nazi struck again: "Get off the grass."

"Do you want me to punch this motherfucker?" Cammy asked.

"No," I said, grabbing his iron forearm.

"That's it, I'm gone," Cammy said, walking away.

"Thanks for fucking up a great interview," I yelled at the Nazi.

As we walked off the field, I heard, "Get off the grass; get off the grass."

My cameraman nudged me and pointed to the Padres' dugout where Cammy was motioning to us to follow him into the clubhouse. With Cammy leading the blocking, we blew past security and did a great interview in front of his locker.

In April 2000, the Padres faced the Astros in Houston. Playing for Houston, Ken Caminiti hit two homers and drove in five runs against his former team. During the telecast, I mentioned that Cammy had been a San Diego icon, an MVP, and had helped the Padres get into the World Series in 1998.

Returning to my hotel room, my phone's message light flashed like a police car's cherry. "Mel, Larry, call me," said the voice mail.

Larry Lucchino had never criticized my work, never told me what to say, and had trusted that I was a pro.

"Hi, Larry?"

"Mel, what the fuck were you doing tonight? Who made you president of the Ken Caminiti fan club?"

"Larry, Cammy had a great game. He's a beloved former Padre, and I was just trying to give him his due."

"Damn it, do you know how many times we kept him out of trouble with the drugs and other things?"

"Well, no, I don't . . ."

"Shit Mel," he said, slamming down the phone.

Wonderful. I had just pissed off the best executive in baseball, someone who'd had my back for 20 years. I sat up for hours, rehashing what I'd said during the broadcast. I'd been fair to Ken Caminiti and the Padres. Larry Lucchino's tirade seemed completely out of character. The next day, still reeling from Larry Lucchino's call, I walked into manager Bruce Bochy's office. General Manager Kevin Towers was also there. "What's the matter with you?" K. T. asked. "You look like you've seen a ghost."

I pulled up a chair and told them about Larry Lucchino's phone call. Both laughed and said they'd gotten similar calls. They said Larry's assistant told them that the boss had a medical problem and his doctor had prescribed steroids. They said he wouldn't even remember the phone call the next day. Roid rage in the front office.

Throughout his career Caminiti had battled drug and alcohol abuse and after his retirement, admitted he'd used steroids. Ken Caminiti died of a drug overdose in 2004.

Country star Garth Brooks came to the Padres' spring training in 1998. A former javelin thrower at Oklahoma State, Garth was in good shape and worked hard, hitting in the cage, fielding ground balls, running, and doing everything the players did. But as a hitter, he went just 1 for 22, with 1 RBI, and wisely kept the guitar gig.

Joining us one night at a local bar, with his baseball cap pulled down low so he wouldn't be recognized, over beers, Garth told us where his career began. "In a place just like this," he said. "The Tumbleweed, in Stillwater, Oklahoma. I'd take my guitar and sing and pretty soon they asked me to perform."

With Garth Brooks in spring training (photo courtesy Mel Proctor)

Larry Lucchino and Charles Steinberg were promotional geniuses. Larry had palm trees planted around the outfield fence, transforming drab Qualcomm Stadium into Shangri-La on TV, and every Saturday night, the Padres handed out quality giveaways. Everything Lucchino tried was a success. Well, almost everything.

In spring training, Larry asked the public address announcer to embellish the plate umpire's calls when the Padres were hitting. When the umpire yelled, "Ball!" the announcer sheepishly added, "Ball 1 . . . just a little outside." The crowd groaned, and the umpire glanced over his shoulder at the press box.

Next pitch, a strike. "Fastball for a strike . . . looked a little low," said the PA guy, getting into this. The crowd booed. The umpire pulled off his mask and glared at the press box.

"Strike two," said the umpire. "Oh, that was outside," whined the PA announcer.

Timeout. The umpires huddled, and then the angry crew chief phoned the press box. The PA announcer explained that he was under orders from Larry Lucchino. Even Lucchino agreed this wasn't working.

Just before spring training in 2000, when the Padres acquired outfielder Al Martin from the Pirates, Larry Lucchino, a Pittsburgh native, said his mom had called saying, "You got a good guy son, everybody here loves Al." A Steel City columnist wrote about Martin being a clubhouse leader, captain of "Al's Army" for kids, and a man who donated 20,000 Pirates tickets and weeks of service to his community.

Just before Martin arrived, his mug shot replaced his smiling baseball photo in the sports pages as Martin was involved in a domestic abuse incident with a woman who said she and Martin had been married in Las Vegas. That was a problem. Martin already had a wife, making this a case of bigamy. Martin told police he didn't think the Vegas ceremony was legitimate. He was later placed on probation.

When I interviewed Al Martin, he told me he'd gone to USC to play football but had accompanied his high school teammate Dave Hansen to an Atlanta Braves tryout camp. As Hansen was being evaluated, a Braves scout asked about his athletic-looking friend in the stands. Hansen said he was Al Martin, a USC football player. Martin said the scout asked him to try out and decided he was a prospect too. The Braves drafted Martin in the eighth round in 1985.

I loved Martin's football stories about his uncle Rod Martin, a former linebacker with the Oakland Raiders, and his own exploits as a strong safety at USC. But Martin turned out to be the Great Imposter.

A reporter discovered that USC had no record that Martin ever played football or even attended the university. So who was Al Martin? I have no idea.

By 1998, promotionally, everything was in place. Fans lined up on Saturday nights to get free T-shirts, autographed baseballs, Trevor Hoffman clocks, baseball gloves, or team pictures. Players sometimes greeted ticket holders at the front gate, and Channel 4 humanized the players. The Padres reached out to the Hispanic community, providing bus service from Mexico. The Padres' attendance had increased from fewer than a million in 1995 to over 2 million in 1997. Now, all they needed was a winner.

General Manager Kevin Towers acquired pitcher Kevin Brown from the world champion Florida Marlins. With a 95 mph fastball and the best sinker in the game, Brown won 18 games, followed by Andy Ashby with 17. Greg Vaughn, the Padres' most valuable player, hit a career-high 50 homers and drove in 119 runs. Tony Gwynn hit .321.

The defense was solid with Gold Glover Ken Caminiti at third, steady Chris Gomez at shortstop, Quilvio Veras at second, and Wally Joyner at first. Catcher Carlos Hernandez was a fiery leader, and the outfield of Greg Vaughn, Steve Finley, and Tony Gwynn was reliable. The Padres also managed to stay healthy. All eight of the regular position players started at least 127 games. When the Padres had the lead in a close game in the late innings, it was "Trevor Time."

When manager Bruce Bochy left the dugout, began his gimpy-kneed walk to the mound, and pointed to the bullpen, video screens went dark. *Bong, bong, bong* echoed through Qualcomm Stadium, as the frenzied crowd got worked up to AC/DC's "Hell's Bell's." "Now pitching for the Padres, number 51, Trevor Hoffman!" proclaimed the public address announcer. In 1998 Hoffman led the majors with 53 saves in 54 save situations and should have won the Cy Young Award, which went to Atlanta's Tom Glavine.

On September 12, 1998, 60,823 fans packed Qualcomm Stadium hoping to see the Padres clinch the NL West against the Los Angeles Dodgers, who quieted the crowd early, taking a 7–0 lead.

In the Padres' fifth, Wally Joyner homered and Chris Gomez singled in two runs to make it 7–3. In the sixth, Greg Vaughn led off with a single, and Dodger reliever Dave Mlicki walked Ken Caminiti.

The crowd began to stir.

Wally Joyner walked to load the bases.

The cheering got louder.

Greg Myers walked to force in a run and make it 7–4 Dodgers.

The decibel level climbed higher.

Sean Maloney relieved Mlicki.

The cheering throng sensed hope.

With the crowd roaring, you could feel Maloney tense up as he hit Andy Sheets, forcing in Caminiti to make it 7–5.

By now, the crowd had taken on a life of its own.

I've never seen a crowd intimidate big-league pitchers like it did that night. With the bases loaded, Maloney walked Chris Gomez, scoring Joyner: 7–6, Dodgers. Jeff Kubenka relieved Maloney for the Dodgers, taking over with the bases loaded.

The crowd noise was deafening; the stadium trembled.

Quilvio Veras's sac fly tied the score at 7–7, and then Greg Vaughn lined a base hit to center field as the Padres took an improbable 8–7 lead.

Fans were delirious, jumping up and down and stomping their feet.

Trevor Hoffman pitched a scoreless ninth, and the Padres won 8–7 to clinch the NL West. Wow, what a night!

The Padres went 98–64 to win the NL West, drawing over 2.5 million fans, a club record, and then faced Houston in the NLDS. In the first game, San Diego's Kevin Brown and Houston's Randy Johnson, two of the best pitchers in baseball, went head to head. Brown struck out an LDS-record 16 batters in eight innings, and Trevor Hoffman saved the Pads' 2–1 victory. The Padres won the series, 4–1. Next stop, Atlanta.

Ken Caminiti's tenth-inning home run gave the Padres a 3–2 win in Game 1 of the NLCS. Georgia native Kevin Brown pitched a three-hit shutout and struck out 11 in Game 2 as the Padres won, 3–0.

Leading the series 2–0 and back in San Diego, over 60,000 fans watched the Padres win, 4–1. No team had ever come back from a 3–0 deficit to win a seven-game series. In Game 4, Andrés Galarraga's grand slam home run powered the Braves to an 8–3 win. It was now 3–1 San Diego.

In Game 5, the Padres led 4–2 in the seventh inning when Bruce Bochy made an unorthodox move, bringing Kevin Brown in as a reliever. Brown retired all three hitters he faced in the eighth, but in the ninth, Atlanta's Michael Tucker belted a three-run homer and Atlanta won, 7–4. The Padres now led, 3–2.

With Kevin Brown spent in relief, in Game 6, Bruce Bochy handed the ball to left-hander Sterling Hitchcock, who held the Braves to two hits as San Diego won 5–0 to capture the National League pennant. Hitchcock was named MVP of the series.

Then it was on to New York to face the Yankees in the World Series. The outcome of the 1998 World Series turned on one pitch, in the seventh inning of Game 1. With the score tied 5–5, Padres left-hander Mark Langston replaced reliever Donnie Wall with a runner at first and one out. Langston got the second out but then walked Bernie Williams and Chili Davis to load the bases. Tino Martinez stepped in. With the count 2 and 2, Langston threw a pitch that looked like strike three, but plate umpire Rich Garcia called it a ball. The Padres went berserk. Langston's next pitch found the fat part of Martinez's bat as the Yankee first baseman launched a grand slam into the upper deck in right and the Yankees won, 9–5. They went on to sweep the Padres in four games.

After the final game in San Diego, as the dejected Padres headed for the clubhouse, 64,000 fans stayed, stood, and cheered. After several minutes, the players returned, shaking hands with fans, throwing baseballs into the stands, and yelling thank-yous to their faithful.

With a spectacular 1998 season and a World Series appearance, owner John Moores convinced Padres fans to vote yes on the construction of a new downtown ballpark. After voters approved the ballpark, they watched the NL champs crumble as Kevin Brown, Greg Vaughn, Ken Caminiti, Steve Finley, and Carlos Hernandez left for other teams.

In 1999, despite a club-record 14-game winning streak in June, the Padres finished fourth, 26 games out of first place. In 2000, they were dead last, 21 games out.

With my contract expiring at the end of 2001, Dan Novak suggested we have lunch to talk about an extension. No rush. Despite the Padres' decline, our ratings were among the highest in baseball, and Dan and I had developed a workable relationship. How quickly things can change.

Late in the season, the Padres held a press conference. Team owner John Moores stood in front of a microphone and with a straight face announced that team president Larry Lucchino was being reassigned to planning and development of the new ballpark. How gullible did Moores think the media was? Larry Lucchino had been fired.

Then Moores introduced new team president Bob Vizas: wrinkled shirt, blue jeans, filthy tennis shoes. Was this guy California cool or a slob? It turned out he was John Moores' spy, who had looked over Lucchino's shoulder and told Moores that Lucchino was spending too much money on ballpark planning. Hello? Larry Lucchino is the same man who helped get Camden Yards built. Petco Park is a wonderful venue, but if Larry Lucchino had stayed it would have eclipsed Camden Yards as the most beautiful park in baseball.

I walked up to Larry, not knowing what to say. I had worked with this man for 20 years and considered him the best executive in sports. I'd moved my family to San Diego because of Larry. As we shook hands, Larry said, "I'm about ready to cry. You know how much I love you. We'll talk later."

When I got home, my wife Julie, who is much more perceptive than I am, asked, "Will Larry's leaving affect you?"

"I don't think so," I said.

Still, I called Dan Novak to arrange a meeting. Dr. No said no. "We're going to wait until the end of the season to evaluate everything. Not just you but the whole broadcast team." Uh-oh. Since Sut and Mud had a year left on their contracts, I was the one being "evaluated."

During telecasts, we'd been promoting "the Padres Cruise," which Julie and I had gone on the year before. All of a sudden, the copy I read had changed from "Join Mel Proctor" to "Join Mark Grant." Not good.

It was about money and power, as it usually is. With Larry Lucchino gone, Channel 4 saw a chance to unload my salary, which they thought was excessive. During a previous negotiation, they told my agent that I should be careful or I might price myself out of the market. I think they also felt that Lucchino had bulldozed them into hiring me. I was "Larry's guy," and with Lucchino gone, I was too.

My suspicions were confirmed when Matt Vasgersian, the Milwaukee Brewers broadcaster, called to tell me Dan Novak had offered him my job. Of course, publicly, Dr. No said I was doing a great job and nothing had been decided.

While on a road trip to Atlanta, reeling from my impeding job loss, my wife called to say that our daughter Maile had been admitted to the psychiatric ward at a San Diego hospital.

About to step on the team bus to Turner Field, I thought, *I'm losing my job and my daughter is in the hospital.* Fuck this. I asked Jerry Coleman and Bob Chandler to fill in on TV and caught the first flight to San Diego. I met my wife and daughter at the hospital. I couldn't take much more. My daughter was in the hospital for 10 days, and I was losing a job I loved. Things come in threes.

My son Billy called. "Dad, are you watching TV?"

"No."

"The United States has just been attacked. A plane has crashed into the World Trade Center in New York. Put the TV on." For the rest of the day, I sat, in my pajamas, transfixed, watching 9/11 unfold. Baseball wisely canceled games for a few days, but finally play resumed. Nobody wanted to work, but we all needed a distraction. As I drove up Highway 5 to Los Angeles where the Padres resumed play, I saw people standing on overpasses, holding banners that read "God Bless America" or "We Will Survive." American flags were waving everywhere. I cried all the way to L.A.

Trying to get my mind back on baseball, I concentrated on the final weeks of Tony Gwynn's career and Rickey Henderson's pursuit of 3,000 hits. Then I got the most asinine e-mail from Dr. No, Dan Novak. "I know it's been a tough year, with the Tony and Rickey things, your daughter's illness, and 9/11, but you've done a great job." Unfuckingbelievable. This moron was firing me and had the nerve to put the worst tragedy in America's history and my daughter's health in the same sentence with baseball.

October 7, 2001. Tony Gwynn's last game. My final game. I wanted to thank the fans who'd been loyal to us for five years, but this was Tony's day, and I didn't want to detract from it. Every time Tony Gwynn came to the plate, fans stood and cheered. Tony played his final game, Rickey Henderson got his 3,000th hit, and my eyes filled with tears as I said goodbye to Padres fans.

Dr. No didn't have the balls to fire me in person. He and Padres exec Mike Dee double-teamed me on the phone. "We're going in another direction," Dan Novak said.

Where did this fucking line "We're going in another direction" come from? Which direction? North, South, East, West, up, down, sideways, out of the country, to another planet? Suits lie. They fire you because you're making too much money or they don't like you.

While he was running Channel 4, Dan Novak wiped out most of our original broadcast team, getting rid of me, producer Scott Hecht, and Rick Sutcliffe, who became a superstar at ESPN.

Larry Lucchino became president, CEO, and part owner of the Boston Red Sox and took most of his loyal employees with him. Although this insane business had taken me from Colorado to Philadelphia to Hawaii to Washington, D.C., to Arlington, Texas, to New Jersey, back to D.C., and to San Diego, I didn't want to move again. But I hoped the Red Sox would hire me. My "friends" never called.

I was job hunting at the 2001 World Series in Anaheim, when Padres owner John Moores told me, "I just want you to know, I had nothing to do with you losing your job." Right, you're only the team's owner.

Chapter 17
Down and Out in Palm Springs

I'd never been out of work. It was terrifying. With two kids in private colleges and no income, how the fuck was I going to keep them in school? My wife Julie, the eternal optimist, always said, "If Plan A doesn't work, we'll go to Plan B and then to Plan C." But she'd never worked in broadcasting.

Texas needed a TV announcer, so I called my friend, Rangers GM Doug Melvin; he'd been fired that day by team owner Tom Hicks. Bye-bye, Plan A.

But Eric Nadel and John Blake of the Rangers called. Eric and I had been broadcast partners, and Blake was a former PR director for the Orioles. En route to a Fox Network game, I met Blake and Rangers president Jim Lites at the DFW airport. Lites said, "We'll offer you a five-year contract and give you the freedom to work for the networks. We want you to spend the rest of your career with us in Texas. I'll call you next week to draw up a contract." Then he added, "But as a favor to someone, I have to interview one more person." The one-more person got the job. Aloha, Plan B.

Jerry Coleman suggested I call Norman Baer, a CBS radio producer who represented several announcers. Playing phone tag with Norman, I finally reached his home. Norman had just died of a heart attack. Rest in peace, Norman and Plan C.

My friend Jeff Rimmer, hockey announcer for the Florida Panthers, suggested I apply for the vacant Florida Marlins TV job. They went young and cheap. Sayonara, Plan D.

I called Peter Angelos in Baltimore, who asked, "Why did you leave the Orioles?" I explained that with the uncertain status of HTS and the lure of Larry Lucchino and the San Diego Padres, it seemed like the right move. I said I'd love to come back to Baltimore.

I flew to Baltimore and was treated like a king. A stretch limo, a studio stop with old friends saying, "Come back," and lunch with Comcast execs. "We'll call you next week," they said. I'm still waiting for their call. So much for Plan E.

The Colorado Rockies had a radio play-by-play job open. Denver. My hometown. My family still lived there. What could be better? I flew to Denver and had dinner with KOA's program director Don Martin and Rockies announcer Jeff Kingery. The next day, we had lunch with Rockies execs, and I was introduced to everyone at KOA from GM Lee Larsen to the janitor. God, please let me come home.

Several days later, a Denver sportswriter called. "I hear you're going to get the Rockies job, so how about an interview?"

"Oh, no. Don't say that. That's the kiss of death."

The next day, Don Martin called to tell me I was number two. Goodbye to Plan F, for "fucked."

I hadn't expected to work my way through the whole fucking alphabet. I applied for every job I heard about, contacted everyone I knew in the business, and worked the Internet job sites. Not a fucking thing. I didn't feel like making another phone call, sending another e-mail, or mailing another tape.

I'd been unemployed for seven months. Then I saw a job listing on tvjobs.com. A startup television station in Palm Springs needed a sports director. Palm Springs was a small market, and the job wouldn't pay much, but when broadcasters got sacked in L.A., they often camped in the desert until they found a job.

"Call them," Julie said. "What have you got to lose?"

I drove to Palm Springs for an interview with Erin Gilhuly, news director of KPSP-TV, Channel 2, a new CBS affiliate.

"You're overqualified," said Erin.

"I know, but I'm bored and I love to work."

While most stations hired the young and the cheap, Channel 2 wanted veterans, who'd hopefully appeal to the older demographics in Palm Springs. Channel 2 hired me. My salary was $46,000, a pay cut of a mere $254,000 from my previous job.

I hadn't anchored TV sports in 28 years, since the Hawaii days. The business had changed. A small-market reporter was now a one-man band who shot camera, edited video, and wrote scripts. Everything was computerized or digital. I was a Tyrannosaurus rex, stumbling through the desert.

Thank God for the "kids," Drew Johnson and Serene Branson. Drew was the weekend sportscaster and Serene was a gorgeous blonde just out of college. They saved my ass. I was fine on air, looking into the camera and reading the teleprompter, but editing and putting my rundown into the computer was totally foreign.

Sport coats and ties were required on newscasts, but I was broke and only had two blue blazers. Fortunately, I discovered Angel View Vintage Clothing, where people donated the most garish sport coats imaginable. I worked out a trade with Angel View. I'd plug their charities if they'd let me wear their sport coats.

Checked, striped, spotted, purple, green, leather, corduroy—the uglier the better. Viewers called to critique my taste in fashion and some dropped off sport coats to wear.

"Mel," Erin Gilhuly said, "People love your sport coats and the goofy things you do. It's great. Go crazy on the air—use your imagination, be creative, and have fun." Erin had just handed me the keys to the funhouse.

In 2001, the California Angels headed to the World Series, and the "Rally Monkey" had become a star. As the Angels continued to win, fans brought stuffed monkeys to games, the team began to market their own, and the Rally Monkey became a phenomenon. Our talented production staff created a monkey with my face superimposed. So, the Rally Monkey delivered the sports each night. One time, I pretended like the Rally Monkey was being attacked by other team mascots. I fell behind the news desk after being beat up by the Phillie Fanatic. I rolled around on the floor, mussed up my hair, and then, totally disheveled, crawled to my chair to say good night. People loved it.

I knew that retired major league manager Gene Mauch lived nearby. "The Little General" had managed the star-crossed 1986 California Angels, who were one pitch away from the

World Series when Boston's Dave Henderson homered in the ninth and the Red Sox won in extra innings and went on to win the series. In 1988 Gene Mauch retired, the winningest manager in baseball history never to manage in the World Series.

I figured Gene would be a bitter old man, trying to forget the past. I called him, and he invited me to his house, on a golf course in Rancho Mirage. Gene played golf every day, taped baseball telecasts, and at night, had a cocktail or two and watched the games. Gene still loved baseball. His mind was sharper than a Samurai's sword, and he admired Angels manager Mike Scioscia and was happy for his old team's success.

I asked Gene to join me as an analyst for the World Series between the Angels and San Francisco Giants but explained that as a start-up operation, Channel 2 couldn't pay him. "Just get me a gross of blue-dot golf balls, and I'll do it," he said. I worked a trade out with a local golf store, and Gene got his golf balls.

I treasured my time with Gene Mauch. In the dugout, he'd been a fierce competitor and a loud bench jockey. Off the field, he was a classy gentleman. His World Series analysis was brilliant. Between newscasts, we'd go to his house and talk baseball. I asked him if he missed managing. "I don't miss the travel, but the two and a half hours in the dugout managing I miss every day."

The Frank Sinatra Golf Tournament is a big deal. Organized by Barbara Sinatra, Frank's widow, the star-studded tourney raises money for charities. Walking around the Renaissance Esmeralda Resort, I saw Andy Williams, Tony Bennett, Smokey Robinson, Pat Boone, Steve Garvey, Don Sutton, and others. I interviewed some of them for the nightly sports show.

As I walked toward the head table, security men whispered into their walkie-talkies, "Unknown person approaching." As I saw them closing in, someone yelled, "Mel Proctor . . . is that you? What the hell are you doing here?" It was Jimmy Borges, a jazz singer and friend from Hawaii. Jimmy and I hugged as the security people backed off. Barbara Sinatra had invited him to Palm Springs to sing some of Frank's songs. Ole Blue

Eyes liked Jimmy's interpretations of his songs, and over the years, Jimmy had maintained a friendship with the Sinatra family. Jimmy put his arm around my shoulder. "I want you to meet my friends, Dick Van Dyke, Mike Connors, and Robert Wagner." Jimmy explained that I was a sportscaster for Channel 2 in Palm Springs, and with that Wagner held up two fingers. I knew what he meant; he had played "Number Two" in three Austin Powers movies. Either that or he was telling me I had again finished second for a sportscaster's job.

I was having fun in Palm Springs but was making little money, was separated from my family, and had disappeared from the broadcast world. One day, driving to work, I heard an ESPN talk show host, Chuck Wilson, who asked, "Whatever happened to Mel Proctor? He was one of the best play-by-play guys around. I'm amazed he's not calling games for some pro team."

I pulled off to the side of the road, called ESPN, and was immediately put on the air. I explained I was in Palm Springs, hoping to find a big-league job somewhere but not knowing if I would be stuck in the desert forever.

The Los Angeles Clippers trained at the College of the Desert, a junior college in Palm Springs. Ralph Lawler, the longtime voice of the Clippers, invited me to training camp. "I think I have some games for you," Ralph said. When Ralph did televised games, the Clippers needed someone to do 30 radio games.

Thank God for Ralph Lawler, who helped me get back in the NBA. The pay was terrible, but I was happy to be back in a sport I loved. That began the most frenetic time of my life. I'd anchor two sportscasts per night on Channel 2 and then drive to L.A. for a Clippers game or fly with them to road games. If I had a weekend off, which was rare, I drove home to San Diego late Friday night and stayed until Sunday when I'd return to the desert. Thankfully, Erin Gilhuly granted me flexibility.

Between all the jobs, I managed to piece together an income of about $100,000, but I was wearing out physically and so were the tires on my Toyota 4Runner.

The Clippers eventually increased their television coverage, which freed up 60 games for me on radio. I left the wonderful people at Channel 2 to go with the Clippers.

I spent three losing seasons with the Clippers, but finally in 2003–04, there was hope as Mike Dunleavy was hired as coach. Dunleavy and his assistants worked harder than any NBA staff I'd seen. The team improved each year, and of course, the year after I left, 2005–06, they had a great season, going 47–35 before losing to Phoenix in the Western Conference Semifinals.

I was making only $60,000 with the Clippers, far below the league average, but I loved the NBA and treasured my time with Clippers announcers Ralph Lawler and Mike Smith and many good people in the organization. If they'd paid me a decent salary, I would have stayed forever.

Norm Nixon, who'd played for both the Lakers and Clippers, regularly attended Clips games. Occasionally I interviewed him at halftime, and we'd always say hello. During halftime of a game, Norm Nixon stopped by, we shook hands, and he said, "I'm looking forward to being your partner."

What?

Norm explained that team president Andy Roeser had hired him as an analyst for the rest of the season. Wouldn't it have been nice if the Clippers had at least run this idea past me? Norm is a bright guy but had virtually no on-air experience, and I sensed he was using this job as an entrée to a coaching job or front-office position.

During a game with several European players, I said, "Norm, I guess when you played, you didn't face many Euros. I mean, was Drazen Petrovic even in the league then?"

"Well, I don't know," Norm said, "but I did play against Havlicek and Maravich." Huh.

Norm and I went to practice and shootarounds on the road, and Norm would often pull a player like Corey Maggette aside and give him advice. I watched Mike Dunleavy's face flush every time this happened. The players were too polite to say no to Norm, but I could sense Mt. Dunleavy was about to erupt.

On a flight, Dunleavy asked me to sit with him. "You've got to do something about your partner. I can't have Norm on the court talking to my players. It's a distraction. Who knows what he's telling them? Can you talk to him?"

I told Mike that I'd talk to Norm but that this was really an issue between him and Norm. I tried to explain to Norm that Dunleavy didn't want his input. Norm was hurt, saying he was just trying to help.

Remember when I said that doing play-by-play for the Los Angeles Lakers has been my lifelong dream? Well, I received a letter from the Los Angeles Lakers' law firm, saying that the Lakers had spoken to the Clippers, requesting permission to talk to me about their vacant radio position, my dream job. The Clippers had said no. What the fuck? I called Lakers GM Mitch Kupchak who said he couldn't talk because it would be tampering, but another Lakers exec candidly told me that my boss, Christian Howard, told the Lakers to back off because the Clippers loved my work, were going to give me a long-term contract, and would take care of me financially, which, of course, they didn't do. When I confronted Howard, he denied he'd had any conversation with the Lakers. I had been Clipperized.

Chapter 18
Back to the Nation's Capital

In 2005, the Montreal Expos moved to Washington, D.C., became the Washington Nationals, and with Opening Day approaching, needed a TV announcer. Since I'd spent 19 years in the Baltimore-Washington market, I figured I had a shot at the job. I called Frank Robinson, the Nationals manager and longtime friend, who put in a good word for me. Before I flew to New Orleans for the Clippers' final game, I learned that I was in the top five for the Washington job. If I got the job, I'd go to Washington. If I didn't get it, I'd fly home to California. I told my wife, "I might be back in two days or six months."

Bob Whitelaw, general manager of the Mid-Atlantic Sports Network, called, offering me a one-year contract for $300,000 to do play-by-play for the Washington Nationals. "Take it or leave it," he said. The money was fine, but his attitude sucked. What happened to "Welcome aboard, this is going to be an exciting year, and we're glad to have you with us?"

I flew to Washington, D.C., and took a taxi to RFK Stadium, where the Nats worked out before flying to Philadelphia to open the 2005 season. I shook hands with Frank Robinson, who asked who my partner was. When I said I didn't know, he laughed and shook his head.

Frank and I were standing behind the batting cage when a chunky guy in a shiny suit walked up, Tony Tavares, Nationals president. I extended my hand, "Hi Tony, Mel Proctor." He stared at my hand and said, "The only reason you're here is because of Frank Robinson" and walked away.

I looked at Frank. "That's Tony," he said.

We bussed to BWI Airport, flew to Philadelphia, took another bus to the Four Seasons Hotel, and then grabbed a taxi to dinner with our production crew. I still didn't know who my partner was. The next morning, on game day, I opened the door of a taxi, slid in, and recognized former New York

Mets pitcher Ron Darling entering from the other side. My partner? I'd never met Ron. As we shook hands, Bob Whitelaw pulled up in his rental car and asked us to join him, saying we'd have a production meeting on the way to Citizens Bank Park. We should have stayed in the cab because Whitelaw got lost and what was normally a 20-minute ride took an hour. I quickly realized Whitelaw was clueless.

Thank God for producer Chip Winfield, director Doug Yalacki, and our incredible crew; their energy level was high, and everyone pooled their talents to produce a helluva first telecast, despite the Nat's 8–4 loss to the Phillies. We met in the hotel bar to celebrate, figuring our boss, Bob Whitelaw, would compliment everyone and pick up the tab, but he said nothing. I had to ask him what he thought of the telecast. "I thought it really went well considering you guys just met," he said with no emotion. That was the last positive comment we got from him all year.

We were pumped—new team, new season, national publicity. In the season home opener, outfielder Brad Wilkerson had the first Nationals hit and in the second game became the first Nationals player to hit for the cycle, but nobody in D.C. saw it. After several doses of truth serum in the hotel bar, our producer Chip Winfield admitted that fans couldn't see most of the weekday telecasts. MASN, trying to circumvent Comcast, the largest cable carrier in the Baltimore-Washington area, was trying to sell the package to regional cable outfits and a new entity, DIRECTV. Comcast had been so sure they'd carry the games that billboards all over D.C. proclaimed, "Follow the Nationals on Comcast." Comcast was shut out, and so were 3 million angry fans who couldn't see most weekday games.

D.C. mayor Anthony Williams expressed his outrage, fans were furious, and I was pissed. Why didn't Bob Whitelaw tell us the truth? Weren't we in this together? Instead, Whitelaw let Ron Darling and I prepare for games, put on sport coats and ties, and broadcast to nobody. I realized that Ronnie and I had fallen into the most bizarre situation in the history of sports broadcasting.

With a team in D.C., Baltimore Orioles owner Peter Angelos was worried that the Nationals would cut into the O's attendance, TV ratings, and profits. Angelos, a street-smart Greek, had made millions in class action suits, and frightened that Angelos would sue MLB, Commissioner Bud Selig handed him the keys to Ft. Knox. The Orioles agreed to share their territory with the Nationals in return for the ability to televise Nationals games on the Mid-Atlantic Sports Network. The Orioles owned 90 percent of MASN, and MLB paid the Orioles $75 million for 10 percent of the network. Over the next 23 years, the Nationals' stake in the network would increase to 33 percent. This was unprecedented, the owner of one major league team controlling the television destiny of another franchise. Unfuckingbelievable.

Since the Nationals opened on the road, Ronnie and I had little time to look for housing. Fortunately, I found a condo downtown, and since Ronnie had no place to stay, he slept on my couch for a month. It was like being in college again. We had lunch together, cocktails after games, and bonded, talking about baseball, families, and life. We both knew we were in broadcast hell and agreed to watch each other's back.

As baseball returned to the nation's capital after a 35-year absence, 45,956 fans packed RFK Stadium for the home opener. The Nationals had slapped makeup and lipstick on the old girl and she looked good. Before the game, Bob Wolff, the TV announcer for the old Washington Senators, congratulated me on being selected as the Nats' announcer, saying, "You're the best possible choice." Coming from one of the classiest men in broadcasting, that meant a lot to me.

As I sat in the booth filling out my scorecard, I watched thousands of fans enter RFK Stadium, including countless fathers and sons, Dad wearing an old Washington Senators hat and son sporting a brand-new red Nationals cap. I imagined the stories fathers must have been sharing with their sons and thought of my dad. I was excited and proud to be part of this history-making day, until I went to the Nationals' clubhouse.

"Do you know what I don't like about you?" said Nationals president Tony Tavares, pulling me off to the side.

"Well, no . . ."

"You're too much like an ESPN announcer." I figured that was a compliment. "You're the Nationals' announcer. You need to see things from the Nationals' standpoint. We don't care about the other team. Don't get excited when the other team hits a home run, but if a Nationals player does it, go crazy."

Are you shitting me? This glorified bean counter wanted a homer, a shill for the team. I started to explain that when a baseball is hit deep, there is drama for both teams. Will the ball leave the yard for a home run, or will it be caught? But I realized Tavares wasn't listening.

I felt like I'd been sucker punched as I tried to block Tavares out of my mind and concentrate on the excitement of the Nats' home opener. President George W. Bush threw out the first ball, Liván Hernández pitched a strong $8^1/_3$ innings, and Vinny Castilla went 3–3 with four RBIs as the Nationals beat Arizona, 5–3.

After the game, in Frank Robinson's office, we shared the excitement of this historic day, but when I told him about the pregame blast I'd taken from Tony Tavares, Frank stood up. "Hold it," he said. "Buf (Don Buford), Mac (Tom McCraw), and the rest of you," Frank yelled, "into my office now." With his coaching staff crowded into his tiny office, Frank asked me to repeat the Tavares story. As I did, Nationals general manager Jim Bowden walked past the door. I figured he'd join us, but he didn't.

Frank Robinson and Tony Tavares hated each other. Tavares had tried to fire Frank in Montreal, but Frank had been hired by his friend, baseball commissioner Bud Selig, and told Tavares to take a flying leap.

"What were you doing in Frank Robinson's office?" yelled Bob Whitelaw on the phone the next day.

"Bob, in all the years I've broadcast baseball, I've always gone to the manager's office after games."

"Well, I heard you said some uncomplimentary things about the Nationals' front office." Jim Bowden.

I explained what we talked about and added, "I've known Frank Robinson for nearly 30 years. If I want to go to his office and talk to him, I will."

Because the Nationals were run by MLB, Tony Tavares and Jim Bowden, like competing gorillas, pounded their chests, each trying to show prospective owners that they were responsible for the team's success and should be rewarded with a job. Frank Robinson suggested that if they all worked together, everyone would benefit. Of course, nobody listened.

Like summer humidity in D.C., fear hung in the air. Nationals employees were afraid of Tony Tavares, and our producer and director were scared of Bob Whitelaw, who was terrified of Peter Angelos. Ronnie and I looked at each other in disbelief and kept doing the games, whether anybody was watching or not.

With little offense but good defense and solid pitching, the Nats found ways to win, and with rookie reliever Chad Cordero piling up more saves than a *Baywatch* lifeguard, the Nats moved into first place in June. After games, Ronnie and I sat in our booth, waiting for increasingly larger crowds to leave RFK Stadium, and wondered how the Nats had pulled out another victory. Then we'd get pissed, remembering that many of these thrillers had gone unseen. So I said, on the air, "We've heard nobody is watching these games. Here's my cell phone number: 760-857-1234. If anyone is watching, please call me. Not a single viewer called. The only call I got was from a coworker in our production truck who said, "Go Nats" and hung up. *Washington Post* writer Barry Svrluga thought the incident was hilarious and interviewed me for a story that ran the next day.

"Insubordination!" yelled Bob Whitelaw on the phone. "You're undermining the product."

First of all, I didn't realize I was in the military and subject to court martial, and second, how could we influence anyone since NOBODY COULD SEE THE FUCKING GAMES?

Although we were the Washington Nationals' announcers, our paychecks, which arrived late, had the Orioles' bird logo on them. Bob Whitelaw warned us about mentioning the Orioles too often. Are you kidding? Nationals manager Frank

Robinson was an Orioles icon, coaches Tom McCraw, Don Buford, and Jack Voigt were former Orioles, and I had spent 12 years broadcasting Orioles games.

After Whitelaw's reprimand, when the *Washington Post* showed the Nationals were outdrawing the Orioles, I said, "Ronnie, did you notice that the Nationals' attendance is better than that team from the north's, you know, the ones with wings and beaks?" Ronnie was speechless.

"Whitelaw wants to know if you have a death wish," said our producer. Are you shitting me? I was quickly learning that Whitelaw had the people skills of an Auschwitz guard.

Balls that were home runs on the road were caught on the warning track at RFK Stadium, and veterans like Vinny Castilla, Jose Vidro, and José Guillén were convinced the dimensions were wrong. Arriving at RFK early, I saw Frank Robinson and several players with their caps on backward, squinting into surveying equipment. Other players stretched out a tape measure from home plate to the outfield wall, trying to find out just how far away the fences were. This would be great TV. I asked our producer to tape it, and he put together a great piece. Unfortunately, he ran it past Whitelaw for approval. Don't run it, Whitelaw said, because it made the Nationals' front office look bad. As it turned out, the power alleys in left center and right center, both listed at 380 feet, were actually 395 feet from home plate. No wonder the players were pissed off.

On a WTOP radio show, Tony Tavares ripped Ronnie and me. What the fuck! If Tavares had a problem, why didn't he come to us? When I told Bob Whitelaw that I was going to confront Tavares, he said no, he would talk to him, which, of course, he never did.

When Ronnie had to fly to California for his son's high school graduation, I suggested we use Nationals coach Jack Voigt as a fill-in. When Jack was an Oriole, I nicknamed him "Mr. Baseball" because he talked baseball 24 hours a day, and I knew he wanted to get into broadcasting. Although a coach, Voigt wasn't in uniform during games, instead serving as the "eye in the sky" from the press box.

As GM Jim Bowden talked to the media after a press conference to announce a contract extension for José Guillén, I approached Tony Tavares. I thought about opening with, "Do you know what I don't like about you?" but instead asked if Jack Voigt could fill in for Ron Darling in an upcoming series in Toronto. Fine, said Tavares, but then I said, "But Tony, as a courtesy to Frank Robinson, I think I should run it by him because we are borrowing one of his coaches."

"What the fuck?" Tavares yelled. "You don't have to clear a damned thing with Frank Robinson. Frank Robinson is a fucking employee just like everybody else, although he doesn't think so. If I say you can use Jack Voigt, then use him."

"But Tony . . ." As our argument heated up, I saw our producer slink out the door.

"You're pissing me off," he yelled. "Don't you know there is a chain of command here, and do you know who's at the fucking top?"

"Yes, Tony, you are."

Dumbfounded by Tavares' explosion, I went to the clubhouse to tell Jack Voigt we wanted him to fill in as an analyst.

"I can't," Jack said.

"Why not?"

"It wouldn't be fair to Frank. I'm one of his coaches."

"Jack, I went to bat for you. You said you wanted to do this, and now you're backing out on me."

As I walked into the dugout, I saw Jim Bowden. "What were you and Tavares arguing about?" he asked.

I explained and asked, "What the hell is wrong with Tavares? I've never had anybody talk to me like that."

"Well, maybe he's upset because he wasn't at the podium for José Guillén's press conference."

Then Jack Voigt walked into the dugout.

"Jack, do you want to do the telecasts?" asked Bowden.

"Yes, but . . ."

"Then do them," said Bowden. "I'll talk to Frank."

Jack Voigt filled in for Ron Darling in a three-game series in Toronto and was fantastic. I'm surprised he hasn't pursued a broadcasting career.

Before a game in Toronto, Curt Smith, author of *Voices of the Game* and *The Storytellers,* asked if he could join us to talk baseball and promote his new book, *Voices of Summer,* in which he selected the 100 best baseball announcers of all time. Curt was a great interview, discussing the history of baseball broadcasting in Washington and mentioning that he had picked me among his top 100. It was great publicity for me, baseball in Washington, MASN, and the Nationals.

"You have to clear all interviews, in advance, with me," said Bob Whitelaw, again bothering me with an early phone call. I tried to explain that most interviews are catch-as-catch-can. If you see John Kruk, Barry Levinson, or Brooks Robinson walk by the booth, you grab them for an interview. But I'd realized this moron just didn't get it. So I blew off a number of interviews I would loved to have done.

In Washington, Phil Wood, a friend and former coworker at WTOP, asked if he could promote his wonderful book *Nationals on Parade,* about the history of baseball in Washington, D.C. Normally, I would have asked Phil to join us, but since I had to clear interviews with this dork I worked for, I called Bob Whitelaw.

"No," said Whitelaw. "If we let him plug his book, we'll have to give everyone a chance to promote their book."

"Ronnie, this is how you hold a microphone" (photo courtesy Mel Proctor)

As I started to point out that this wasn't an election, we didn't have to give equal time, and that Phil Wood's credentials were impeccable, I realized I was again banging my head against the Washington Monument.

Since neither Ronnie nor I had a car, you'd think our thoughtful employers would've provided us with transportation to and from RFK Stadium, but no. So we took the train. Washington, D.C., is a swamp in the summer; so humid that for each game, I brought two shirts, the one I wore on the train and another to wear on camera.

We named our booth air-conditioner "Sometimes" because sometimes it worked and sometimes it didn't. We wanted to keep the windows open so we could hear the crowd and experience the ambience, but often it was so hot and humid that we closed the windows and prayed the air-conditioning worked. One weekend, the air-conditioning conked out. The booth thermometer read 108 degrees. Unbearable. I told Bob Whitelaw, who assured me the problem would be fixed. Of course, it wasn't.

The next day, after sweating through another game, I told Ronnie, fuck this, tomorrow we'll wear shorts. Who gives a shit; they only see us from the chest up anyway when we're on camera. We actually wore long pants with shorts underneath, and when we found the booth was still the Amazon Jungle, we went with shorts.

"You can't wear shorts," yelled Bob Whitelaw on the phone, while watching the studio feed during a commercial break. "That's unprofessional."

"Bob, nobody can see us wearing shorts. Relax. It's 108 degrees in the booth. For two days, we've asked for somebody to repair the air-conditioning. What do you expect us to do?"

"Tomorrow, we'll send up fans, just in case."

The only fans that showed up were the ones who bought tickets.

We felt like we were working against our employers instead of with them. I wanted to help Ronnie more than I could, but I spent so much time pissing on brushfires that all I could do was prepare for the games, take the train to the park, and do the telecasts.

Baseball games are three, sometimes four, hours long, and every announcer has been challenged to keep his energy level up. One time, Ronnie was running late, had taken a cab to the game, ran up the ramps to the booth, and arrived breathless. It was the best game he'd ever done. Our producer, director, and I agreed, "Yes, Ronnie, that's the energy we need."

Ronnie had done studio shows for Fox but had never broadcast games. He got absolutely no help from the Nationals, MASN, or the media. I often asked for a DVD of a game so that Ronnie and I could watch, but my requests were denied. Hell, I don't have a single telecast from the Nationals' historic season.

By early June, over 320,000 fans had poured into RFK Stadium, as the Nationals moved into first place, winning 10 in a row, including sweeps of the Florida Marlins, Oakland A's, and Seattle Mariners.

The streak ended in the first game of a road trip, as the Nats lost to the Angels, 11–1. In the second game of the series, with the Angels leading 3–1 in the seventh inning, manager Mike Scioscia brought in reliever Brendan Donnelly. Nationals outfielder José Guillén had played for the Angels and knew Donnelly used pine tar, an illegal substance he applied to the ball. The information was passed to manager Frank Robinson, and as Donnelly warmed up, Robinson asked the umpires to check the pitcher's glove. They found pine tar, and Donnelly was ejected. Angels manager Mike Scioscia stormed out of the dugout and got into a heated argument with the still-fiery 69-year-old Robinson. The Nationals players raced onto the field to support their skipper, and José Guillén had to be restrained as the teams engaged in a near bench-clearing brawl. In the eighth inning, Guillén swung in anger and hammered a home run to left. Tying the game, he dropped his bat and slowly circled the bases. The Nationals won, 6–3, and the incident seemed to enhance the Nationals' team chemistry.

The Nationals were winning thrillers and fans loved it. I called Gene Mauch in Palm Springs to share the excitement, and when I told him the Nationals were an amazing 24–9 in one-run games, Mauch said, "Most one-run games are lost." Mauch meant that if a team, like the red-hot Nationals, was winning one-run games, eventually fortunes would turn. Sure enough, in July the Nats lost 10 straight one-run games and fell out of first place. The Magic was gone.

After going 50–31 in the first half of the season, the team went 31–50 in the second half and finished last. Injuries to key players like Nick Johnson, Ryan Church, Vinny Castilla, and Liván Hernández hurt, but José Guillén had become a divisive factor in the clubhouse and blew up the team's chemistry set. "It was like someone turned off a switch," said Frank Robinson.

Ronnie and I didn't know if we'd be back in 2006. Bob Whitelaw said the new owners would select the announcers. I thought I'd be okay because Stan Kasten, whom I knew well, was about to be named team president and had already told me he looked forward to us working together in Washington.

As spring training neared, the team hadn't been sold. Tony Tavares and Bob Whitelaw let us hang until it was too late to find another job and then told us they weren't renewing our contracts.

"I don't know who's a bigger asshole, Tony Tavares or Bob Whitelaw," I said to Ron Darling.

"They're the same person," he said.

As so often happens with these egomaniacs, they derail careers, damage families, and then, without an ounce of guilt, move on. None of the Three Stooges are still in baseball. Tony Tavares bit the dust when new ownership hired Stan Kasten as team president. Before Tavares left, the team's former director of ticket sales filed suit, claiming Tavares slapped him in the face.

Eventually, Bob Whitelaw was fired as MASN's general manager. When I think back to Whitelaw, he was such a zero, a nondescript person, that I can't remember what he looked like and wouldn't recognize his voice if I heard it.

In 2009, Jim Bowden resigned as Nationals general manager under the cloud of a federal investigation for skimming the signing bonuses of Latin American prospects.

Ron Darling was fortunate to get hired by his old team, the New York Mets, but during his interview, he heard that our Washington employers had bashed our reputations. In a nurturing environment, he got help from his bosses, regained his confidence, and his career took off, as I knew it would. In addition to broadcasting Mets games on SNY-TV in New York, he does network telecasts for TNT.

I wanted to find another play-by-play job, but opportunities are limited. My Washington employers had poisoned the waters, damaging a reputation I'd built up over nearly 40 years, and in this economy, more than ever, employers are hiring the young and the cheap. So, where did that leave my career as a sportscaster?

Chapter 19
Now What?

Without a job, I was now a freelancer, which means I was doing a little of this, a little of that, but not enough of anything. And with the stagnant economy, networks stopped using freelance announcers, instead forcing their staff voices to work harder.

When you're successful, you have more "friends" than you can count, but when you're out of the picture, most of those people disappear. They're always there when they need tickets to a game or a player's autograph, but now the phone had stopped ringing.

I had to laugh. I was riding my bicycle down the Pacific Coast Highway, trying to forget my problems, when my cell phone rang. "Hey Mel, how are you?" asked some guy I'd known slightly. "Can you get me a couple of tickets to the Nationals game tonight?" I shook my head in disbelief and explained I no longer worked for the Nats but was riding my bike down Highway 101. I never heard from this clown again.

My son Billy worked for the Big Ten Network in Chicago. Probably because he was there and with the kindness of coordinating producer Tim Sutton, I did basketball play-by-play. One day, sitting in Sutton's office, we talked about how raw and inexperienced many of the network's announcers were. Most of the play-by-play announcers were young, and many of the analysts had no experience.

It's always amazed me that networks spend millions of dollars on rights fees and production, but little time or money goes to helping young announcers. NBC had been an exception. While I was doing football there, executive producer Michael Weisman hired veteran play-by-play announcer Marty Glickman to be the broadcast coach. He would critique the work of the network's announcers, mostly neophyte analysts and some budding play-by-play types. His suggestions helped improve the performance of many of NBC's talents. I asked Marty why he didn't critique my work, and he told me I already knew what I was doing.

I'd been amazed that no other network followed suit. Tim Sutton suggested that I submit a proposal to the Big Ten Network. The network liked the idea, and I became the "coach." I loved helping these wonderful young people get better. Many of them told me how much I'd helped them, and several veterans said they'd never gotten that kind of help. It was very satisfying.

When Tim Sutton asked if I'd ever called track and field, of course I said yes. I'd never called a track meet in my life, but I needed the work. So I was assigned to cover the 2008 Big Ten Women's Track and Field Championships. I immediately called veteran NBC announcer Charlie Jones, whom I had worked with nearly 40 years ago at NFL Films. Like me, Charlie lived in San Diego and we shared the same agent, Martin Mandel. Charlie had called many track and field events, including several Olympics, and gladly gave me some pointers.

Remember, I'd covered NBA Finals, Super Bowls, the World Series, Cal Ripken's record-breaking 2,131st consecutive game, and Tony Gwynn's 3,000th hit. So you probably think women's track and field wouldn't be in my top five. But over the years I've learned that some of the most exciting moments in sports sometimes come from the most unexpected sources.

The night before the meet, I had dinner with our producer, director, and analysts Kevin Sullivan and Suzy Favor Hamilton. We discussed our game plan to cover the events the next day at the University of Minnesota Fieldhouse.

The telecast was smooth, and Kevin, Suzy, and I meshed. Kevin and Suzy had both competed in the Olympics, but what we saw that day knocked our socks off. Minnesota's Heather Dorniden was the most decorated track athlete in school history. As a freshman, she won the 800 meter championship and was an eight-time All-American. She was the obvious favorite in a 600 meter finals heat.

As the runners ended the second lap, with only 200 meters to go, Dorniden, running second, began to pass the leader, Penn State's Fawn Dorr, as the partisan Minnesota crowd roared. But Dorr accidently stepped on the back of Dorniden's leg. Heather fell hard to the track, skidding on her stomach, as the three other competitors blew past her.

As the crowd gasped, I said, "Oh no. Dorniden is falling down—but gets up quickly—that's going to cost her. She's lucky she wasn't injured."

Dorniden quickly bounced up and began to sprint. She was 30 meters behind the nearest runner.

"Dorniden . . . flying down the back stretch!" yelled Kevin Sullivan.

"She's catching up!" shouted Suzy Favor Hamilton.

"She's going to catch Fawn Dorr and may catch the leaders," said Kevin.

"Wow," I managed to say. Pretty insightful stuff.

"She's got Fawn," Suzy said as Dorniden flew past Fawn Dorr.

"This is a gutsy effort by Dorniden . . . can she pull it off?" I asked.

"Unbelievable," said Suzy.

As Dorniden continued her amazing all-out sprint, I said, "She's moved into third. Dorniden's coming down the stretch . . . on the outside . . . Dorniden coming on strong." As she crossed the finish line, I shouted, "Dorniden goes all the way . . . she did it. Wow! Unbelievable."

It was an incredible moment. Go to YouTube and search for 2008 Big Ten 600m. The video has since become part of many motivational films.

Suzy and I weren't flying out until the next day so we had dinner. We talked about the incredible event we'd described, our work, families, and life. She seemed like the All-American wife and mother. She was beautiful, intelligent, kind, and funny. Suzy lived in Wisconsin, worked in real estate, and gave motivational speeches. Her topics included depression and suicide, which had touched both of our families. Suzy and I worked together several times and became friends.

Can you imagine my surprise when in December 2012 a website revealed that during the past year, Suzy Favor Hamilton had worked for an escort service in Las Vegas using the name "Kelly Lundy"? She was a $600-per-hour and $6,000-per-day escort—a prostitute, a hooker. Suzy said that depression and marital problems had driven her to this bizarre point in her life. I couldn't believe it. I e-mailed her, saying I hoped she was okay. Through social media, she apologized and promised to be a better wife, mother, daughter, and friend. I guess you just never know.

In 2009 Leon Schweir, former executive producer of the Big Ten Network but now in the same job with the Versus Network, called me. "Mel, I know you live in San Diego and Junior Seau also lives there. He's going to host a show called *Sports Jobs with Junior Seau.* He doesn't have any experience, and I was wondering if you'd be willing to tutor him. Versus is a new network, and this show is important to us."

Leon explained that each week Junior would perform a different sports-related job, such as an MMA corner man, a batboy for the Los Angeles Dodgers, a rodeo clown, or a member of a NASCAR pit crew. In addition to interacting with his coworkers, Junior would also narrate the program.

I told Leon I'd be glad to work with Junior, whom I'd never met. I knew Junior Seau was a San Diego icon, having played linebacker for the Chargers for 13 years before moving on to Miami for three seasons and New England for his final four. Twenty years in the NFL. Amazing. Seau had been a 10 time All-Pro, was selected for 12 Pro Bowls, and was named to the NFL's Team of the Decade for the 1990s. He owned two Seau's restaurants, and his foundation raised millions of dollars to educate and empower young people through the support of child abuse prevention and drug and alcohol awareness. I had lunch with Junior at the La Costa Country Club and outlined the program I had devised for him.

Over the next two months, three times a week, I'd go to Junior's house, across from the beach in Oceanside where he'd grown up. I met his girlfriend and his pit bull Rock, ever present at our sessions.

We worked on pronunciation, enunciation, word emphasis, and reading aloud. I gave Junior a tape recorder and asked him to do the drills I'd devised, over and over.

At first, I think Junior thought I was an idiot. Here's a big, strong All-Pro being asked to say "Fah, fah, fah, blah, blah, blah." I tried to put my instructions in football terms, explaining that these were warm-up exercises similar to the ones he did before a game. Junior gave me a strange look when I had him do tongue twisters like "Amos Ames, the amiable astronaut, aided in an aerial enterprise at the age of eighty-eight."

I've learned that great athletes like Junior Seau are perfectionists. They don't want to look bad at anything. Junior took the same approach as he did to football, doing the exercises religiously. His improvement was astounding.

After our sessions, Junior and I sat around and talked about sports, life, and our families. We agreed that the best things in our lives were our kids. I asked him if upon retirement he might consider coaching in the NFL, but he said that life was too unstable.

Once, Junior and I went to lunch. We had to walk down the Strand, a popular stretch of beach, to get to his car. It was like walking with a god. Everyone knew him. *Hi, Junior, how are you. Junior, we love you. Junior, we miss you.* People stopped their cars, rolled down their windows, and said hi. It was amazing.

Lunch was a Subway sandwich and Jamba Juice, and we sat outside and talked. Occasionally, another side of Junior surfaced. He said he was going to Las Vegas and admitted that he was a big-time gambler. He said one of the casinos would send a charter plane to pick him up and that he would be comped at Caesar's Palace and Bellagio, where he bet thousands playing blackjack. He was such a big player that the casinos closed off his table, leaving just Junior and the dealer. Do you know how much money you must bet to get this treatment?

Junior's biggest test came when we went to the studio to record the voiceover to accompany the video. I knew Junior was serious when he pulled his shirt off and flexed his muscles. It was apparent that Junior still had some difficulty reading long sentences, so here's what we did. I would read a line like, "In the brutal and bloody world of the MMA, the corner man is the fighter's guru . . . training the fighter, studying opponents'

Sports Jobs with Junior Seau *(photo by Versus)*

techniques, and keeping the fighter in shape," emphasizing words the way I thought they should be said. Then Junior would read the same line. With two producers in the studio and a Versus exec on the phone the whole time, offering suggestions and corrections, we worked our way through the half-hour script. Then through the magic of editing, my lines were removed and Junior's were pieced together. It worked, sounding like Junior had simply read the text. It was a tedious, intense session, and I was surprised when Junior snapped at me as he walked out the door.

But we got results. Andy Meyer, the Versus exec overseeing the project, was so impressed that he sent me a bonus check. That kind of kindness is unheard of in broadcasting.

Versus was pleased with *Sports Jobs with Junior Seau,* and we all figured the show would return for a second season. But then Versus was purchased by NBC and the show slipped through the cracks.

I saw Junior after he'd retired. He was looking forward to the future—spending time with his kids, running his restaurant and foundation, surfing, working out, and learning to play the ukulele. But in October 2010 Junior was arrested for domestic violence after an incident reported to police by his girlfriend. Hours later, after being bailed out, his SUV plunged down a 100-foot cliff, landing on the beach below. Junior's injuries weren't serious, and he convinced everyone that he'd just fallen asleep at the wheel. All of us should have seen this incident as a warning sign.

When I tried to call Junior, his cell phone number had been changed. I figured he just wanted to avoid publicity about the incident. Then, in May 2012, I heard that Junior Seau had committed suicide. It was one of those times like the Kennedy assassination, 9/11, or the shootings in Connecticut—events our limited minds just can't comprehend.

With his girlfriend at the gym, Junior put a shotgun to his chest and killed himself. Of course everyone wondered why. Junior seemed to have it all: wealth, fame, wonderful kids, and his restaurant and foundation to occupy his time.

Never in my life have I seen such an outpouring of public emotion for a famous athlete. It had been 10 years since Junior had played for the San Diego Chargers, but he was still regarded as the greatest player in franchise history. Junior Seau's death was front-page material for two weeks in the *San Diego Union Tribune.*

Fans and family stood outside Junior's beachside home, the same place I'd spent so much time with him, placing leis and signs reading "We love you Junior. Rest in Peace." Someone purchased a billboard near Highway 5 with a picture of Junior Seau.

Gradually, we learned that there were two Junior Seaus: his public persona and the other side hidden by his ever-present smile.

After seemingly endless celebrations of his life, it was revealed that Junior's world had collapsed on him. Without football, he had no structure and purpose. He had countless empty hours to ruminate about his escalating problems. His restaurant was losing money, his investments turned sour, and his gambling losses at Las Vegas casinos continued to mount. He began to drink heavily and overdo the use of prescription drugs.

Later, a study of Junior Seau's brain revealed that he suffered from chronic traumatic encephalopathy (CTE), a disease triggered by multiple concussions that's linked to memory loss, dementia, and depression. Junior was one of several CTE sufferers who had committed suicide. In January 2013, Junior Seau's family sued the NFL for concealing information linking football-related injuries to long-term brain damage. Seau's suit was one of 4,000 that had been filed against the league for the same reasons.

Junior Seau was the second friend I'd lost to suicide within a year. Like Seau, Mike Flanagan, former Baltimore Orioles pitcher and one of my broadcast partners, had also shot himself. Those two deaths ripped into my soul because my family had a history of depression and suicide.

What I've learned over the years, working with these fascinating sports personalities, is that we're all just human beings with strengths and weaknesses. We all have a dark side and make mistakes. I think with the rich and famous there may be even more pressure to succeed. When I think back on my career, it's not the game-winning shots or walk-off home runs I remember, but the people I have worked with and the athletes whose actions I have described. Despite dealing with an occasional asshole wearing a suit, I've loved my work and career.

So today I look back on a fascinating career beginning with Colorado College and a taste of the corporate world. I embraced my passion for sports, found my career path behind a microphone, met my mentor in Hawaii, swam with sharks, watched the greatest athletes in the world, helped build a start-up network, lived in America's favorite city, stepped on a landmine, rehabbed in the desert, and watched the roller coaster climb back up, only to plummet again. As one of my bosses once said, "You jump into this business and have no control over where it will take you. You just hold on and try to enjoy the ride before it spits you out at the end." I've enjoyed the ride, more than anyone could imagine.